BRAIN LATERALIZATION AND DEVELOPMENTAL DISORDERS

Brain Lateralization and Developmental Disorders provides a comprehensive review of key findings and speculations from previous research on atypical cerebral lateralization in the most common neurodevelopmental disorders: stuttering, dyslexia, autism and intellectual disability. Emphasis is placed on recent studies, as well as descriptions of the author's personal research which will provide a promising new direction for future research on these issues.

In this text, Asenova presents four separate studies aiming to examine hemispheric asymmetries in neurodevelopmental disorders. These include the subtypes of developmental stuttering, the subtypes of developmental dyslexia, mild, non-syndromic intellectual disability with comorbid speech and language deficits and autism spectrum disorder with comorbid severe language impairment. The use of uniform research methods, including dichotic verbal perception tasks and lateral preference performance tests, has led to findings that suggest that this new approach could be a key factor in overcoming the ambiguity of findings from previous studies.

By focusing on the discussion of key issues concerning the role of atypical laterality in the genesis of neurodevelopmental psychopathology in both past research and Asenova's own studies, *Brain Lateralization and Developmental Disorders* is a valuable reading for students and researchers in neurodevelopmental psychopathology, as well as in developmental neuropsychology and developmental neuroscience.

Ivanka V. Asenova, PhD, is an Associate Professor of Neuropsychology at South-West University "Neofit Rilski" in Blagoevgrad, Bulgaria.

BRAIN LATERALIZATION AND DEVELOPMENTAL DISORDERS

A New Approach to Unified Research

Ivanka V. Asenova

LONDON AND NEW YORK

First published 2018
by Routledge
2 Park Square, Milton Park, Abingdon, Oxon OX14 4RN

and by Routledge
711 Third Avenue, New York, NY 10017

Routledge is an imprint of the Taylor & Francis Group, an informa business

© 2018 Ivanka V. Asenova

The right of Ivanka V. Asenova to be identified as the author of this work has been asserted by her in accordance with sections 77 and 78 of the Copyright, Designs and Patents Act 1988.

All rights reserved. No part of this book may be reprinted or reproduced or utilised in any form or by any electronic, mechanical, or other means, now known or hereafter invented, including photocopying and recording, or in any information storage or retrieval system, without permission in writing from the publishers.

Trademark notice: Product or corporate names may be trademarks or registered trademarks, and are used only for identification and explanation without intent to infringe.

British Library Cataloguing-in-Publication Data
A catalogue record for this book is available from the British Library

Library of Congress Cataloging-in-Publication Data
Names: Asenova, Ivanka V., author.
Title: Brain lateralization and developmental disorders : a new approach to unified research / Ivanka V. Asenova.
Description: Abingdon, Oxon ; New York, NY : Routledge, 2018. | Includes bibliographical references and index.
Identifiers: LCCN 2017036306 (print) | LCCN 2017038522 (ebook) | ISBN 9781315147598 (Ebook) | ISBN 9781138551480 (hardback : alk. paper) | ISBN 9781138551503 (pbk. : alk. paper) | ISBN 9781315147598 (ebk)
Subjects: | MESH: Dominance, Cerebral | Neurodevelopmental Disorders—etiology
Classification: LCC QP385.5 (ebook) | LCC QP385.5 (print) | NLM WL 335 | DDC 612.8/25—dc23
LC record available at https://lccn.loc.gov/2017036306

ISBN: 978-1-138-55148-0 (hbk)
ISBN: 978-1-138-55150-3 (pbk)
ISBN: 978-1-315-14759-8 (ebk)

Typeset in Bembo and Stone Sans
by Florence Production Ltd, Stoodleigh, Devon, UK

 Printed in the United Kingdom by Henry Ling Limited

CONTENTS

Abbreviations   *vii*

Introduction   1

1 Functional specialization of the brain (general theoretical framework)   7

Introduction   7
Empirical basis for the concept of the functional specialization of the brain   7
Anatomical data for differences in the structure of the cerebral hemispheres   8
Data from neuropsychological assessment of brain-damaged patients   10
Neurophysiological data for differences in the bioelectric activity of the cerebral hemispheres   11
Data from functional neuroimaging studies of healthy subjects   12
Data from behavioral studies of healthy subjects   13
Genesis of the functional specialization of the human brain   14
A general theoretical framework of the modern concept of functional specialization of the brain   18
Theoretical models of the mechanisms underlying perceptual asymmetry   19
Theoretical models of the mechanisms of hemispheric interaction   21
Contemporary models of language organization   23
The relation of language lateralization and handedness   24
References and further reading   26

2 Developmental stuttering   39

Introduction   39
About the birth of the theory of atypical cerebral dominance for speech as a cause of developmental stuttering   40

Developmental stuttering and left-handedness	*41*
Developmental stuttering and lateralization of language functions	*42*
Empirical evidence supporting the Cerebral Dominance Theory of developmental stuttering	*43*
Theoretical models of stuttering as a result of atypical cerebral lateralization of speech and language functions	*52*
Current perspectives on the defining and studying of developmental stuttering	*53*
Personal research data	*56*
References and further reading	*68*

3 Developmental dyslexia — 77

Introduction	*77*
Atypical cerebral dominance as an etiological factor of developmental dyslexia	*77*
Current perspectives in defining the deficit underlying developmental dyslexia	*88*
Current issues and perspectives in studying developmental dyslexia	*94*
Personal research data	*100*
References and further reading	*114*

4 Intellectual disability — 127

Introduction	*127*
Handedness and intellectual disability	*128*
Language lateralization and intellectual disability	*130*
Personal research data	*132*
References and further reading	*137*

5 Autism spectrum disorder — 141

Introduction	*141*
Handedness and autism spectrum disorder	*142*
Language lateralization and autism spectrum disorder	*144*
Autism and Asperger syndrome – separate clinical entities or not?	*151*
Personal research data	*152*
References and further reading	*158*

Conclusion — 165

Index — 175

ABBREVIATIONS

ADHD	Attention deficit hyperactivity disorder
APA	American Psychiatric Association
ASD	Autism spectrum disorder
CNS	Central nervous system
CV	Consonant-vowel
DD	Developmental dyslexia
DI	Developmental instability
DRC	Dual Route Cascaded model
DS	Developmental stuttering
DSM-IV	Diagnostic and Statistical Manual – Fourth Edition
DSM-V	Diagnostic and Statistical Manual – Fifth Edition
DTI	Diffusion tensor imaging
EEG	Electroencephalography
EPs	Evoked potentials
ERPs	Event-related potentials
fMRI	functional magnetic resonance imaging
fNIRS	functional near infrared spectroscopy
fTCD	functional transcranial doppler ultrasonography
HSS	Hereditary subtype of stuttering
ICD-10	International Classification of Diseases, Tenth Edition
ID	Intellectual disability
LD	Learning disabilities
LEA	Left-ear advantage
LH	Left hemisphere
LHA	Left-hemisphere advantage
LQ	Laterality quotient
MDS	Mixed dyslexia subtype

MEG	Magnetoencephalography
MRI	Magnetic resonance imaging
NEA	No-ear advantage
NS-ID	Non-syndromic intellectual disability
15O-PET	15Oxygen positron emission tomography
OSS	Organic subtype of stuttering
PDD-NOS	Pervasive developmental disorder-not otherwise specified
PDS	Phonological dyslexia subtype
PET	Positron emission tomography
PSS	Psychogenic subtype of stuttering
QMA	Quotient of manual asymmetry
REA	Right-ear advantage
RH	Right hemisphere
RHA	Right hemisphere advantage
SDS	Surface dyslexia subtype
SLD	Specific learning difficulties
SLI	Specific language impairment
SPECT	Single positron emission computed tomography
TSD	Transcranial Doppler sonography
VBM	Voxel-based morphometry

INTRODUCTION

Human language is a complex communication system processed in most people by specialized brain systems in the left cerebral hemisphere [5]. The notion that developmental speech, language and literacy disorders might be due to a failure to develop a dominant language hemisphere belongs to Orton [28]. Almost a century ago, he suggested that the lack of normal cerebral lateralization can cause difficulties in speech, language and reading.

Since then, atypical laterality has been studied not only in developmental language and literacy disorders including dyslexia [11, 21, 33], stuttering [3, 12, 22] and specific language impairment (SLI) [7, 8], but also in other developmental disorders and pathological conditions such as autism [8, 30, 31], attention deficit hyperactivity disorder (ADHD) [17, 18], learning disabilities [25], intellectual disability (ID) [24], Down syndrome [16, 19], Rett syndrome [27], Turner syndrome [13], Klinefelter syndrome [14], Williams syndrome [23], fragile-X syndrome [10], schizophrenia [9, 11], cerebral palsy [6] and epilepsy [32].

My intention when writing this book was to discuss and integrate findings from research on atypical cerebral lateralization in the most common neurodevelopmental disorders – developmental stuttering (DS), developmental dyslexia (DD), non-syndromic intellectual disability (NS-ID) and autism spectrum disorder (ASD), including my own research in which I have used dichotic verbal perception tasks and lateral preference performance tests, with the set of applied research methods being identical for all studies.

All these non-syndromic, neurodevelopmental disorders are behaviorally-defined disorders with multifactorial aetiology most probably involving multiple genes and environmental risk factors [1, 4, 5].

A number of theories have been proposed to account for the observed underlying differences in hemispheric asymmetry between each of these developmental disorders and control populations; yet studies conducted to investigate these relationships have received widely varying results. Among the most frequently discussed reasons for the inconsistency of research findings are the use of different research methods and developmental disorders definitions [16, 22, 30, 31], differences in characteristics of the studied subjects, such as gender, handedness, age, etc., known as factors initiating individual differences in the pattern of brain laterality [4, 20] and heterogeneity of populations suffering from these developmental disorders [4, 8, 33].

The organization and planning of my own research on the relation between these developmental disorders and atypical hemispheric asymmetries was based on the following theoretical assumptions and conceptions:

1. Non-syndromic developmental disorders are heterogeneous and include distinct subtypes [4, 8, 33].
2. The aetiology of non-syndromic developmental disorders is polygenic and multifactorial [1, 4, 5, 12].
3. There is a relationship between handedness and language dominance, and it is a natural phenomenon [26]. Therefore, handedness disturbances may reflect an abnormal pattern of cerebral lateralization [2, 15].

Two main hypotheses underlie my research. The first one states that each developmental disorder is heterogeneous in terms of language lateralization and manual asymmetry (or handedness), and atypical patterns of lateralization (probably different) can most likely be seen only in one, or several, subtypes of the disorder, but not in all of its subtypes. The second hypothesis states that atypical language laterality could be the cause for the emergence and persistence of only specific subtypes of developmental disorders.

The book consists of six chapters. In Chapter 1 I discuss the contemporary conceptualization of functional specialization of the human brain and its empirical support provided by an impressive amount of clinical observations and experimental studies using a wide variety of research methods.

The next four chapters are dedicated to different developmental disorders: Chapter 2 to DS, Chapter 3 to DD, Chapter 4 to NS-ID and Chapter 5 to ASD. Each of the chapters is organized in three parts. In the first part, after a short definition and discussion of the most contentious issues concerning the disorder, I present theoretical analyses and overviews of empirical evidence regarding the association between atypical cerebral lateralization and the disorder. In the second part, I hereby present the results of my personal research on functional asymmetries in children suffering from the disorder comparing them to an age- and gender-matched control group of typically developing children.

Finally, analysis and interpretation of the received results are presented in the last part. Here, I also make assumptions about the new findings and propose a hypothetical model for accounting the observed deviations in hemispheric asymmetries and their implications on the origin of the developmental disorder.

In the final chapter, Conclusion, I briefly summarize the findings presented in the previous chapters of the book and their implications on our understanding of the relationship between developmental disorders and atypical cerebral lateralization. Finally, I discuss the contribution of laterality research in seeking answers on the outstanding issues concerning aetiology and neuropsychology of developmental disorders.

The main hypotheses of my research are highly supported by analysis of findings from different studies. Based on results received from studying a stutterers sample and a dyslexics sample, I come up with the supposition that atypical language lateralization may act as a causal factor for the emergence and persistence only of certain subtype(s) of developmental speech, language or literacy disorders.

Based on results received from studying the sample with NS-ID and the one with ASD, I come up with the supposition that in developmental disorders which are not essentially linguistic in nature but have comorbid early language impairment, the lack of normal cerebral lateralization could be causally associated with the comorbid language deficit rather than with the developmental disorders themselves.

I believe this book will be useful to students, researchers and practitioners who have an interest in the field of developmental neuropathology. Also, I presume that the assumptions and hypotheses discussed in this book will attract the attention and research interest of scholars and provoke them to undertake research in order to verify or develop them further.

References and further reading

1 Andrews, G., Craig, A., Feyer, A. M., Hoddinott, S., Howie, P. & Neilson, M. (1983). Stuttering: A review of research findings and theories circa 1982. *JSHD, 48*(3) 226–246.
2 Annett, M. (2002). *Handedness and brain asymmetry: The right shift theory.* Hove, UK: Psychology Press.
3 Beal, D. S., Gracco, V. L., Lafaille, S. J. & Nil, L. F. (2007). Voxel-based morphometry of auditory and speech related cortex in stutterers. *Neuroreport, 18*(12), 1257–1260.
4 Bishop, D. V. M. (2009). Genes, cognition, and communication: Insights from neurodevelopmental disorders. *Ann. N. Y. Acad. Sci., 9*(1156), 1–18.
5 Bishop, D. V. M. (2013). Cerebral asymmetry and language development: Cause, correlate or consequence? *Science, 340*(6138): 1230531.
6 Brizzolara, D., Pecini, C., Brovedani, P., Ferretti, G., Cipriani, P. & Cioni, G. (2002). Timing and type of congenital brain lesion determine different patterns of language lateralization in hemiplegic children. *Neuropsychologia, 40*(6), 620–632.
7 De Guibert, C., Maumet, C., Jannin, P., Ferré, J.-C., Tréguier, C., Barillot, C. . . . Biraben, A. (2011). Abnormal functional lateralization and activity of language brain areas in typical specific language impairment (developmental dysphasia). *Brain, 134*(10), 3044–3058.
8 De Fossé, L., Hodge, S., Makris, N., Kennedy, D., Caviness, V., McGrath, L., . . . Harris, G. J. (2004). Language-association cortex asymmetry in autism and specific language impairment. *Ann. Neurol., 56*(6), 757–766.
9 Collinson, S., Mackay, C. E., James, A. C. & Crow, T. J. (2009). Dichotic listening impairments in early onset schizophrenia are associated with reduced left temporal lobe volume. *Schizophr. Res., 112*(1–3), 24–31.

10 Cornish, K. M., Pigram, J. & Shaw, K. (1997). Do anomalies of handedness exist in children with fragile-X syndrome? *Laterality, 2*(2), 91–101.
11 Edgar, J. C., Yeo, R. A., Gangestad, S. W., Blake, M. B., Davis, J. T., Lewine, J. D. & Cañive, J. M. (2006). Reduced auditory M100 asymmetry in schizophrenia and dyslexia: Applying a developmental instability approach to assess atypical brain asymmetry. *Neuropsychologia, 44*(2), 289–299.
12 Foundas, A., Corey, D., Angeles, V., Bolich, A., Crabtree-Hartman, E. & Heilman, K. (2003). Atypical cerebral laterality in adults with persistent developmental stuttering. *Neurology, 61*(10), 1378–1385.
13 Ganou, M. & Grouios, G. (2008). Cerebral laterality in Turner syndrome: A critical review of the literature. *Child Neuropsychol., 14*(2), 135–147.
14 Ganou, M., Grouios, G., Koidou, I. & Alevriadou, A. (2010). The concept of anomalous cerebral lateralization in Klinefelter syndrome. *Appl. Neuropsychol., 17*(2), 144–152.
15 Geschwind, N. & Galaburda, A. (1987). *Cerebral lateralization.* Cambridge, MA: MIT Press.
16 Grouios, G., Ypsilanti, A. & Koidou, I. (2013). Laterality explored: Atypical hemispheric dominance in Down syndrome. In Subrata Kumar Dey (Ed.), *Down syndrome* (pp. 209–236). Rijeka, Croatia: InTech
17 Hale, T. S., McCracken, J. T., McGough, J. J., Smalley, S. L., Philips, J. M. & Zaidel, E. (2005). Impaired linguistic processing and atypical brain laterality in adults with ADHD. *Clin. Neurosci. Res., 5*(5–6), 255–263.
18 Hale, T. S., Smalley, S. L., Walshaw, P. D., Hanada, G., Macion, J., McCracken, J. T. . . . Loo, S. K. (2010). Atypical EEG beta asymmetry in adults with ADHD. *Neuropsychologia, 48*(12), 3532–3539.
19 Heath, M. & Elliott, D. (1999). Cerebral specialization for speech production in persons with Down syndrome. *Brain Lang., 69*(2), 193–211.
20 Hellige, L. (1993). *Hemispheric asymmetry.* Cambridge, MA: Harvard University Press.
21 Illingworth, S. & Bishop, D. (2009). Atypical cerebral lateralisation in adults with compensated developmental dyslexia demonstrated using functional transcranial Doppler ultrasound. *Brain Lang., 111*(1), 61–65.
22 Ingham, R. J. (2001). Brain imaging studies of developmental stuttering. *J. Commun. Dis., 34*(6), 493–516.
23 Jackowski, A. P., Rando, K., Maria de Araújo, C., Del Cole, C. G., Silva, I. & Tavares de Lacerda, A. L. (2008). Brain abnormalities in Williams syndrome: A review of structural and functional magnetic resonance imaging findings. *Eur. J. Paediatr. Neurol., 13*(4), 305–316.
24 Leconte, P. & Fagard, J. (2006). Lateral preferences in children with intellectual deficiency of idiopathic origin. *Dev. Psychol., 48*(6), 492–500.
25 Obrzut, J. (1988). Deficient lateralization in learning disabled children. In D. Molfese & S. Segalowitz (Eds.), *Brain lateralization in children* (pp. 567–589). New York: Guilford.
26 Ocklenburg, S., Beste, C., Arning, L., Peterburs, J. & Güntürkün, O. (2014). The ontogenesis of language lateralization and its relation to handedness. *Neurosci. Biobehav. Rev., 43,* 191–198.
27 Olsson, B. & Rett, A. (1986). Shift to right-handedness in Rett syndrome around age 7. *Am. J. Med. Genet., 24,* 133–141.
28 Orton, S. (1928). A physiological theory of reading disability and stuttering in children. *NEJM, 198,* 1045–1052.
29 Paquette, C., Bourassa, M. & Peretz, I. (1996). Left-ear advantage in pitch perception of complex tones without energy at the fundamental frequency. *Neuropschologia, 34*(2), 153–157.

30 Philip, R. C., Dauvermann, M. R., Whalley, H. C., Baynham, K., Lawrie, S. M. & Stanfield, A. C. (2012). A systematic review and meta-analysis of the fMRI investigation of autism spectrum disorders. *Neurosci. Biobehav. Rev.*, *36*(2), 901–942.
31 Preslar, J., Kushner, H. I., Marino, L., & Pearce, B. (2014). Autism, lateralisation, and handedness: A review of the literature and meta-analysis. *Laterality*, *19*(1), 64–95.
32 Slezicki, K. I., Cho, Y. W., Yi, S. D., Brock, M. S., Pfeiffer, M. H., McVearry, K. M. . . . Motamedi, G. K. (2009). Incidence of atypical handedness in epilepsy and its association with clinical factors. *Epilepsy Behav.*, *16*(2), 330–334.
33 Zadina, J., Corey, D., Casbergue, R., Lemen, L., Rouse, J., Knaus, T. & Foundas, A. (2006). Lobar asymmetries in subtypes of dyslexic and control subjects. *J. Child Neurol.*, *21*(11), 922–931.

1
FUNCTIONAL SPECIALIZATION OF THE BRAIN (GENERAL THEORETICAL FRAMEWORK)

Introduction

There are obvious functional differences between the cerebral hemispheres of the human brain which has been assumed for a long time to be beneficial to its functioning [86]. The distribution of functions between the left hemisphere (LH) and the right hemisphere (RH) is referred to as hemispheric lateralization or functional asymmetry of the cerebral hemispheres [93, 129, 195, 199].

The issue of functional differentiation of LH and RH has been studied since the time of Broca and Wernicke (1861–1874) [196], and is becoming one of the most studied areas in cognitive science today.

It was considered at the beginning that while in right-handers the LH is absolutely dominant in all cognitive processes and the RH is entirely subordinate (for that reason it was called 'subdominant'), in left-handers these relationships are absolutely opposed (for a review, see [37, 38]). Over the years, these initial speculations underwent multiple changes to reach the current conception of the functional specialization of the cerebral hemispheres and their close collaboration in the processing of any complex mental activity [2, 37, 38, 40, 209, 213, 214].

Empirical basis for the concept of the functional specialization of the brain

Contemporary conceptions of functional specialization of the human brain are based on an impressive amount of empirical data generated from clinical observations and experimental studies that use a wide variety of research methods.

Main approaches to characterizing hemispheric specialization may be summarized as following [190]: (a) post-mortem studies of human brains which focus on structural differences between homotopic regions of the two cerebral hemispheres; (b) in vivo studies of both structural and functional brain asymmetries using a variety of techniques: electroencephalography (EEG), magnetoencephalography, evoked potentials (EPs), magnetic resonance imaging (MRI) morphometry, functional MRI (fMRI), positron emission tomography (PET), transcranial Doppler sonography (TSD), functional TSD (fTSD), single positron emission computed tomography; (c) neuropsychological assessment of patients with focal brain lesions or split-brain patients and (d) neuropsychological assessment of hemispheric performance differences using tachistoscopic visual or dichotic auditory stimulus presentation techniques.

Unfortunately, regardless of the impressive advances in our understanding of functional lateralization of the human brain over the past two to three decades, the knowledge for the causes behind the functional asymmetries remains limited [28, 194, 199].

Anatomical data for differences in the structure of the cerebral hemispheres

The observed anatomical differences between the two cerebral hemispheres in both adults and children [16, 95, 194], even in foetuses [110] and infants [66], have underlaid the proposal that anatomical asymmetries in the human brain could reflect, or even be a significant factor for, the formation of functional hemispheric asymmetries [78, 93, 208].

In healthy subjects, a number of structural asymmetries in terms of cortical matter volume, surface area size, cortical thickness or white matter properties have been found (for a review, see [194]). It has been established that in most people the planum temporale in the LH (that roughly corresponds to Wernicke's area) is typically larger compared to the RH [65, 75, 85, 111, 112, 121, 162, 191]. Similar left-right anatomical asymmetries have been found for Heschl's gyrus [65, 85, 111, 121], planum parietale [162], Broca's area [65, 112], pars triangulais [75], pars opercularis (but not in pars triangulais) [4] and hippocampal formation [85].

Structural differences have also been found in the following areas of the LH and RH, especially in right-handers: deeper cortical sulci of the inferior parietal regions in the LH [1]; leftward asymmetry of Sylvian fissure [74]; larger sizes in the LH than in the RH of the 3rd and 5th layers of Brodmann areas 44 and 45, as well as the pyramidal cells of Betz located within the 5th layer of Brodmann area 4 (the primary motor cortex) [113]; greater extent of higher order dendritic branching in certain speech areas of the LH than in homologous areas of the RH [177]; larger grey matter volume than white matter volume only in the LH [90]; more pronounced leftward structural asymmetries of the insula [26, 112] accompanied by greater left-hemisphere dominance for gesture and language [26]; deeper superior temporal sulcus in the RH in the area ventral of Heschl's gyrus, irrespective of gender, handedness and language lateralization [126].

Morphological differences have been found in some subcortical structures of the two cerebral hemispheres, such as globus pallidus, putamen, hippocampus and thalamus (for a review, see [88]), as the asymmetry in thalamic nuclei associated with speech functions has been most pronounced [for a review, see [45] and [113]).

An overall rightwards volumetric asymmetry of the cerebellum has been reported (as the interaction is in rostral/caudal plane (in the rostral part: right > left and in the caudal plane: left > right) which follows the pattern of those in the neocortex and is more pronounced in right-handers) [182]. In contrast, a recent large study found that these cerebellar asymmetries had no significant associations to handedness and had some significant (but weak) associations to cerebral cortical asymmetries (including the asymmetry of cerebellar region I.IV with the asymmetry of Heschl's gyrus) [111].

Studies of the associations of these structural asymmetries with handedness, language dominance and gender have produced conflicting findings. For example, Foundas et al. [75] have found that structural asymmetries of planum temporale and pars triangulais, determined by MRI, are associated with language dominance and handedness, as right-handers with left-hemispheric language lateralization (determined by selective hemispheric anaesthesia or Wada testing) have a significant leftward asymmetry of these cortical regions while left-handers do not. Good et al. [85] have reported a significant main effect of sex, but not of handedness on structural asymmetry of planum temporale and Heschl's gyrus, but Steinmetz et al. [191] have reported the opposite – a significant main effect of handedness, but not of sex on structural asymmetry of planum temporale. Dorsaint-Pierre et al. [65] have found that leftward structural asymmetries of the planum temporale, do not relate to language lateralization, those of the inferior frontal gyrus (pars opercularis, corresponding functionally to Broca's area) are related to language lateralization, and for Heschl's gyrus this structure–function relationship is not obligatory.

Keller et al. [112] have observed no relationship between the volume asymmetry of Broca's area or planum temporal and language lateralization, but instead a robust relationship between volume asymmetry of the insula and language lateralization.

Kulynych et al. [121] have found larger left planum temporale in males than in females, but not Foundas et al. [74]. According to the observations of Amunts et al. [4], although area 44 (but not area 45) has been left-over-right asymmetrical in both male and female brains, cell density was higher on the left side than on the right side in all studied men but only in a minority of women.

A recent study using diffusion tensor imaging (DTI) among a large sample of youths has revealed unique sex differences in brain connectivity during the course of development. It has been discovered that males have greater within-hemispheric connectivity, as well as enhanced modularity and transitivity, while females have greater between-hemispheric connectivity and cross-module participation [105].

To sum up, although the structural hemispheric asymmetries are well documented in healthy individuals and demonstrate a degree of correspondence with functional hemispheric specialization, with the LH being dominant for language and manual preference and the RH being dominant for spatial abilities, face processing and emotional expression [16, 17, 35, 95, 155, 194], there is a lack of clear-cut evidence for direct links between structure and function [16, 17, 95, 112], which in turn leaves it unclear how such structural differences are related to language development [87].

Results like those from studies that have observed no relationship between the structural asymmetry of Broca's area [112] or planum temporale [65, 112] and language lateralization challenge the view that structural hemispheric asymmetries are a reliable predictor of functional asymmetry of language, leave the issue of the strength of the relationship between structure and function open and support the view of multifactorial determination of the functional cerebral lateralization [16, 17, 95, 128].

Data from neuropsychological assessment of brain-damaged patients

Studies of patients with focal brain damage have historically provided major insights into the relationships between brain structure and cognitive functions [84, 193], and despite the continuous dispute how lawful and reasonable it is to use this data for making generalizations and conclusions regarding the functions of the intact brain, the outcomes of clinical observations and neuropsychological assessments of patients with focal brain lesions are the basis of most contemporary conceptions concerning the relationships between different aspects of mental activity and brain function.

Classical lesion tests and newer imaging techniques (mostly voxel-based imaging) have been used over the past one to two decades to detect lesion-deficit relationships. No doubt, classical lesion studies are unique in the kinds of inference they permit but are limited in their generalization and specificity because of typically small sample sizes (usually single case studies) and large lesions [84]. The neuroimaging techniques surpass lesion analysis in examining functional networks and when applied in large samples, these techniques provide a powerful statistical tool to identify brain regions necessary for particular cognitive processes [84], which makes them increasingly preferred.

So, using classical or neuroimaging-based lesion symptom mapping in brain-damaged patients (mainly after a stroke or a traumatic brain injury) or epilepsy patients undergoing presurgical evaluation, it has been evidenced through various cognitive tasks that the LH is responsible for the planning and production of complex and automatic motor skills [129, 136] of speech and language functions including phonological, morphological and syntactic processing [25, 113, 202]; verbal memory [55] and language comprehension ([84, 179], and for a review, see [9, 45]). LH is also related to working memory [84], arithmetic [140] linguistic thought, analytic reasoning and problem-solving [19]. Difficulties in lexical-semantic, discursive, pragmatic-inferential and/or prosodic processing [53], however, are associated with RH brain damages. Also, the RH is associated with conceptual knowledge [55] and perceptual organization [84] and is responsible for attention [109], visual-spatial perception and spatial manipulation [76, 109] and body schema [33]. The RH dominates emotion processing, especially the perception and expression of facial emotions [124, 168], lexical emotion [34] and emotional prosodic perception (see [217] for a review).

Neurophysiological data for differences in the bioelectric activity of the cerebral hemispheres

EEG is one of the most widely used methods for studying neurophysiological aspects of cerebral laterality. Alpha rhythm is considered to indicate relative deactivation of brain areas over which it is recorded, and regional alpha power at rest has been found to be inversely correlated with cerebral blood flow as measured by PET and fMRI (for a review, see [132]).

Previous studies have unequivocally shown that the asymmetries in EEG activity depend on the nature of the applied stimulation. Basically, while performing intellectual and verbal activities, a more expressed depression of the alpha rhythm in amplitude, index or total energy has been observed in the LH than in the RH, and while performing non-verbal perceptive activities (perception of non-verbal acoustic and visual stimuli), the opposite pattern has been registered [2, 14, 57, 132, 156]. Left-hemispheric asymmetry of theta (4–8 Hz) and beta (13–30 Hz) rhythms during word processing (phonological, semantic and orthographic) has also been observed at left frontal sites specifically during the phonological task [188]. Something more – it has been found that the different stages of the verbal and perceptive processing are characterized by a specific spatially–temporal organization of the bioelectric impulses: when performing verbal activities, except for the temporal and parietal regions of the LH that play a special role in language processing, many different regions of both hemispheres are involved; while during visual imaging processing, although the leading part is played by the posterior regions of the RH, the frontal and central regions of the LH also take part [158]. In this regard, Sviderskaya [192] concludes that "the specifics of the interhemispheric relationships consists not only in the degree of activity of any of the regions but also in the sequence of inclusion of the different cortical areas, as well as in the stability of the processes inside" (p. 92).

Studies assessing EEG activity (especially in the alpha band: 8–13 Hz) have shown that the left- and right-anterior cortical regions are differently involved in emotional and motivational processes, as higher depression levels of the EEG alpha rhythm in the left frontal regions is linked to positive and approach-related emotion whereas in the reciprocal areas of the RH – with negative and withdrawal-related emotion [2, 48]. The same pattern of brain asymmetry in emotion-related constructs has been observed in 10-month-old infants [58]. Parallel to the changes of the alpha rhythm, there were registered changes of the beta rhythm and the total energy, but with opposite sign [2].

The method of EPs is another widely applicable electrophysiological technique in the study of functional hemispheric asymmetries. It has been found that hemispheric asymmetries of the EPs can be clearly observed during mental activity, have a regional character and depend on the nature of the performed activity [156]. Regarding motor EPs, a lower threshold for the LH than for the RH has been observed. This asymmetry has also been shown to correlate with some characteristics of manual praxis such as speed, proficiency and less power, as the lower threshold of motor EPs of the preferred hand (irrespective of right or left hand) has been in higher correlation with its larger skills [197].

In psychophysiological studies, special attention is paid to the late components of the EPs [149], also entitled event-related potentials (ERPs), where changes have demonstrated a dependence on the type of cognitive tasks. Hemispheric asymmetries in multiple components of ERPs during word recognition [149, 178], speech sound perception [69], face perception [183], selecting pictures of objects and words [120] and perception of approach- and withdrawal-related emotional stimuli [1] have been reported. These asymmetries have been reflected in a greater negative wave and a smaller positive wave in posterior regions of the directly stimulated hemisphere.

Data from functional neuroimaging studies of healthy subjects

Findings from studies regarding the functional differences between the two cerebral hemispheres that have used traditional and established methods have been confirmed by data generated in studies using modern higher resolution techniques of functional neuroimaging.

In general, changes in the cerebral blood flow reflect changes in the cerebral metabolism due to cerebral activation [194]. Studies of regional variations in the distribution of cerebral blood flow through PET or 15oxygen PET [150-PET] during linguistic and non-linguistic processing have found that words, syllables [103, 154] and story listening [198] provoke greater neuronal activity in the left temporal lobe; musical stimuli and sounds from the environment lead to stronger activation of the right temporal lobe [103, 154] and listening to and repeating sentences increase frontal-temporal blood flow significantly more in the LH than in the RH [146]. Also, a PET study has observed that simultaneous piano playing and musical notation reading are mainly LH activities which, similar to sign language, include both cortical planning and peripheral motor manual activity [150].

When measuring changes in arterial blood flow rate provoked by cognitive activity using the technique of bilateral TSD, the LH dominance for verbal tasks have been found [41, 87, 91, 205], as the tasks requiring active or creative verbal processing, such as sentence construction or word fluency, elicited the most asymmetric activation [205]. Also, there has been RH dominance for visuospatial tasks [87, 205], inconsistent or lack of RH dominance for tasks requiring spatial visualization and mental rotation of complex figures [31, 41] and RH dominance in analyzing complex musical stimuli [206].

Many studies using event-related fMRI (a technique based on changes in oxygen consumption) have also found predominantly LH activation for various verbal tasks [68, 100, 119, 163, 179, 193, 202, 215].

Most of these PET, TSD and fMRI studies evaluating language lateralization, among other findings, have reported that language lateralization in the brain depends on age ([68, 100, 179, 193]; but see [87, 205]), personal handedness [119,

163, 193, 198, 202], family history of handedness [193] and pathology ([119]; but see [202]), but not on sex ([202, 205] and for a meta-analysis, see [184]).

fMRI studies of verbal and non-verbal memory processes especially, have revealed that the verbal task activated the left medial temporal lobe, whereas the non-verbal task activated the right medial temporal lobe [21]. Another fMRI study has observed left hemispheric lateralization for verbal working memory, most notably in frontal and parietal cortices, and RH lateralization for spatial working memory, seen in frontal and temporal lobes [147]. Furthermore, the appearance of the left-right hemispheric dissociation of verbal and spatial working memory by early adolescence, as well as age-related changes of brain activity during both verbal and spatial memory, have also been found [147].

Regarding the lateralization of non-verbal functions, fMRI studies have found RH dominance for spatial selective attention and target detection [52]. Two studies have observed age-related changes in lateralization of activation associated with visuospatial function. The first study found that the typical RH asymmetry of visual search functions increase in frontal and parietal regions between the ages of 8 and 20 [68]. The second study found that RH lateralization of visuospatial memory function not only continues to increase with age but is also stronger in males [87]. Another fMRI study has found that the parietal and frontal cortex of the RH and the LH play differential roles in mental arithmetic, as their functional non-equivalences have been modulated by task demands: the intraparietal and prefrontal activation was more important in the RH during the comparison task in the LH during the multiplication task and was intensely bilateral during the subtraction task [47]. A recent study using fTSD has shown again that the performance of multiplication operations preferentially activate the LH, but the performance of subtraction operations is not lateralized [49].

A systematic review of functional neuroimaging studies on lateralization of amygdala activation during emotion processing has observed a strong preponderance of left amygdala activation over right amygdala activation [15].

Data from behavioral studies of healthy subjects

Introduction to the research practices of tachistoscopic, dichotic and dihaptic tactile stimulus presentation techniques gave a new impetus for the study of functional differences between the cerebral hemispheres. These are behavioral methods, which use lateralized presentation (unilateral or bilateral) of auditory, visual and tactile stimuli, and are based on the functional division of sensory pathways transmitting sensory information to the hemispheres [117]. The fact that they are non-invasive procedures enabling the study of not only brain-damaged patients but also neurologically healthy individuals makes them preferred research techniques.

The classical method to determine language laterality in hospital conditions is the Wada test – highly invasive and in practice not applicable to healthy subjects. The dichotic listening procedure is the most widely used non-invasive alternative for assessing the language dominant hemisphere among all behavioral methods because of its easy applicability and proven reliability [57, 102, 201]. In this task, two different verbal stimuli are presented simultaneously to the left and right ear, such that each ear receives a different stimulus. The recall may be free or controlled [117].

An impressive amount of studies using dichotic paradigm have found that the majority of people demonstrate right-ear advantage (REA) for dichotic verbal perception (syllables, words or sentences), which indicates the LH dominance for language processing ([42, 57, 69, 98, 103, 125, 144, 215] and see [207] for a meta-analysis). Studies examining the effects of handedness, gender or age on the direction and magnitude of ear advantage have yielded inconsistent findings. The results range from lack of handedness [42, 98], gender [42] and age-related [29] differences to a higher frequency of REA with a stronger asymmetry among right-handers [201] and males ([207] for a meta-analysis and [98] for age-dependent sex-related differences) and an increase in the REA magnitude with increasing age [24, 98].

Also, it has been established that attentional factors play a significant role in the modulation of the REA in dichotic listening (see [161] for a review). A relatively recent observation, however, has evidenced that the top-down influences of attention affect the quantitative asymmetry of the REA and does not alter the qualitative asymmetry of the REA, which suggests that the presence/absence of a REA is a low-level cognitive phenomenon reflecting the LH dominance for language processing, while the magnitude of the REA depends also on cognitive factors, including attention processes [161].

In contrast, studies examining dichotic perception of non-verbal information such as emotions, speech intonation or musical stimuli ([42, 56, 103, 144] and see [207] for a meta-analysis) have found left-ear advantage, indicating RH dominance.

Similar results have been obtained in experiments using tachistoscopic paradigm: right-field/LH advantage in the perception of verbal stimuli: letters, syllables, words or numbers ([125, 150, 165, 170] and [207] for a meta-analysis), and left-field/RH advantage in the perception of non-verbal stimuli such as faces, shapes, images and spatial relations ([89, 170], and [207] for a meta-analysis).

Studies by dihaptic paradigm, although scarce, have also established that the identification of verbal stimuli (letters) is better when feeling with the right hand and the identification of non-verbal stimuli is better when doing it with the left hand [79, 158].

Genesis of the functional specialization of the human brain

How and why do the two cerebral hemispheres of the human brain undergo functional specialization both in phylogenenesis and ontogenesis? This long debated issue in psychology and brain-studying sciences still has no definite answer [22, 199].

With regard to the evolution of the human brain lateralization there are two main suggestions. According to the first one, which is chronologically older and, until recently, the dominant speculation, cerebral asymmetry is a unique and even a defining characteristic of the human species, which has evolved in the course of the evolutionary development of the human brain (for a review, see [22, 50, 51]).

According to the second and more recent speculation, which is becoming increasingly supported, cerebral asymmetry itself is not unique to the human species – left-right asymmetries of brain and behavior are a common feature that is shared with many vertebrate classes [50], which supports the possibility for an early common origin of lateralization in vertebrates [153, 199].

Whether the brain asymmetries in humans are unique or the differences between *Homo sapiens* and other apes are simply a matter of degree is a question that has continued to be discussed for more than a century [50]. Unusual and unique about humans, without any doubt, is that they exhibit the most robust and species-wide lateralization among all primates, especially for language and manual functions [72].

Various evolutionary explanations for this human-specific asymmetry have been proposed. A popular suggestion shared by authors like Annett [7], Crow [54] and McManus [134] is that the asymmetry of the human brain is a unique characteristic resulting from a certain genetic mutation at some point of evolution after the separation of the hominins from the other great apes (for details and a critical review, see [50]). Furthermore, it has even been assumed that this mutation has created *Homo sapiens* by establishing a new 'specific mate recognition system' – the language and other unique human features, such as theory of mind and susceptibility to psychosis [54].

Accumulation of evidences for a LH presentation of conspecific vocalization in a wide variety of mammalian species, and some non-mammalian vertebrate species (e.g. frogs) (for a review, see [153]), suggesting a phylogenetically early emergence of the left hemispheric specialization for vocal communication [36], challenges the view that lateralization of cognitive functions, including language, has emerged during human evolution, and supports the alternative hypothesis that LH dominance for language is due to the LH dominance for the perception of the temporal and spectral characteristics of species-typical communicative sounds or their production [36]. In other words, there is a hypothesis that left-right asymmetries of basic perceptual and motor functions that have appeared phylogenetically early may have underlaid the complex cognitive functions, some of which, like language, are unique to *Homo sapiens* and incorporated into their functional architecture [131].

Evidently, functional specialization of the brain is a manifestation of adaptation supported by the evolution that has allowed more efficient use of cortical resources and has contributed a clear benefit to the overall processing capacity of the human brain [93, 127, 199]. Most significantly, perhaps, the emergence of language is thought to provoke the lateralization of cortical functions and the specialization of the two cerebral hemispheres to an extent that is unique to humans. Furthermore, the emergence and improvement of the language have become prerequisites for the emergence of numerous new and more complex cognitive abilities, as the cerebral lateralization has allowed their development without the need for increasing cortical size [93, 128, 129].

Nowadays it becomes increasingly clear that development of cerebral lateralization in the human brain is driven by the complex interactions of genetic and non-genetic factors [50, 128, 176, 199].

Genetic theories of laterality have focused on human handedness and its relation to language lateralization. The most popular among the single-gene theories are the Right Shift Theory of Annett [6] and the Dextral/Chance Theory of McManus [133, 134]. Both postulate a shared genetic background for handedness and language lateralization. Annett proposed that in humans only, one gene with two alleles exists, one being dominant (RS+) and the other being recessive (RS–), which induces a shift to right-handedness and LH advantage for language and speech functions. This gene, called the "right shift factor", can be located in either maternal or paternal genes. In the later formulation of her model, Annett [6] proposed that the bias is cerebral rather than manual, so that it is more correctly, the right shift to be described as a left shift.

Annett's model provides a satisfactory account of atypical cerebral dominance by allowing the existence of naturally occurring aberrant brain organization and pathologically occurring aberrant brain organization. In naturally occurring aberrant brain organization, individual differences in brain laterality are associated with natural variation in this gene: the dominant allele selects for right-handedness (RS+), while the recessive allele (RS–) selects for both right- and left-handedness. Conversely, all the factors that cause abnormal early development (e.g. in subjects with cerebral palsy, ID, pathological left-handedness) can affect the expression of RS+ gene and thus provoke a pathologically aberrant brain organization, which would explain the higher incidence of atypical brain laterality and left-handedness among these populations, irrespective of the presence or absence of brain lesions in the areas specifically involved in the control of speech and dominant hand [6].

In the McManus theory [133, 134], similar to the Annett model, handedness depends on a two-allele gene, with a dextral (D) allele specifying right-handedness and a chance (C) allele leaving handedness to chance. All DD subjects develop right-handedness, 75 percent of CD subjects develop right-handedness and the remaining 25 percent develop left-handedness, while CC subjects have a 50:50 probability of being right- or left-handed.

Although single-gene models can provide good fit to phenotypic data, the fact that this putative gene has not yet been located impedes their widespread acceptance [50]. Also, recent genome-wide association studies of handedness exclude simple genetic models [10, 169]. Based on the meta-analysis of these studies, McManus et al. [135] estimated that at least forty loci, but possibly up to a hundred, are involved in determining handedness. Similar findings increase the acceptance of the multifactorial models as better suited than monogenic models to explain the development of handedness and language lateralization [152, 169].

Another popular model to account for biological mechanisms underlying cerebral lateralization is the Geschwind-Behan-Galaburda Theory which links it with prenatal testosterone exposure: foetal testosterone slows down the development of

LH language and handedness areas in the cortex and modifies cerebral lateralization, leading to less asymmetrical and even anomalous patterns of hemispheric organization [77, 78, 83].

Birth trauma [18], cultural influences [137] or social-interaction pressures [199] are among the environmental factors that have been proposed as playing a role in determination of handedness and brain asymmetry.

Over the past two to three decades, there have been huge advances in our understanding not only of the evolution of human lateralization but also of its ontogenetic development, especially language lateralization.

Apparently, lateralization of the function between the two hemispheres in humans is done gradually, mainly after birth and, according to most researchers, the deadline for the establishment of the mature pattern of the cerebral lateralization coincides with the final maturation (both structural and functional) of the specific human cortical areas [38, 50, 129, 195]. Since the maturation of cortical areas occur in sequence, with the phylogenetically older cortical areas that underlie the most basic functions, such as senses and movement, maturing first, the areas involved in spatial orientation and language following around the age of early adolescence and the areas with the most complex and integrative functions, such as integration of sensory information, reasoning and other executive functions maturing last, in late adolescence (for a review see [195]), it is most probable that the process of the age-associated maturation of cerebral lateralization also ends in late adolescence (for a review, see [5, 43]).

It is considered that the lateralization of the cortical functions is the final stage in shaping the mature pattern of structural and functional organization of the human cortex in the individual ontogenesis [38]. If, as suggested, the specialization of the cortical areas on the one hand and the specialization of the cerebral hemispheres on the other, is what makes the human brain a highly differentiated functional system [129], it is logical that any delay or disruption of these processes could provoke some kind of disturbance (varying in type and intensity) in the system's functioning.

At present, it is well-known that hemispheric lateralization is not a sustained, static phenomenon but undergoes changes under the influence of genetic and environmental factors throughout a lifespan [28]. These factors act through the mechanisms of neural plasticity – the property of the human brain to reorganize itself in response to environmental pressure, experience or injury [82]. Its basic mechanisms are neurogenesis, programmed cell death and activity-dependent synaptic plasticity [82].

It is well documented that lateralization of the brain function which evolves from childhood and adolescence to young adulthood most likely relates to both the natural brain structural maturation and cognitive maturation that take place during this period [68, 87, 100, 142]. Also, throughout adulthood and mostly throughout elderly age, processes related to aging and cortical decline cause changes of the functional hemispheric lateralization mainly in the direction of its reduction [43].

Besides these age-related changes, functional lateralization of the brain can also undergo plastic changes induced by long-term (vocational) training in cognitive skills or by brain injury. Studies of subjects with different occupations have evidenced obvious differences in the pattern of functional asymmetries (motor, sensory or cognitive) between professional musicians and non-musicians [138, 185], musicians and painters [92], highly qualified judo wrestlers and beginners [141], subjects with high ability in mathematics and subjects with high ability of pictorial art [11], proficient bi- and multilinguals and monolinguals [12], etc.

With regard to the plastic changes in brain lateralization following brain injury, it is well documented by neuroimaging studies (using PET or fMRI) that both early [146, 189] and late [146, 164] left lesions lead to rightward shifts in the asymmetry of language activations, which tend to be stronger as a consequence of early lesions in comparison to late lesions [146].

Undoubtedly, neuroplasticity is a vital process and is usually related to adaptation and benefits, both during normal development and throughout recovery after brain damage [82]. Sometimes, however, it can be maladaptive and associated with negative consequences [82]. For example, maladaptive plasticity has been described in early sensory (auditory or visual) deprivation, which resulted in an aberrant neural organization and permanent auditory and visual deficits, respectively. Another example includes the emergence of new onset epilepsy as a complication of cerebral trauma several months after the insult. Moreover, the suggestion that brain plasticity may define the manifestations of human disease has led to the assumption that neuroplasticity may also mediate the emergence of pathological symptomatology of neurodevelopmental disorders, such as autism, schizophrenia, and attention-deficit/hyperactivity disorder (ADHD) (for a review and details, see [82]). Gazzaniga [82] has hypothesized that "the processes of neural plasticity themselves can be normal, but may act upon an abnormal nervous system as a consequence of genetic or specific environmental factors. Alternatively, the mechanisms of plasticity themselves may be abnormal, potentially compounding the consequences of an abnormal substrate on the basis of a genetically determined 'starting point' or environmental insult" (p. 147). This draws attention to the possibility of improving intervention and overcoming pathological symptomatology by modulating neuroplasticity [82].

A general theoretical framework of the modern concept of functional specialization of the brain

The main postulates of the modern concept of functional specialization of the brain could be briefly summarized as follows:

1. The functional brain asymmetry is seen as different in character and unequal in importance with regard to participation of LH and RH in the realization of mental functions. The functional asymmetry of the two cerebral hemispheres is partial rather than global [28, 87, 113]. Three main types of hemispheric

asymmetries can be differentiated: motor (upper and lower limbs, etc.), sensory (auditory, visual, olfactory, etc.) and mental (perceptive, mnemonic, attentional, intellectual, etc.), as each one is subdivided into many partial subtypes [72, 113, 194]. Combinations of these types of asymmetries form numerous profiles of functional asymmetry [113].
2. Any concrete form of asymmetry is characterized by a certain size, and based on the quantitative indicators, we can talk about strong or weak asymmetry [7, 113].
3. The degree of brain lateralization in humans is subject to inter- and intra-individual differences [7, 97, 102, 104].
4. Hemispheric lateralization of function is associated with improved cognitive ability [7, 46, 86, 97].
5. The functional specialization of the cerebral hemispheres is a product of biological and social mechanisms [50, 153, 199].

Nowadays, the functional specialization of the brain is seen as a problem including two aspects: one is that of hemispheric asymmetries and the second is that of hemispheric interactions in various mental functions [38, 80, 82, 95, 101, 113].

Theoretical models of the mechanisms underlying perceptual asymmetry

Among the numerous attempts for explaining lateralized performance of various cognitive tasks, three theoretical models are the most popular [3]. They are designed mainly on the basis of data from studies of perceptive asymmetries using dichotic listening or tachistoscopic paradigms.

The first model considers the functional differences between the LH and RH in the framework of the verbal/non-verbal dichotomy. According to this model, each hemisphere is specialized in different kinds of information processing, as the LH is more effective in perception and production of verbal stimuli and the RH is specialized in processing non-verbal, visual spatial and musical stimuli. Hemispheric specialization is absolute. That is, for a given task only one hemisphere is competent, which imposes transcallosal transfer of information [186]. Therefore, the differences between the visual fields/auditory channels reflect the "costs" of interhemispheric transfer to the dominant hemisphere, if the stimuli have been presented to the subdominant hemisphere. These costs may include the time delay and the degradation effects on the stimuli due to the transcallosal information transfer [114, 145, 218].

This model is based on the Kimura's sensorimotor theory of language lateralization [115] (see [117] for a recent update) and represents the first attempt to account for the hemispheric asymmetries in the performance of lateralized tasks by bottom-up stimulus-driven effects on auditory language laterality [3, 102]. The model is well supported by studies using various research methods (for a review, see [102, 104]).

The second theoretical model is based on the holistic/analytical dichotomy as the functional differences between the cerebral hemispheres are explained with the differences in their information processing strategies: RH is more efficient in the global or holistic processing and LH is more efficient in the local or analytic processing; RH carries out the immediate perception of the whole (gestalt perception) and the individualized identification of the objects, and is more effective in the synthesis of the information, while LH carries out the analysis of information, classifications of features of objects and their categorical recognition [37, 94]. It is assumed that LH is involved in sequential information processing and RH is involved in simultaneous information processing, and that the opposite principles of information processing used by the hemispheres are the cause of their unequal participation in the different mental functions, since the latter requires unequal involvement of analytical and synthetic processes. According to this model, hemispheric specialization is relative, not absolute, that is each kind of information can be processed by both hemispheres but with a different degree of accuracy. Therefore, performance asymmetries in lateralized studies may be due to the hemispheric differences in processing efficiency. For example, if verbal stimuli are presented in the right field or right ear, they will be processed by the highly effective LH, but if they are presented in the left field or left ear, they will be processed more slowly and less precisely by the less effective RH (for details, see [3, 40]).

This model has been described in the framework of analytic-synthetic theory of language lateralization, proposed by Levy [127]. It has received inconsistent empirical support [30, 94, 167].

Theoretical models described above are an illustration of structural approach in neuropsychology. With slight differences, both are based on the assumption that asymmetries in visual/auditory fields during perception of verbal/non-verbal stimuli are the result of fixed structural differences in the pathways connecting the processing centres in the cerebral hemispheres with the left and right visual/auditory fields, respectively (for a review, see [104, 117]).

The third model, known as the attentional model, has been developed by Kinsbourne [118] (see [99] for a recent update of the theory). In this model, asymmetrical perception is attributed to a dynamic imbalance in the activation of the two hemispheres. Asymmetries in the performances of lateralized perceptual tasks are explained with an attentional bias to the corresponding hemispace, due to the activation of the hemisphere primarily involved in the processing of submitted information. At rest, the hemispheres are in a state of reciprocal inhibitory balance, which results in equal distribution of attention between the left and right hemispaces. However, when one hemisphere is activated by an act or an expectation of processing certain classes of stimuli, attentional resources will subsequently be deployed to the contralateral hemispace. Therefore, hemispheric asymmetries in the performance of lateralized tasks in Kinsbourne's attentional model are attributed to top-down cognitive effects.

Although the attentional model of perceptual asymmetry has been supported by many studies (for literature review, see [104]), the reports of evidence that failed to support it indicate the uncertainty surrounding it [60, 150]. Recent studies clearly show that the attention processes have modulating effects on perceptual asymmetries without being identical to them [13, 71, 103, 161].

None of the models reviewed above can fully account for perceptual asymmetry observed in the performance of lateralized perceptual tasks. As Hiscock and Kinsbourne [99] point out, it is not excluded that the implementation of an integrated approach is the key to the explanation of a truly comprehensive model of perceptual asymmetry. Such an attempt has already been made with the recently proposed two-component model by Hugdahl and co-workers for accounting the REA in dichotic listening [102, 104, 161, 201, 215]. Trying to combine both the structural and the attentional explanations of REA and LH asymmetry for auditory language processing, the model postulates that the REA, or lack of it, in any experimental condition depends on the interaction between bottom-up, stimulus-driven and top-down, instruction-driven aspects of hemispheric asymmetry. Therefore, the interaction of perceptual factors (stimulus properties like sound intensity or frequency) with cognitive factors (attention bias) shapes asymmetry of auditory language information processing.

Theoretical models of the mechanisms of hemispheric interaction

Although equally important, the second aspect of the issue of the functional specialization of the brain concerning hemispheric interaction is much less studied, mostly due to the fact that for many years, data on the nature and mechanisms of hemispheric interactions has been drawn mainly from cases with congenital or acquired pathology of the corpus callosum or split-brain studies [64, 218].

Today, the study of interhemispheric communication relies not only on split-brain methodology but also on neuroimaging and recently developed dynamic, network-based analysis techniques, which enables the studying of dynamic changes in the brain's functional connectivity and the decoding of the interaction between the two hemispheres in both the damaged and the intact brain [64, 203].

Neuropsychological and neuroimaging studies of patients with damaged or total or partial resection of the corpus callosum [64, 70, 101, 139, 218], as well as of healthy subjects [70, 172], have shown that the corpus callosum displays a functional topographic organization and represents a differentiated system whose different sections perform strictly defined roles in the mechanisms of the hemispheric interactions. Since the corpus callosotomy blocks the interhemispheric transfer of information, studies of callosotomized patients provide insight into brain lateralization and interhemispheric interaction, enabling the evaluation of the independent functioning of the two hemispheres (for a review, see [80]). These studies have demonstrated that basic perceptual processes are a function which is duplicated between the hemispheres, with the RH being dominant in various perceptual functions, such as visuospatial and complex auditory processing, perceptual grouping, mirror image discrimination, episodic memory, part-whole relations, spatial relations, motion detection, mental rotation, spatial matching, reflexive joint attentional processes and others, and the LH being specialized in intelligence, hypothesis formation, semantic memory and many aspects of speech and language (for reviews, see [80, 81, 203]).

It is determined that corpus callosum is especially important for lateralized processes that require interhemispheric cooperation, as evidenced by the absolute inability to perform tasks such as combining sensory information entering the RH with the LH localized speech processes in the case of the complete removal of the corpus callosum [203]. It is considered that lateralization of specialized areas can require interhemispheric transfer and cooperation, and as evidenced by studies in healthy subjects, interhemispheric transfer and cooperation increases along with task complexity and task difficulty (for a review, see [212, 213]).

A widely shared view is that there are both costs and benefits of the interhemispheric interaction [212]. The costs are related to greater time and energy required for the interhemispheric transfer and degradation effects on the stimuli due to the transcallosal information transfer. The benefits of interhemispheric interaction refer to increasing efficiency of the performance of complex tasks by allowing the LH and the RH to use their processing resources as needed [212]. Therefore, interaction of the cerebral hemispheres becomes beneficial when the processing demands overload the resources of one hemisphere and bilateral processing outweighs the costs of transfer – a view supported by fMRI studies that have found a greater bilateral activity in complex tasks versus simple tasks and thus a reduction in asymmetry [213], and greater interhemispheric coordination when lexical information is introduced to the RH and must subsequently be transferred to the LH for language processing than when it is directly introduced to the language-dominant LH [64]. Furthermore, based on these findings, it is suggested that selection of the most efficient processing mode depends on the online processing demands posed by the task rather than arising from previous experience with performing this kind of task, which, in turn, would allow for efficient processing even of unfamiliar or less familiar tasks [213].

All these findings evidence that the corpus callosum is not just a channel for the automatic exchange of information between the two hemispheres but rather allows for dynamic and flexible interhemispheric interactions, necessary for more-efficient and cost-effective stimulus processing [64, 203, 214].

Mohr et al. [143] have reviewed the hypothesized possibilities to account for hemispheric interaction in the cognitive processing in the intact brain:

- Both hemispheres can operate independently so that processing in the intact brain is comparable to that in the split brain.
- The two cerebral hemispheres are independent processors that mutually inhibit. This might explain why simultaneous processing in both hemispheres

sometimes leads to delays in responses and to disruption of performances in comparison to the condition when only one hemisphere processes.
- The LH and the RH cooperate and if both have access to the same stimulus information, the performance will improve in comparison to the condition when only one hemisphere processes all information by itself. If this is the case, either both hemispheres process the same information and this redundancy leads to improvement of the performance or the hemispheres divide the processing thus reducing their workload which might be especially beneficial for complex tasks requiring relatively large numbers of computations.
- The cerebral hemispheres are not only independent, mutually inhibited and collaborative but also interactive. Hemispheric interactions have both the inhibitory and facilitatory aspects, which is a complex way to exchange information and control over the results.

As Mohr et al. [143] have suggested, these possibilities reflect different processing modes and most probably, not all are possible patterns of hemispheric interactions in the intact brain during information processing. Also, it is assumed that the choice of the precise mode of hemispheric interaction in the processing of each task will depend on a number of factors, such as the type of stimulus materials or task specifics [101, 143, 213].

Confirming this suggestion, findings of a recent study have challenged our fundamental understanding of how the LH and RH of the human brain interact by establishing that the two hemispheres have qualitatively different biases in how they dynamically interact with one another. These biases are associated with their functional specialization, such as LH regions that are specialized in processing language and motor functions are biased to interact more strongly within the same hemisphere and RH regions that are specialized in visuospatial and attentional processes interact more strongly with both hemispheres [86].

Contemporary models of language organization

Briefly, the classical models of cortical language organization, which really represent a family of models, referred to as the "Broca-Wernicke-Lichtheim-Geschwind Model", or simply the "Wernicke-Lichtheim Model" [45, 196], postulate that speech and language functions are associated with two separate centres – Broca's area located in the inferior frontal gyrus and Wernicke's area located in the superior temporal gyrus and the connections between them (arcuate fasciculus), with the Wernicke's area being crucial to language comprehension and Broca's area crucial to language expression [196].

Advancement in the field of language neurobiology, neurophysiology and neuropsychology has provided a more detailed description of the functional neuroanatomy of language and new insights into the underlying mechanisms of the different aspects of speech and language processing. This has led to the shaping of modern network-based models of language processing composed of parallel and interconnected streams involving both cortical and subcortical areas [45].

Two recent models of cortical language organization, often referred to as "Dual Stream Model of Language" [45], have been proposed: the model of Hickok and Poeppel [96] and the model of Rauschecker and Scott [166].

Both models are based on the modern theories of dual streams of auditory processing of language information [96, 166], and although they have some differences, they also share many key features. According to the main postulates of the Dual Stream Model, auditory processing of language information is performed in "dorsal" and "ventral" pathways, which mediate phonological and semantic processing, respectively. Phonological processing starts with spectro-temporal and phonological analysis of speech sounds carried out by the Wernicke's area and continues with the sensorimotor integration by mapping phonological information onto articulatory motor representations. The dorsal pathway encompasses the posterior frontal lobe and the Sylvian parietotemporal region, and is likely left-dominant.

The ventral pathway runs from the anterior and middle temporal lobe to the basal occipitotemporal cortex with anterior connections and carries out the speech recognition and the representation of lexical concepts. Dorsal stream for sensorimotor integration is mostly dominant while ventral stream for speech comprehension is bilateral.

Chang et al. [45] have highlighted three important differences between the two models: while the model of Hickok and Poeppel [96] claims that speech perception is bilaterally processed, the model of Rauschecker and Scott [166] argues that it is processed only in the language-dominant hemisphere; models differ in the localization of intermediate nodes in the dorsal stream; also, both models claim that the Sylvian parietotemporal region is important for auditory sensorimotor integration, but the model of Rauschecker and Scott argues that this region is also engaged in processing of auditory spatial information.

The relation of language lateralization and handedness

A widely shared view since the studying of hemispheric specialization of the human brain began is that handedness and hemispheric specialization for language are interrelated [7, 54, 134].

Ocklenburg et al. [152] have reviewed the classic and contemporary conceptualizations about phylo- and ontogenesis of language lateralization and its relation to handedness, and have discussed their strengths and weaknesses.

Regarding the phylogenetic development, the widely supported view today is that limb preferences represent a common characteristic in all vertebrates, and although they are far less expressed in animals, they could be the evolutionary predecessor of human handedness [152].

Regarding the evolution of language lateralization, there are two major views: one is that lateralization of conspecific vocalization seen in some animals could be the evolutionary predecessor of human language. Thus, "language lateralization in humans may have resulted from an inherited dominance of the left hemisphere for those aspects of human language that are similar to the sensory or motor properties of conspecific vocalization in animals" [152, p. 193]. It is important to note that this hypothesis predicts factors that might be involved in the evolution of human language lateralization, but not handedness, therefore the development of the two traits most probably depend on different ontogenetic factors.

According to the other major view regarding the phylogenetic development of language lateralization, gestural communication in primates could be the predecessor of language lateralization. The initial form of language has been based on a gestural system of communication with dominance of the right hand that has provided the neural base for vocal articulation [51]. Therefore, this hypothesis predicts that handedness and language lateralization are influenced by some common ontogenetic factors, but nevertheless are largely independent of each other [152].

With regard to ontogenetic development of manual preference and language lateralization, the classic single-gene models assume that the two traits are monogenic and are determined by the same single gene [6, 7, 133, 134]. Current empirical evidence, however, which indicates multiple non-identical genetic influence factors for both traits [135, 151], as well as growing evidence for several different non-genetic factors that influence the ontogenesis on both traits [176], increase the acknowledgement for the multifactorial models as better suited than monogenic models to explain the development of handedness and language lateralization [152, 169].

Summarizing the results from the analyses of a number of recent studies that indicate a medium correlation between the two traits, some non-shared genetic influences and shared candidate genes (e.g. genes involved in the formation of the corpus callosum or myelin), Ocklenburg and co-workers conclude that the only model that could correctly describe the complex ontogenetic relationship between handedness and language lateralization is "a partial pleiotropy model that assumes several shared and several unique influence factors provides the best fit with current empirical evidence" [152, p. 196].

Although brief, the above-mentioned overview of contemporary theoretical perspectives concerning the issue of functional specialization of the human brain and their empirical basis provides insight into the nature and multifactorial determination of this complex phenomenon which is deep-rooted in the evolution of vertebrate species.

Currently, it is considered that the complex interactions of multiple genetic and non-genetic influence factors contribute to the development and changes of cerebral lateralization across the lifespan.

Handedness is supposed to be the main biological factor underlying individual differences in cerebral lateralization, especially language lateralization. Although the connection between hand preference and language lateralization is far from being fully understood, there is growing evidence that the association between the two traits derives from a longstanding evolutionary origin and is determined by the interactions of many genetic and environmental influence factors.

Evidently, functional hemispheric asymmetry and interaction during cognitive processing represent a complex function depending on many variables such as interhemispheric differences in the level of activation, structural differences in the pathways linking the periphery with the processing networks in LH and RH, task specifics, degree of participation of memory processes, distribution of attention between the right and left hemispace, and individual characteristics of the subjects. Therefore, in evaluating the patterns of the lateralization of brain functions, perceptual or expressive, verbal, spatial or musical, it should always be taken into account that the effect of hemispheric specialization is not exempted from the effects of each of the above variables, and this undoubtedly makes their study a difficult and delicate task.

Cerebral specialization is a fundamental principle in the human brain function and a marker of successful development, and it is entirely possible that the formation of an aberrant pattern of hemispheric asymmetry and interaction is related to some form of cognitive dysfunction. While currently an indisputably established fact is that LH and RH lesions lead to specific disorders of higher cortical functions, the assumption that the development of atypical patterns of hemispheric lateralization could become a cause of various forms of mental pathology is still under discussion and the target of comprehensive studies.

References and further reading

1 Adolph, D., von Glischinski, M., Wannemüller, A. & Margraf, J. (2017). The influence of frontal alpha-asymmetries on the treatment of approach- and withdrawal-related stimuli – A multichannel psychophysiology study. *Psychophysiology, 54*(9), 1295–1310.
2 Ahern, G. & Schwartz, G. (1985). Differential lateralization for positive and negative emotion in the human brain: EEG spectral analysis. *Neuropsychologia, 23*(6), 745–756.
3 Allen, M. (1983). Models of hemispheric specialization. *Psychol. Bull., 93*(1), 73–104.
4 Amunts, K., Schleicher, A., Burgel, U., Mohlberg, H., Uylings, H. B. & Zilles, K. (1999). Broca's region revisited: Cytoarchitecture and intersubject variability. *J. Com. Neurol., 412*, 319–341.
5 Andonova, Y. (2015). *Ontogenetic dynamics of the lateralization of the attention in school age: Effects on academic success and intelligence.* PhD thesis. Blagoevgrad, Bulgaria: South-West University "Neofit Rilski" Publishing House.
6 Annett, M. (1985). *Left, right hand and brain: The right shift theory.* London: Erlbaum Associate.
7 Annett, M. (2002). *Handedness and brain asymmetry: The right shift theory.* Hove, UK: Psychology Press.
8 Annett, M. & Alexander, M. (1996). Atypical cerebral dominance: Predictions and tests of the right shift theory. *Neuropsychologia, 34*(12), 1215–1227.
9 Ardila, A., Bernal, B. & Rosselli, M. (2016). How localized are brain areas? A review of Brodmann areas of involvement in oral language. *Arch. Clin. Neuropsychol., 31*(1), 112–122.
10 Armour, J. A. L., Davison, A. & McManus, I. C. (2014). Genome-wide association study of handedness excludes simple genetic models. *Heredity (Edinb), 112*(3), 221–225.

11 Asenova, I. (2011). Professional training and language lateralization: A comparative study of mathematicians and painters [in Russian]. *Voprosy psikhologii, 3,* 113–120.
12 Asenova, I. (2011). A comparative dichotic listening study of verbal perception in subjects with different levels of knowledge of a foreign language [in Bulgarian]. In S. Djonev & P. Dimitrov (Eds.), *Proceedings of the VI National Congress of Psychology* (pp. 12–17). Sofia, Bulgaria: Sofia University "St. Kliment Ohridski" Publishing House.
13 Atchley, R. & Atchley, P. (1998). Hemispheric specialization in the detection of subjective objects. *Neuropsychologia, 36*(12), 1373–1386.
14 Auzou, P., Eustache, F., Etevenon, P., Platel, H., Rioux, P., Lambert, J. . . . Baron, J. C. (1995). Topographic EEG activations during timbre and pitch discrimination tasks using musical sounds. *Neuropsychologia, 33*(1), 25–37.
15 Baas, D., Aleman, A. & Kahan, R. S. (2004). Lateralization of amygdala activation: A systematic review of functional neuroimaging studies. *Brain Res. Rev., 45*(2), 96–103.
16 Badzakova-Trajkov, G., Corballis, M. C. & Häberling, I. S. (2015). Complementarity or independence of hemispheric specializations? A brief review. *Neuropsychologia, 93* (Pt B), 386–393.
17 Badzakova-Trajkov, G., Häberling, I. S. & Corballis, M. C. (2010). Cerebral asymmetries in monozygotic twins: An fMRI study. *Neuropsychologia, 48*(10), 3086–3093.
18 Bakan, P. (1971). Handedness and birth order. *Nature, 229*(5281), 195.
19 Baldo, J. V., Paulraj, S. R., Curran, B. C. & Dronkers, N. F. (2015). Impaired reasoning and problem-solving in individuals with language impairment due to aphasia or language delay. *Front Psychol., 6,* 1523.
20 Banich, M. (1998). The missing link: The role of interhemispheric interaction in attentional processing. *Brain Cogn., 36*(2), 128–157.
21 Banks, S. J., Sziklas, V., Sodums, D. & Jones-Gotman, M. (2012). FMRI of verbal and nonverbal memory processes in healthy and epileptogenic medial temporal lobes. *Epil. Behav., 25*(1), 42–49.
22 Barrett, C. (2013). A hierarchical model of the evolution of human brain specializations. In G. F. Striedter, J. C. Avise & F. J. Ayala (Eds.), *In the Light of Evolution. Volume VI: Brain and Behavior* (pp. 313–333). Washington, D.C.: National Academy of Sciences.
23 Bates, E., Wilson, S. M., Saygin, A. P., Dick, F., Sereno, M. I., Knight, R. T. & Dronkers, N. F. (2003). Voxel-based lesion-symptom mapping. *Nat. Neurosci., 6,* 448–450.
24 Bellis, T. J. & Wilber, L. A. (2001). Effects of aging and gender on interhemispheric function. *JSLHR, 44*(2), 246–263.
25 Bhatnagar, S., Mandybur, G., Buckingham, H. & Andy, O. (2000). Language representation in the human brain: Evidence from cortical mapping. *Brain Lang., 74*(2), 238–259.
26 Biduła, S. P. & Kroliczak, G. (2015). Structural asymmetry of the insula is linked to the lateralization of gesture and language. *Eur J Neurosci., 41*(11), 1438–1447.
27 Bishop, D. V. M. (1990). *Handedness and developmental disorder.* Oxford, UK: Blackwell.
28 Bishop, D. V. M. (2013). Cerebral asymmetry and language development: Cause, correlate or consequence? *Science, 340*(6138), 1230531.
29 Bissell, J. C. & Clark, F. (1984). Dichotic listening performance in normal children and adults. *Am. J. Occup. Ther., 38*(3), 176–183.
30 Blanca, M. J. & López-Montiel, G. (2009). Hemispheric differences for global and local processing: Effect of stimulus size and sparsity. *Span. J. Psychol., 12*(1), 21–31.

31 Blonder, L., Bowers, D. & Heilman, K. (1991). The role of the right hemisphere in emotional communication. *Brain, 114* (Pt 3), 1115–1127.
32 Bode, S. & Curtiss, S. (2000). Language after hemispherectomy. *Brain Cogn., 43*(1–3), 135–138.
33 Boisson, D. & Luaute, J. (2004). Somatoparaphrenia. *Ann. Med. Psychol., 162*(1), 55–59.
34 Borod, J. C., Rorie, K. D., Haywood, C. S., Andelman, F., Obler, L. K., Welkowitz, J. ... Tweedy, J. R. (1996). Hemispheric specialization for discourse reports of emotional experience: Relationships to demographic, neurological and perceptual variables. *Neuropsychologia, 34*(5), 351–359.
35 Bourne, V. J. (2008). Examining the relationship between degree of handedness and degree of cerebral lateralization for processing facial emotion. *Neuropsychology, 22*(3), 350–356.
36 Böye, M., Güntürkün, O. & Vauclair, J. (2005). Right ear advantage for conspecific calls in adults and subadults, but not infants, California sea lions (*Zalophus californianus*): Hemispheric specialization for communication? *Eur. J. Neurosci., 21*(6), 1727–1732.
37 Bradshaw, J. & Nettleton, N. (1983). *Human cerebral asymmetry*. Englewood Cliffs, NJ: Prentice-Hall.
38 Bragina, N. N. & Dobrohotova, T. A. (1981). *Human functional asymmetry* [in Russian]. Moscow, Russia: Meditsina.
39 Bryden, M. (1986). Dichotic listening performance, cognitive ability, and erebral organization. *Can. J. Psychol., 40*(4), 445–456.
40 Bryden, M., Ley, R. & Sugarman, J. (1982). A left ear advantage for identifying emotional quality of tonal sequences. *Neuropsychologia, 20*(1), 83–87.
41 Bulla-Hellwig, M., Vollmer, J., Götzen, A., Skreczek, W. & Hartje, W. (1996). Hemispheric asymmetry of arterial blood flow velocity changes during verbal and visiospatial tasks. *Neuropsychologia, 34*(10), 987–991.
42 Bulman-Fleming, M. & Bryden, M. (1994). Simultaneous verbal and affective laterality effects. *Neuropsychologia, 32*(7), 787–797.
43 Cabeza, R. (2002). Hemispheric asymmetry reduction in older adults: The HAROLD Model. *Psychol. Aging, 17*(1), 85–100.
44 Cantello, R., Gaanelli, M., Bettucci, D., Civardi, C., De Angelis, M. & Mutani, R. (1991). Parkinson's disease rigidity: Magnetic motor evoked potentials in a small hand muscle. *Neurology, 41*(9), 1449–1456.
45 Chang, E. F., Raygor, K. P. & Berger, M. S. (2015). Contemporary model of language organization: An overview for neurosurgeons. *J. Neurosurg., 122*(2), 250–261.
46 Chiarello, C., Welcome, S. E., Halderman, L. K. & Leonard, C. M. (2009). Does degree of asymmetry relate to performance? An investigation of word recognition and reading in consistent and mixed handers. *Brain Cogn., 69*(3), 521–530.
47 Chochon, F. & Cohen, L. (1999). Differential contribution of the left and right inferior parietal lobules to number processing. *J. Cogn. Neurosci., 11*(6), 617–622.
48 Coan, J. A. & Allen, J. J. B. (2004). Frontal EEG asymmetry as a moderator and mediator of emotion. *Biol. Psychol., 67*(1–2), 7–49.
49 Connaughton, V. M., Amiruddin, A., Clunies-Ross, K. L., French, N. & Fox, A. M. (2017). Assessment of hemispheric specialization for the processing of arithmetic skills in adults: A functional transcranial Doppler ultrasonography (fTCD) study. *J. Neurosci. Methods, 283*, 33–41.
50 Corballis, M. C. (2009). The evolution and genetics of cerebral asymmetry. *Philos. Trans. R. Soc. Lond. B Biol. Sci., 361*, 867–879.
51 Corballis, P., Funnell, M. & Gazzaniga, M. (2000). An evolutionary perspective on hemispheric asymmetries. *Brain Cogn., 43*(1–3), 112–117.

52 Corbetta, M., Kincade, J. M., Ollinger, J. M., McAvoy, M. P. & Shulman, G. (2000). Voluntary orientation is dissociated from target detection in the human posterior parietal cortex. *Nat. Neurosci.*, *3*(3), 292–297.
53 Côté, H., Payer, M., Giroux, F. & Joanette, Y. (2007). Towards a description of clinical communication impairment profiles following right-hemisphere damage. *Aphasiology*, *21*(6,7,8), 739–749.
54 Crow, T. J. (2002). Sexual selection, timing, and an X–Y homologous gene: Did *Homo sapiens* speciate on the Y chromosome? In T. J. Crow (Ed.), *The speciation of modern Homo sapiens* (pp. 197–216). Oxford, UK: Oxford University Press.
55 Damasio, H., Trane, D., Grabowski, T., Adolphs, R. & Damasio, A. (2004). Neural systems behind word and concept retrieval. *Cognition*, *92*(1–2), 179–229.
56 Davidson, R. (1993). Cerebral asymmetry and emotion: Conceptual and methodological conundrums. *Cogn. Emotion*, *7*(1), 115–138.
57 Davidson, R. J. & Hugdahl, K. (1996). Baseline asymmetries in brain electrical activity predict dichotic listening performance. *Neuropsychology*, *10*(2), 241–246.
58 Davidson, R. & Schaffer, C. (1983). Affect and disorders of affect: Behavioural and electrophysiological studies. In P. Flor-Henery & J. Gruzelier (Eds.), *Laterality and psychopathology* (pp. 249–268). Amsterdam, The Netherlands: Elsevier Science.
59 De Lacoste, M., Horvath, D. & Woodward, D. (1991). Possible sex difference in the developing human fetal brain. *J. Clin. Exp. Neuropsychol.*, *13*(6), 831–846.
60 Demakis, G. J., Harrison, D. W. & Campen, M. (1993). A test of Kinsbourne's selective activation model. *Int. J. Neurosci.*, *72*(3–4), 201–207.
61 Demonet, J. & Puel, M. (1994). Aphasie et correlate cerebraux des functions linguistiques. In X. Seron & M. Jeannerod (Eds.), *Neuropsychologie humaine* (pp. 336–359). Liege, Belgium: Mardaga.
62 De Renzi, E., Perani, D., Carlesimo, G., Silveri, M. & Fazio, F. (1994). Prosopagnosia can be associated with damage confined to the right hemisphere – An MRI and PET study and a review of the literature. *Neuropsychologia*, *32*(8), 893–902.
63 Dingman, S. (1996). Differences between Caucasians and American Indians on the cognitive laterality battery. *Neuropsychologia*, *34*(7), 647–660.
64 Doron, K. W., Bassett, D. S. & Gazzaniga, M. S. (2012). Dynamic network structure of interhemispheric coordination. *Proc. Natl. Acad. Sci. USA*, *109*(46), 18661–18668.
65 Dorsaint-Pierre, R., Penhune, V. B., Watkins, K. E., Neelin, P., Lerch, J. P., Bouffard, M. & Zatome, R. J. (2006). Asymmetries of the planum temporale and Heschl's gyrus: relationship to language lateralization. *Brain*, *129*(Pt 5), 1164–1176.
66 Dubois, J., Hertz-Pannier, L., Cachia, A., Mangin, J. F., Le Bihan, D. & Dehaene-Lambertz, G. (2009). Structural asymmetries in the infant language and sensori-motor networks. *Cereb. Cortex*, *19*(2), 414–423.
67 Duecker, F., Formisano, E. & Sack, A. (2013). Hemispheric differences in the voluntary control of spatial attention: Direct evidence for a right-hemispheric dominance within frontal cortex. *J. Cogn. Neurosci.*, *25*(8), 1332–1342.
68 Everts, R., Lidzba, K., Wilke, M., Kiefer, C., Mordasini, M., Schroth, G. . . . Steinlin, M. (2009). Strengthening the laterality of verbal and visuospatial functions during childhood and adolescence. *Hum. Brain Mapp.*, *30*(2), 473–483.
69 Eichele, T., Nordby, H., Rimol, L. M. & Hugdahl, K. (2005). Asymmetry of evoked potential latency to speech sounds predicts ear gain in dichotic listening. *Cogn. Brain Res.*, *24*, 405–412.
70 Fabri, M., Pierpaoli, C., Barbaresi, P. & Polonara, G. (2014). Functional topography of the corpus callosum investigated by DTI and fMRI. *World J. Radiol.*, *6*(12), 895–906.

71 Fink, G., Marshall, J., Halligan, P. & Dolan, R. (1999). Hemispheric asymmetries in global/local processing are modulated by perceptual salience. *Neuropsychologia, 37*(1), 31–40.
72 Fitch, W. F. & Braccini, S. N. (2013). Primate laterality and the biology and evolution of human handedness: A review and synthesis. *Ann. N. Y. Acad. Sci., 1288*, 70–85.
73 Foundas, A. L., Corey, D. M., Hurley, M. M. & Heilman, K. M. (2006). Verbal dichotic listening in right and left-handed adults: Laterality effects of directed attention. *Cortex, 42*(1), 79–86.
74 Foundas, A. L., Faulhaber, J. R., Kulynych, J. J., Browning, C. A. & Weinberger, D. R. (1999). Hemispheric and sex-linked differences in Sylvian fissure morphology: A quantitative approach using volumetric magnetic resonance imaging. *Neuropsychiatry Neuropsychol. Behav. Neurol., 12*(1), 1–10.
75 Foundas, A. L., Leonard, C. M. & Heilman, K. M. (1995). Morphologic cerebral asymmetries and handedness. The pars triangularis and planum temporale. *Arch Neurol., 52*(5), 501–508.
76 Funnell, M., Corballis, P. & Gazzaniga, M. (1999). A deficit in perceptual matching in the left hemisphere of a collosotomy patient. *Neuropsychologia, 37*(10), 1143–1154.
77 Galaburda, A., Corsiglia, J., Rosen, G. & Fherman, G. (1987). Planum temporale asymmetry, reappraisal since Geshwind and Levitsky. *Neuropsychologia, 25*(6), 853–868.
78 Galaburda, A. & Habib, M. (1987). *Cerebral dominance: Biological associations and pathology (discussions in neurosciences)*. Geneva, Switzerland: Foundation FESN.
79 Gautt-Gentry, C. & White, H. (1994). Laterality effects in Cherokee and Anglo children. *J. Gen. Psychol., 155*(1), 123–131.
80 Gazzaniga, M. S. (2000). Cerebral specialization and interhemispheric communication: Does the corpus callosum enable the human condition? *Brain, 123*(Pt 7), 1293–1326.
81 Gazzaniga, M. S. (2005). Forty-five years of split-brain research and still going strong. *Nat. Rev. Neurosci., 6*(8), 653–659.
82 Gazzaniga, M. S. (2009). *The cognitive neurosciences.* (4th ed.). Cambridge, MA: MIT Press.
83 Geschwind, N. & Behan, P. O. (1982). Left-handedness: Association with immune disease, migraine, and developmental learning disorder. *Proc. Natl. Acad. Sci. USA, 79*(16), 5097–5100.
84 Gläscher, J., Tranel, D., Paul, L. K., Rudrauf, D., Rorden, C., Hornaday, A., ... Adolphs, R. (2009). Lesion mapping of cognitive abilities linked to intelligence. *Neuron, 61*(5), 681–691.
85 Good, C. D., Johnsrude, I., Ashburner, J., Henson, R. N., Friston, K. J. & Frackowiak, R. S. (2001). Cerebral asymmetry and the effects of sex and handedness on brain structure: A voxel-based morphometric analysis of 465 normal adult human brains. *Neuroimage, 14*(3), 685–700.
86 Gotts, S., Jo, H. J., Wallace, G. L., Saad, Z. S., Cox, R. V. & Martina, A. (2013). Two distinct forms of functional lateralization in the human brain. *Proc. Natl. Acad. Sci. USA, 110*(36), 3435–3444.
87 Groen, M. A., Whitehouse, A. J. O., Badcock, N. & Bishop, D. V. M. (2012). Does cerebral lateralization develop? A study using functional transcranial Doppler ultrasound assessing lateralization for language production and visuospatial memory. *Brain Behav., 2*(3), 256–269.
88 Guadalupe, T., Mathias, S. R., vanErp, T. G. M., Whelan, C. D., Zwiers, M. P., Abe, Y. . . . Francks, C. (2016). Human subcortical brain asymmetries in 15,847 people worldwide reveal effects of age and sex. *Brain Imaging Behav.*, 1–18. Advance online publication.

89 Guseva, M. V., Dodonova, N. A., Zal'tsman, A. G. & Meyerson, Y. M. (1987). Functional hemispheric asymmetry in the classification of nonverbal images [in Russian]. *Fiziol Cheloveka*, *13*(2), 179–184.

90 Habib, M. & Galaburda, A. (1994). Fondements neuroanatomiques et neurobiologiques du langage. In X. Seron & M. Jeannerod (Eds.), *Neuropsychologie humaine* (pp. 320–335). Liege, Belgium: Mardaga.

91 Hartje, W., Ringelstein, B., Kistinger, B., Fabianek, D. & Willmes, K. (1994). Transcranial Doppler ultrasonic assessment of middle cerebral artery blood flow velocity changes during verbal and visiospatial cognitive tasks. *Neuropsychologia*, *32*(12), 1443–1452.

92 Hassler, M. (1990). Functional cerebral asymmetries and cognitive abilities in musicians, painters, and controls. *Brain Cogn.*, *13*(1), 1–17.

93 Hellige, L. (1993). *Hemispheric asymmetry*. Cambridge, MA: Harvard University Press.

94 Hellige, J. B. (1996). Hemispheric asymmetry for visual information processing. *Acta. Neurobiol. Exp. (Wars)*, *56*(1), 485–497.

95 Herve, P. Y., Zago, L., Petit, L., Mazoyer, B. & Tzourio-Mazoyer, N. (2013). Revisiting human hemispheric specialization with neuroimaging. *Trends Cogn. Sci.*, *17*(2), 69–80.

96 Hickok, G. & Poeppel, D. (2004). Dorsal and ventral streams: A framework for understanding aspects of the functional anatomy of language. *Cognition*, *92*(1–2), 67–99.

97 Hirnstein, M., Hugdahl, K. & Hausmann, M. (2014). How brain asymmetry relates to performance – A large-scale dichotic listening study. *Front Psychol.*, *4*, 997.

98 Hirnstein, M., Westerhausen, R., Korsnes, M. S. & Hugdahl, K. (2013). Sex differences in language asymmetry are age-dependent and small: A large-scale, consonant-vowel dichotic listening study with behavioral and fMRI data. *Cortex*, *49*(7), 1910–1921.

99 Hiscock, M. & Kinsbourne, M. (2011). Attention and the right-ear advantage: What is the connection? *Brain Cogn.*, *76*(2), 263–275.

100 Holland, S. K., Vannest, J., Mecoli, M., Jacola, L. M., Tillema, J.-M., Karunanayaka, P. R. . . . Byars, A. W. (2007). Functional MRI of language lateralization during development in children. *Int. J. Audiol.*, *46*(9), 533–551.

101 Hoptman, M. & Davidson, R. J. (1994). How and why do the two cerebral hemispheres interact? *Psychol. Bull.*, *16*(2), 195–219.

102 Hugdahl, K. (2000). What can be learned about brain function from dichotic-listening? *Revista Espanola De Neuropsichologia*, *2*(3), 62–84.

103 Hugdahl, K., Bronnick, K., Kyllingsbaek, S., Law, I., Gade, A. & Paulson, O. B. (1999). Brain activation during dichotic presentations of consonant-vowel and musical instrumental stimuli: A ^{15}O- PET study. *Neuropsychologia*, *37*(4), 431–440.

104 Hugdahl, K. & Westerhausen, R. (2016). Speech processing asymmetry revealed by dichotic listening and functional brain imaging. *Neuropsychologia*, *93*(Pt B), 466–481.

105 Ingalhalikar, M., Smith, A., Parker, D., Satterthwaite, T. D., Elliott, M. A., Ruparel, K. . . . Verma, R. (2014). Sex differences in the structural connectome of the human brain. *Proc. Natl. Acad. Sci. USA*, *111*(2), 823–828.

106 Johnsen, B. & Hugdahl, K. (1994). Brain asymmetry and autonomic conditioning sensitization control. *Integr. Psychol. Behav. Sci.*, *29*(4), 395–406.

107 Kaplan, R. F, Meadows, M. E., Verfaellie, M., Kwan, E., Ehrenberg, B. L., Bromfield, E. B. . . . Cohen, R. A. (1994). Lateralization of memory for the visual attributes of objects: Evidence from the posterior cerebral artery amobarbital test. *Neurology*, *44*(6), 1068–1073.

108 Karapetsas, A. (2002). Accuracy and speed of processing verbal stimuli among subjects with low and high ability in mathematics. *Educational Psychology*, *22*(5), 613–619.

109 Karnath, H. O., Ferber, S. & Himmelbach, M. (2001). Spatial awareness is a function of the temporal not the posterior parietal lobe. *Nature, 411*(6840), 950–953.

110 Kasprian, G., Langs, G., Brugger, P. C., Bittner, M., Weber, M., Arantes, M., & Prayer, D. (2011). The prenatal origin of hemispheric asymmetry: An in utero neuroimaging study. *Cereb. Cortex, 21*(5), 1076–1083.

111 Kavaklioglu, T., Guadalupe, T., Zwiers, M., Marquand, A. F., Onnink, M., Shumskaya, E. . . . Francks, C. (2017). Structural asymmetries of the human cerebellum in relation to cerebral cortical asymmetries and handedness. *Brain Struct. Funct., 222*(4), 1611–1623.

112 Keller, S. S., Roberts, N., Garcia-Fiñana, M., Mohammadi, S., Ringelstein, E. B., Knecht, S., & Deppe, M. (2011). Can the language-dominant hemisphere be predicted by brain anatomy? *J. Cogn. Neurosci., 23*(8), 2013–2029.

113 Khomskaya, E. D. (1987). *Neuropsychology* [in Russian]. Moscow, Russia: Moscow University Press.

114 Kimura, D. (1961). Some effects of temporal lobe damage on auditory perception. *Canad. J. Psychol., 15*(3), 156–165.

115 Kimura, D. (1966). Dual function asymmetry of the brain in visual perception. *Neuropsychologia, 4*(3), 275–285.

116 Kimura, D. (1987). Are men's and women's brains really different? *Canad. Psychol., 28*(2), 133–147.

117 Kimura, D. (2011). From ear to brain. *Brain Cogn., 76*(2), 214–217.

118 Kinsbourne, M. (1974). Mechanisms of hemispheric interaction in man. In M. Kinsbourne & W. L. Smith (Eds.), *Hemispheric disconnection and cerebral function* (pp. 260–285). Oxford, IL: Thomas.

119 Knecht, S., Jansen, A., Frank, A., van Randenborgh, J., Sommer, J., Kanowski, M. & Heinze, H. J. (2003). How atypical is atypical language dominance? *Neuroimage, 18*(4), 917–927.

120 Kok, A. & Rooyakkers, J. (1986). ERPs to laterally presented pictures and words in a semantic categorization task. *Psychophysiology, 23*(6), 672–683.

121 Kulynych, J. J., Vladar, K., Jones, D. W. & Weinberger, D. R. (1994). Gender differences in the normal lateralization of the supratemporal cortex: MRI surface-rendering morphometry of Heschl's gyrus and the planum temporale. *Cereb. Cortex, 4*(2), 107–118.

122 Lalova, Y. (1997). Tachistoscopic study of spatial gnosis functions in healthy adults [in Bulgarian]. *The Bulgarian J. Psychol., 1*, 74–80.

123 Lambe, E. K. (1999). Dyslexia, gender and brain imaging. *Neuropsychologia, 37*(5), 521–536.

124 Lane, R., Kivley, L., Bois, A., Shamasundara, P. & Schwartz, G. (1995). Level of emotional awareness and the degree of right hemispheric dominance in the perception of facial emotion. *Neuropsychologia, 33*(5), 528–538.

125 Lawfield, A., McFarland, D. J. & Cacace, A. T. (2011). Dichotic and dichoptic digit perception in normal adults. *J. Am. Acad. Audiol., 22*(6), 332–341.

126 Leroy, F., Cai, Q., Bogart, S. L., Dubois, J., Coulon, O., Monzalvo, K. . . . Dehaene-Lambertz, G. (2015). New human-specific brain landmark: The depth asymmetry of superior temporal sulcus. *Proc. Natl. Acad. Sci. USA, 112*(4), 1208–1213.

127 Levy, J. (1969). Possible basis of evolution of lateral specialization of the human brain. *Nature, 224*(5219), 614–615.

128 Liu, H., Stufflebeam, S. M., Sepulcre, J., Hedden, T. & Buckner, R. L. (2009). Evidence from intrinsic activity that asymmetry of the human brain is controlled by multiple factors. *Proc. Natl. Acad. Sci. USA, 106*(48), 20499–20503.

129 Luria, A. R. (1969). *Higher cortical functions in man*. New York: Basic Books.
130 Macdonnell, R. A., Shapiro, B. E., Chiappa, K. H., Helmers, S. L., Cros, D., Day, B. J., & Shahari, B. T. (1991). Hemispheric threshold differences for motor evoked potentials produced by magnetic coil stimulation. *Neurology, 41*(9), 1441–1444.
131 MacNeilage, P. F., Rogers, L. J. & Vallortigara, G. (2009). Origins of the left and right brain. *Sci. Am., 301*(1), 60–67.
132 Manna, C. B. G., Tenke, C. E., Gates, N. A., Kayser, J., Borod, J. C., Stewart, J. W. ... Bruder, G. E. (2010). EEG hemispheric asymmetries during cognitive tasks in depressed patients with high versus low trait anxiety. *Clin. EEG Neurosci., 41*(4), 196–202.
133 McManus, C. (1985). Handedness, language dominance and aphasia: A genetic model. *Psychol. Med. Monogr. Suppl., 8*, 1–40.
134 McManus, C. (2002). *Right hand, left hand: The origins of asymmetry in brains, bodies, atoms and cultures*. London: Weidenfeld & Nicolson.
135 McManus, I. C., Davison, A. & Armour, J. A. (2013). Multilocus genetic models of handedness closely resemble single-locus models in explaining family data and are compatible with genome-wide association studies. *Ann. N. Y. Acad. Sci., 1288*, 48–58.
136 Mavlov, L. (1976). Premotor cortex, oral praxis and speech functions [in Bulgarian]. In: *Structure and functions of the brain* (Vol. 1, pp. 241–253). Sofia, Bulgaria: BAS.
137 Medland, S. E., Perelle, I., De Monte, V. & Ehrman, L. (2004). Effects of culture, sex, and age on the distribution of handedness: An evaluation of the sensitivity of three measures of handedness. *Laterality, 9*(3), 287–297.
138 Messerli, P., Pegna, A. & Sordet, N. (1995). Hemispheric dominance for melody recognition in musicians and non-musicians. *Neuropsychologia, 33*(4), 395–405.
139 Meyer, B., Roricht, S., Von Einseidel, H., Kruggel, F. & Weindl, A. (1995). Inhibitory and excitatory interhemispheric transfers between motor cortical areas in normal humans and patients with abnormalities of corpus callosum. *Brain, 118*(2), 429–433.
140 Mihulowicz, U., Willmes, K., Karnath, H.-O. & Klein, E. (2014). Single-digit arithmetic processing – Anatomical evidence from statistical voxel-based lesion analysis. *Front Hum. Neurosci., 8*, 286.
141 Mikeev, M., Mohr, C., Afanasiev, S., Landis, T. & Thut, G. (2002). Motor control and cerebral hemispheric specialization in highly qualified judo wrestlers. *Neuropsychologia, 40*(8), 1209–1219.
142 Minagawa-Kawai, Y., Cristià, A. & Dupoux, E. (2011). Cerebral lateralization and early speech acquisition: a developmental scenario. *Dev. Cogn. Neurosci., 1*(3), 217–232.
143 Mohr, B., Pülvermüller, F., Mittelstadt, K. & Rayman, J. (1996). Multiple simultaneous stimulus presentation facilitates lexical processing. *Neuropsychologia, 34*(10), 1003–1013.
144 Morozov, V. P., Vartanyan, I. A., Galunov, V. I., Dmitriyeva, Y. E. S., Zaytseva, K. A., Koroleva, I. V. ... Shurgaya, G. G. (1988). *Speech perception: Questions about functional asymmetry of the brain* [in Russian]. Leningrad, Russian Federation: Nauka.
145 Moscovitch, M. (1986). Afferent and efferent models of visual perceptual asymmetries: Theoretical and empirical implications. *Neuropsychologia, 24*(1), 91–114.
146 Müller, R., Rothermel, R., Behen, M., Muzik, O., Chakraborty, P. & Chugani, H. (1999). Language organization in patients with early and late left-hemisphere lesion: A PET study. *Neuropsychologia, 37*(5), 545–557.
147 Nagel, B. J., Herting, M. M., Maxwell, E. C., Bruno, R. & Fair, D. (2013). Hemispheric lateralization of verbal and spatial working memory during adolescence. *Brain Cogn., 82*(1), 58–68.
148 Nakagawa, A. & Sukigara, M. (2000). Visual word familiarity and attention in lateral difference during processing Japanese Kana words. *Brain Lang., 74*(2), 223–237.

149 Neville, H., Kutas, M. & Schmidt, A. (1982). Event-related potential studies of cerebral specialization during reading. *Brain Lang.*, *16*, 300–315.
150 Nuun, J., Polkey, C. & Morris, R. (1998). Selective spatial memory impairment after right unilateral temporal lobectomy. *Neuropsychologia*, *36*(9), 837–848.
151 Ocklenburg, S., Beste, C. & Güntürkün, O. (2013). Handedness: A neurogenetic shift of perspective. *Neurosci. Biobehav. Rev.*, *37*(10, Pt 2), 2788–2793.
152 Ocklenburg, S., Beste, C., Arning, L., Peterburs, J. & Güntürkün, O. (2014). The ontogenesis of language lateralization and its relation to handedness. *Neurosci. Biobehav. Rev.*, *43*, 191–198.
153 Ocklenburg, S. & Güntürkün, O. (2012). Hemispheric asymmetries: The comparative view. *Front Psychol.*, *3*, 5.
154 O'Leary, D., Anderson, N. C., Hurtig, R. R., Hichwa, R. D., Watkins, G. L., Ponto, L. L. . . . Kirchner, P. T. (1996). A positron emission tomography study of binaurally and dichotically presented stimuli: Effects of level of language and directed attention. *Brain Lang.*, *53*(1), 20–39.
155 Onal-Hartmann, C., Pauli, P., Ocklenburg, S. & Güntürkün, O. (2012). The motor side of emotions: Investigating the relationship between hemispheres, motor reactions and emotional stimuli. *Psychol. Res.*, *76*(3), 311–316.
156 Orbachevskaya, G. & Serbinenko, M. (1985). Spatial-temporal distribution of EEG activation in verbal-logical and visual-imaging activities [in Russian]. *Fiziol Cheloveka*, *11*(3), 436–449.
157 Palmer, R. & Corballis, M. (1996). Predicting reading ability from handedness measures. *Br. J. Psychol.*, *87*(4), 609–620.
158 Pencheva, S. (1988). *Perception and functional cerebral asymmetry in the norm and in focal brain injury* [in Bulgarian]. PhD thesis. Sofia, Bulgaria: BAS "Prof. Marin Drinov" Publishing House
159 Perrine, K., Gershengorn, J., Brown, E., Choi, I., Luciano, D. & Devinsky, O. (1993). Material-specific memory in the intracarotid amobarbital procedure. *Neurology*, *43*(4), 706–711.
160 Plenger, P. M, Breieer, J. I., Wheless, L. W., Ridley, T. D., Papanicolaou, A. C., Brookshite, B. . . . Willmore, L. J. (1996). Lateralization of memory for music: Evidence from the intracarotid sodium amobarbital procedure. *Neuropsychologia*, *34*(10), 1015–1018.
161 Pollmann, S., Maertens, M., Von Cramon, D. Y., Lepsien, J. & Hugdahl, K. (2002). Dichotic listening in patients with spinal and nonsplenial callosal lesions. *Neuropsychology*, *16*(1), 56–64.
162 Preis, S., Jancke, L., Schittler, P., Huang, Y. & Steinmetz, H. (1998). Normal intrasylvian anatomical asymmetry in children with developmental language disorder. *Neuropsychologia*, *36*(9), 849–855.
163 Pujol, J., Deus, J., Losilla, J. M. & Capdevila, A. (1999). Cerebral lateralization of language in normal left-handed people studied by functional MRI. *Neurology*, *52*(5), 1038–1043.
164 Qiu, W. H., Wu, H. X., Yang, Q. L., Kang, Z., Chen, Z. C., Li, K. . . . Chen, S. Q. (2017). Evidence of cortical reorganization of language networks after stroke with subacute Broca's aphasia: a blood oxygenation level dependent-functional magnetic resonance imaging study. *Neural. Regen. Res.*, *12*(1), 109–117.
165 Rastatter, M. & Dell, C. (1987). Vocal reaction times of stuttering subjects to tachistoscopically presented concrete and abstract words: A closer look at cerebral dominance and language processing. *JSHD*, *30*(3), 306–310.
166 Rauschecker, J. P. & Scott, S. K. (2009). Maps and streams in the auditory cortex: Non-human primates illuminate human speech processing. *Nat. Neurosci.*, *12*(6), 718–724.

167 Razumnikova, O. M. & Vol'f, N. V. (2011). Selection of visual hierarchical stimuli between global and local aspects in men and women [in Russian]. *Fiziol Cheloveka*, *37*(2), 14–19.
168 Reilly, J., Stiles, J., Larsen, J. & Trauner, D. (1995). Affective facial expression in infants with focal brain damage. *Neuropsychologia*, *33*(1), 83–99.
169 Rentería, M. E. (2012). Cerebral asymmetry: A quantitative, multifactorial, and plastic brain phenotype. *Twin Res. Hum. Genet.*, *15*(3), 401–413.
170 Resnick, S., Gur, J. & Gur, R. (1997). The stability of tachistoscopic measures of hemispheric specialization. *Neuropsychologia*, *32*(11), 1419–1430.
171 Rogers, L. (1995). Evolution and development of brain asymmetry and its relevance to language, tool use and sex. *Inter. J. Comp. Psychol.*, *8*(1), 1–15.
172 Ross, E. D., Thompson, R. & Yenkosky, J. (1997). Lateralization of affective prosody in brain and the callosal integration of hemispheric language functions. *Brain Lang.*, *56*(1), 27–54.
173 Rugg, M. (1995). La difference vive. *Nature*, *373*(6515), 561–562.
174 Samson, S. & Zatorre, R. (1994). Contribution of the right temporal lobe to musical timbre discrimination. *Neuropsychologia*, *32*(2), 231–240.
175 San Martini, P., De Gennaro, L., Filetti, F., Lombardo, C. & Violani, C. (1994). Prevalent direction of reflective lateral eye movements and ear asymmetries in a dichotic test of musical chords. *Neuropsychologia*, *32*(12), 1515–1522.
176 Schaafsma, S. M., Riedstra, B. J., Pfannkuche, K. A., Bouma, A. & Groothuis, T. G. (2009). Epigenesis of behavioural lateralization in humans and other animals. *Philos. Trans. R. Soc. Lond. B Biol. Sci.*, *364*(1519), 915–927.
177 Scheibel, A. (1985). Differentiality characteristics of the human speech cortex. In D. Benson & F. Zaidel (Eds.), *The dual brain* (pp. 65–74). New York: Guilford.
178 Selpiena, H., Siebert, A. C., Genc, A. E., Besteb, C., Faustmannc, P. M., Güntürküna, O., & Ocklenburg, S. (2015). Left dominance for language perception starts in the extrastriate cortex: An ERP and sLORETA study. *Behav. Brain Res.*, *291*, 325–333.
179 Sepeta, L. N., Berl, M. M., Wilke, M., You, X., Mehta, M., Xu, B. . . . Gaillard, W. D. (2016). Age-dependent mesial temporal lobe lateralization in language FMRI. *Epilepsia*, *57*(1), 122–130.
180 Sergent, J., Zuck, E., Terriach, S. & Mac Donald, B. (1992). Distributed neural network underlying musical sight-reading and keyboard performance. *Science*, *257*(5066), 106–109.
181 Shaywitz, B. A., Shaywitz, S. E., Pugh, K. R., Constable, R. T., Skudlarski, P., Fulbright, R. K. . . . Katz, L. (1995). Sex differences in the functional organization of the brain for language. *Nature*, *373*(6515), 607–609.
182 Snyder, P., Bilder, R., Wu, H., Bogerts, B. & Lieberman, J. (1995). Cerebellar volume asymmetries are related to handedness: A quantitative MRI study. *Neuropsychologia*, *33*(4), 407–419.
183 Sobotka, A., Pizlo, Z. & Budohoska, W. (1984). Hemispheric differences in evoked potentials to pictures of faces in the left and right visual fields. *Electroencephalogr. Clin. Neurophysiol.*, *59*(6), 441–453.
184 Sommer, I. E., Aleman, A., Bouma, A. & Kahn, R. S. (2004). Do women really have more bilateral language representation than men? A meta-analysis of functional imaging studies. *Brain*, *127*(Pt 8), 1845–1852.
185 Spajdel, M., Jariabkova, K. & Riecansky, I. (2007). The influence of musical experience on lateralization of auditory processing. *Laterality*, *12*(6), 487–499.
186 Sparks, R. & Geschwind, N. (1968). Dichotic listening in man after section of neocortical commissures. *Cortex*, *4*, 3–16.

187 Spielberg, J. M., Stewart, J. L., Levin, R. L., Miller, G. A. & Heller, W. (2008). Prefrontal cortex, emotion, and approach/withdrawal motivation. *Soc. Personal Psychol. Compass.*, *2*(1), 135–153.
188 Spironelli, C., Penolazzi, B. & Angrilli, A. (2008). Dysfunctional hemispheric asymmetry of theta and beta EEG activity during linguistic tasks in developmental dyslexia. *Biol. Psychol.*, *77*(2), 123–131.
189 Staudt, M. (2010). Reorganization after pre- and perinatal brain lesions. *J. Anat.*, *217*(4), 469–474.
190 Stefan, K. E., Fink, G. R. & Marshall, J. C. (2007). Mechanisms of hemispheric specialization: Insights from analyses of connectivity. *Neuropsychologia*, *45*(2–4), 209–228.
191 Steinmetz, H., Volkman, J., Janke, L. & Freud, H. (1991). Anatomical left-right asymmetry of language-related temporal cortex is different in left- and right-handers. *Ann. Neurol.*, *29*(3), 315–319.
192 Sviderskaya, N. (1987). *Synchronous electrical activity of the brain and mental processes* [in Russian]. Moscow, Russia: Nauka.
193 Szaflarski, J. P., Holland, S. K., Schmithorst, V. J. & Byars, A. W. (2006). An fMRI study of language lateralization in children and adults. *Hum. Brain Mapp.*, *27*(3), 202–212.
194 Toga, A. W. & Thompson, P. M. (2003). Mapping brain asymmetry. *Nat. Rev. Neurosci.*, *4*(1), 37–48.
195 Toga, A. W., Thompson, P. M. & Sowell, E. R. (2006). Mapping brain maturation. *Trends Neurosci.*, *29*(3), 148–159.
196 Tremblay, P. & Dick, A. S. (2016). Broca and Wernicke are dead, or moving past the classic model of language neurobiology. *Brain Lang. 162*, 60–71.
197 Triggs, W., Calvanio, R. & Levine, M. (1997). Transcranial magnetic stimulation reveals a hemispheric asymmetry correlate of intermanual differences in motor performance. *Neuropsychologia*, *35*(10), 1355–1363.
198 Tzourio, N., Crivello, F., Mellet, E., Nkanga-Ngila, B. & Mazoyer, B. (1998). Functional anatomy of dominance for speech comprehension in left handers vs right handers. *Neuroimage*, *8*(1), 1–16.
199 Vallortigara, G. & Rogers, L. J. (2005). Survival with an asymmetrical brain: advantages and disadvantages of cerebral lateralization. *Behav. Brain Sci.*, *28*(4), 575–633.
200 Van den Noort, M., Specht, K., Rimol, L. M., Ersland, L. & Hugdahl, K. (2008). A new verbal reports fMRI dichotic listening paradigm for studies of hemispheric asymmetry. *Neuroimage*, *40*(2), 902–911.
201 Van der Haegen, L., Westerhausen, R., Hugdahl, K. & Brysbaert, M. (2013). Speech dominance is a better predictor of functional brain asymmetry than handedness: a combined fMRI word generation and behavioral dichotic listening study. *Neuropsychologia*, *51*(1), 91–97.
202 Van der Kallen, B. F., Morris, G. L., Yetkin, F. Z., van Erning, L. J., Thijssen, H. O. & Haughton, V. M. (1998). Hemispheric language dominance studied with functional MR: Preliminary study in healthy volunteers and patients with epilepsy. *Am. J. Neuroradiol.*, *19*(1), 73–77.
203 Van der Knaap, L. J. & van der Ham, I. J. M. (2011). How does the corpus callosum mediate interhemispheric transfer? A review. *Behav. Brain Res.*, *223*(1), 211–221.
204 Van Ettinger-Veenstra, H. M., Ragnehed, M., Hällgren, M., Karlsson, T., Landtblom, A.-M., Lundberg, P., & Engström, M. (2010). Right-hemispheric brain activation correlates to language performance. *Neuroimage*, *49*(4), 3481–3488.

205 Vingerhoets, G. & Stroobant, N. (1999). Lateralization of cerebral blood flow velocity changes during cognitive tasks: A simultaneous bilateral transcranial Doppler study. *Stroke, 30*(10), 2152–2158.
206 Vollmer-Haase, J., Finke, K., Hartje, W. & Bulla-Hellwig, M. (1998). Hemispheric dominance in the processing of J. S. Bach fugues: A transcranial Doppler sonography (TCD) study with musicians. *Neuropsychologia, 36*(9), 857–867.
207 Voyer, D. (2011). Sex differences in dichotic listening. *Brain Cogn., 76*(2), 245–255.
208 Wada, J. A. (2009). Is functional hemispheric lateralization guided by structural cerebral asymmetry? *Can. J. Neurol. Sci., 36*(Suppl 2), S25–S31.
209 Wada, J., Clarke, R. & Hamm, A. (1975). Cerebral hemispheric asymmetry in human. *Arch. Neurol., 32*(4), 239–245.
210 Wada, J., & Rasmussen, T. (1960). Intracarotid injection of sodium for the lateralization of cerebral speech dominance. *J. Neurosurg.*, 17(2), 266–282.
211 Wang, D., Buckner, R. L. & Liu, H. (2013). Cerebellar asymmetry and its relation to cerebral asymmetry estimated by intrinsic functional connectivity. *J. Neurophysiol., 109*(1), 46–57.
212 Weissman, D. H. & Banich, M. T. (2000). The cerebral hemispheres cooperate to perform complex but not simple tasks. *Neuropsychology, 14*(1), 41–59.
213 Welcome, S. & Chiarello, C. (2008). How dynamic is interhemispheric interaction? Effects of task switching on the across-hemisphere advantage. *Brain Cogn., 67*(1), 69–75.
214 Westerhausen, R. & Hugdahl, K. (2008). The corpus callosum in dichotic listening studies of hemispheric asymmetry: A review of clinical and experimental evidence. *Neurosci. Biobehav. Rev., 32*(5), 1044–1054.
215 Westerhausen, R., Kompus, K. & Hugdahl, K. (2014). Mapping hemispheric symmetries, relative asymmetries, and absolute asymmetries underlying the auditory laterality effect. *Neuroimage, 84*, 962–970.
216 Witelson, S., Glezer, I., Kigar, D. (1995). Women have greater density of neurons in the posterior temporal cortex. *J. Neurosci., 15*(5), 3418–3428.
217 Witteman, J., van Ijzendoorn, M. H., van de Velde, D., van Heuven, V. J. & Schiller, N. O. (2011). The nature of hemispheric specialization for linguistic and emotional prosodic perception: A meta-analysis of the lesion literature. *Neuropsychologia, 49*(13), 3722–3738.
218 Zaidel, E. (1983). Disconnection syndrome as a model for laterality effects in the normal brain. In J. Hellige (Ed.), *Cerebral hemispheric asymmetry* (pp. 95–115). New York: Praeger.
219 Zaidel, E. & Schweiger, A. (1984). On wrong hypothesis about the right hemisphere. *Cogn. Neuropsychol., 1*(4), 215–222.

2
DEVELOPMENTAL STUTTERING

Introduction

Verbal communication is a bidirectional process including two main interrelated sub-processes: verbal expression (encoding and generating of verbal messages) and verbal perception (decoding, understanding and interpreting of verbal messages). Each of these two sub-processes itself is a complex, multicomponent cognitive function, whose implementation goes through subsequent, hierarchically organized, but interdependent stages and is supported by different neural structures (large cortical/subcortical neural networks) [47, 54, 64, 91, 92, 159].

Generation of fluent speech depends on the timely temporal synchronization of phonatory and articulatory muscles [8, 16, 44]. Language content modulates this process in a top-down manner, indicating the close interaction between language and speech [88, 91]. This complex function is specifically compromised in developmental stuttering (DS) – one of the most frequent communicative disorders in childhood, with severe clinical characteristics. Although DS can be defined as a speech disorder, its symptoms seem specifically related to language use and become more prominent in emotionally and syntactically demanding speech [16, 76, 86, 90, 97, 154].

DS evolves before puberty, without apparent brain damage or other known causes. Its emergence marks a peak between the age of 3 and 5 and 2–5 percent of preschool children are affected, with a ratio of 3:4 times more frequently occuring in boys than in girls [86, 97, 165–167]. Although its recovery rate (spontaneous or induced by early speech therapy) is up to about 80 percent, in about 1 percent of affected subjects the disorder persists after puberty, more often in men than in women, which is considered as evidence for its genetic basis [1, 5, 10, 55, 86, 85, 113, 117, 164–168]. The high concordance rate between the stutterers' family members (about 70 percent for monozygotic twins [3, 56], about 30 percent for dizygotic twins [3, 56] and 18 percent for siblings of the same sex [3]) and the identification of candidate genes that contribute to stuttering in the population at large are strong arguments in favour of the assumption for the existence of a hereditary component (for a review, see [161]).

Actually, the hereditary component and the early onset of DS provide the strongest support to the hypothesis that some kind of anatomical or neurophysiological predetermination increases the vulnerability for DS (for details, see [3, 24, 82]).

Despite the centuries-long history of studies on DS, its nature remains unknown, undeniable evidence for which is the insufficient therapeutic effectiveness and frequent relapses in many cases. Actually, Hartman [70] has defined DS quite appropriately as "something of a paradox" because, although easy to identify, it has proved to be too difficult to understand and solve.

One of the unsolved problems concerning DS is its aetiology. The long and rich history of theoretical speculations and empirical research of its possible etiological factors is well documented by many authors [15, 23, 41, 67, 70, 97, 145, 160, 167].

From all the existing etiological theories of stuttering, the most popular have always been the theories postulating that DS is a product of a central nervous system (CNS) dysfunction, possibly with genetic origins. One of them is the Cerebral Dominance Model of stuttering proposed by Orton and Travis (1928–1931) early in the last century [110, 149]. As Bloodstein [24] has noted, perhaps the most enduring hypothesis in the scientific literature on neural mechanisms in stuttering is the atypical language and speech lateralization hypothesis.

About the birth of the theory of atypical cerebral dominance for speech as a cause of developmental stuttering

In 1928, Orton [110] first proposed that in some cases, stuttering may be caused by the competition between the two cerebral hemispheres in speech control. Because speech muscles are paired structures, and right-sided muscles receive impulses from the left hemisphere (LH) and left-sided muscles receive impulses from the right hemisphere (RH), the fluency of speech production depends on the synchronization of these impulses. Orton suggested that this synchronization could only occur if there was a "leading" hemisphere that would impose its timing patterns over the other hemisphere. Therefore, the reduced or absent cerebral dominance would induce asynchronous activations of speech muscles and provoke stuttering. In addition, Orton also suggested that the enforced shift from left- to right-handedness would interfere with the development of speech dominant gradient and may cause stuttering [110].

This early speculation found support in the widely accepted view that handedness is a reliable indicator of cerebral lateralization [7, 65, 92, 156], with data showing increased incidence of left-handedness and ambidexterity among stutterers than the general population [17, 97, 145, 156] and in observations of reduced lateralization of speech functions in left-handers and mixed-handers in comparison with right-handers [17, 33, 94, 138, 147, 169].

Only three years later, in 1931, Travis published The Cerebral Dominance Theory of Stuttering. The author's hypothesis for the pathogenetic mechanisms of stuttering was based on the theory of the human body as a dynamic whole, functioning as a unity of hierarchical subordinate centres of psychic dominance [149]. According to this theory, the bigger the differentiation of the organism's structures and functions, the greater the importance of the executive centre of general dominance which integrates the whole unit. The term "psychic dominance" has been used in the sense of control applied by the more active structures towards the less active ones, as in the more active structures the most important excitation processes function with greatest efficiency [149].

Based on his own experimental findings, Travis concluded that stuttering is a profound neuropsychological impairment resulting from a general reduction in the cortical lead control for speech [149]. The neurological basis of stuttering is the lack of a sufficient dominant gradient of excitation in the central nervous system, which impedes the integration of the highest neuropsychological levels of speech processing or predisposes the disintegration of these levels through various exogenous or endogenous factors, such as disease, damage, evolutionary conflict, family factors, etc. In stutterers, the existing nervous energy is driven by two centres with similar potential instead of being retained by the centre with the greatest potential. Therefore, the lack of cerebral dominance for speech causes timing disturbances of motor impulses to bilaterally innervated speech muscles [149].

Right from the beginning, research on this issue was focused in two directions: (1) to study the relationship between DS with left-handedness and its shift and (2) to investigate comparatively the degree and type of hemispheric lateralization of speech mechanisms in stutterers and non-stutterers.

Developmental stuttering and left-handedness

The idea that handedness disturbances in stutterers may reflect their abnormal pattern of cerebral organization of function, is closely related to the assumption of the reliability of handedness as an indicator of cerebral laterality [7, 68, 156].

The wide variety of research findings on the distribution of left-handedness and ambidexterity among the stuttering population, from 2 percent to 21 percent for left-handedness and from 0 percent to 61 percent for mixed-handedness (ambidexterity) (for a review, see [127]), has made the issue of the relationship between stuttering and handedness debatable.

In general, researchers' opinions have grouped around two basic assumptions: first, that the relationship "stuttering–left-handedness" is psychologically based, and second, that this relationship has a neurological basis. Proponents of the first assumption have seen the enforced shift from left- to right-handedness as a psychological trauma having the potential to provoke stuttering [86, 97, 108, 143].

Viewed from this position, the relationship "stuttering–left-handedness" does not depend on brain lateralization and is the result of entirely different processes.

Many researchers of the "stuttering–left-handedness" relationship have united around the hypothesis of its neurological basis [30, 46], but their opinions concerning its origin have been quite different. According to some authors, this relationship is a sign of motor system dysfunction [59]; according to others, it is the result of prenatal exposure of higher testosterone levels leading to a change of the standard pattern of cerebral dominance [68]; according to others still, this relationship is a consequence of pathological effects caused by an early left hemispheric stroke leading to a change of the cerebral hand and speech dominance [17, 42] and a fourth group of researchers postulate the genetic nature of this relationship [7].

Other authors consider that left-handedness has no special role in the occurrence of DS [24, 45, 87, 99, 144, 156].

The inconsistency of scientific literature data concerning the frequency of left-handedness among stutterers has provoked more profound studies of both the type and degree of handedness; studies which results have shown greater frequency of weak handedness among stutterers, regardless of left-handedness or right-handedness [28, 42] and have been interpreted as a sign of weak and insufficient lateralization of the overall cerebral activity of stutterers.

Developmental stuttering and lateralization of language functions

Soon after its emergence, the theory of the atypical cerebral dominance lost its initial popularity mainly due to two reasons: first, failure to clearly demonstrate a lack of cerebral dominance, and second, failure of the therapies targeted at establishing and stabilizing the hemispheric dominance in stutterers [30].

For a certain period, environmental theories of stuttering prevailed. Nevertheless, the basis of the Cerebral Dominance Theory was not rejected or refuted and, when in 1966 Jones [79] announced his findings – four stutterers with bilateral motor speech areas – this theory regained researchers' interest.

In fact, when Jones tested by Wada test four neurological patients who had suffered from stuttering since early childhood, he found evidence of bilateral speech control as they all acquired transient aphasia after Amytal sodium injection in both carotid arteries. After surgical removal of one of the speech centres (by medical prescription), all four patients stopped stuttering without relapse in the period in which Jones was able to monitor them. After surgery, patients underwent Wada retest and this time all of them acquired transient aphasia only after Amytal sodium injection in their un-operated hemisphere. Based on these results, Jones concluded that prior to surgery his patients had bilateral cortical representation of motor speech areas and the removal of one of the two centres led to a normalization of their speech.

The two attempts immediately following to repeat Jones' finding did not have the same success. In the first study, four stutterers without additional brain pathology were tested and only one of them demonstrated bilateral speech presentation while all the rest showed the typical left-hemispheric lateralization [4]. Three patients were tested in the second study and all showed left-hemispheric lateralization of speech functions [93]. The failure of these two studies to repeat Jones' finding, as well as the report of Branch et al. [31] that described patients with bilateral speech representation and lack of stuttering, have become the most serious evidences against the reliability of the bilateral speech control hypothesis.

If these results are interpreted in the context of the approach to DS as a disorder with heterogeneous aetiology and non-unitary nature, then such an argument would lose strength. It is also possible that the inconsistency of the results of these three investigations is due to differences in characteristics of the studied subjects such as gender, handedness, etc., known as factors initiating individual differences in the pattern of brain laterality. For example, ignoring the fact that three of the four Jones' patients have been left-handers supports such an assumption.

Interest towards Cerebral Dominance Theory did not abate after the fading of both the euphoria of Jones' finding and the disappointment of the poor success of the subsequent two attempts to repeat it. To a great extent this has contributed to the arming of researchers with improved non-invasive technologies for investigation of brain structures and functions such as electrophysiological methods (electroencephalography [EEG], evoked potentials [EPs]), behavior methods (dichotic listening, auditory tracking, tachistoscopic investigation) and, most recently, neuroimaging techniques (magnetic resonance imaging [MRI], functional MRI [fMRI], computed tomography [CT]). As Van Borsel et al. [150] has pointed out, in subsequent years, numerous studies were conducted with results ranging from equivocal to the conclusion that there is a bilateral language representation in stutterers, an inverse cerebral dominance, a RH dominance, an interference of the RH with LH activities or more RH speech production but no difference for speech perception.

Empirical evidence supporting the Cerebral Dominance Theory of developmental stuttering

Neuroanatomical evidence

As mentioned previously, in the long history of studying DS, many researchers have shared the assumption that some kind of anatomical and/or neurophysiological predetermination increases the vulnerability for stuttering, the strongest arguments for this conception being the hereditary component, early onset, lack of apparent brain damage or another known cause for the occurrence of this deficit.

The emergence of the theory of atypical cerebral dominance as a cause of DS created huge debate on the hypothesis that atypical anatomy may be associated with atypical functional cerebral laterality, which poses a risk for speech dysfluency. Nevertheless, the examination of anatomical substrates underlying DS is considered as insufficiently detailed [76]. According to contemporary scientific literature, only a few anatomical studies have found brain abnormalities in stutterers. In the earliest of these studies, two left-handed stuttering siblings were examined using CT. The results obtained indicated reduced anatomical asymmetry of the occipital poles [147]. The next two studies used high-resolution MRI [60, 61]. The first one established reduced volumetric asymmetry of the planum temporale – a cortical area with a key role in higher order auditory processing, and other anatomical peculiarities in speech-related areas [60]. The second one revealed reduced asymmetries of the prefrontal and occipital areas in adults with persistent DS, as the reduced volume was associated with slight linguistic deficits in a stutterers' group. These results were interpreted by the researchers as supporting the proposition that the atypical cerebral laterality may be an etiological factor of DS [61].

Using diffusion tensor imaging (DTI), a MRI technique allowing the assessment of white matter ultrastructure, Sommer et al. [139] found an area of decreased white matter tract coherence in the left Rolandic operculum, which was a sign of disconnection of premotor and motor cortices related to the planning and the execution of the speech act, respectively.

Janke et al. [76] used voxel-based morphometry (VBM) and found strong evidence that adults with persistent DS have anomalous anatomy not only in perisylvian speech and language areas but also in prefrontal and sensorimotor areas. The researchers detected increased white matter volumes in a right-hemispheric network including brain structures relevant to language and speech. These areas comprised the superior temporal gyrus (including the auditory areas planum temporale and Heschl's gyrus), the inferior frontal gyrus (including the pars triangularis that is part of Broca's right-sided homologue), the somatosensory area (including the face and mouth representation, as well as the mesial part of the hand representation) and the anterior middle frontal gyrus. In addition, Janke and co-workers found a leftward white matter asymmetry in the auditory cortex in non-stutterers, but symmetric white matter volumes in stutterers due to its atypical enlargement in the right. The researchers explained the findings of regionally increased right hemispheric white matter in stutterers with an increased, and possibly atypical, interhemispheric communication within these areas via association fibres, probably accompanying different processing strategies in the RH in stutterers [76]. Regarding the atypical anatomical lateralization in the auditory cortex in stutterers (expressed as an increased symmetry of white matter volume), it was considered as a crucial peculiarity possibly determining the processing mode of the right auditory cortex and the interaction between both auditory cortices [76]. The reports for dysfunctional auditory system and impaired auditory feedback in stutterers [77, 80, 105–107, 122, 123, 132], as well as the well-known key role of the auditory cortex in the continuous control over self-generated suprasegmental speech features (duration, intensity, stress), are in support of this assumption.

In a subsequent study using the same method (VBM), Beal et al. [13] revealed significant differences not only in white matter densities of LH and RH regions involved in auditory processing and speech production, but also in grey matter densities of these regions.

Structural anomalies of the corpus callosum among adults who stutter were recently reported by Choo et al. [39]. The researchers found a larger overall corpus callosum in stutterers compared to non-stutterers and concluded that this size difference could be linked to atypical brain function.

All these brain imaging studies have examined adults with DS. But now it is well known that the establishment of the neural correlates of stuttering is not reliable enough when examining adults only, since some of the brain structure differences observed in adults who stutter for decades may have occurred as a result of stuttering, that is they may reflect some compensatory mechanisms that have become hard-wired in the brain [32, 63, 76]. The studies that have established that the intensive practice of different skills and activities may change the functional organization of the brain [2, 10, 95, 96], as well as its structural organization at micro-anatomical level [50, 104], are in support of such an assumption.

This makes the studies of children who stutter really critical. Unfortunately, they are very few in numbers. Chang and co-authors have conducted several studies on this subject. In the first of them, Chang et al. [34] used an optimized VBM to compare grey matter volume and DTI to measure fractional anisotropy in white matter tracts in three groups: children with persistent stuttering, children who have recovered from stuttering and fluent peers. Both the persistent stuttering and recovered groups had reduced grey matter volume compared to controls in the left inferior frontal gyrus and bilateral temporal regions. Reduced fractional anisotropy was found in the left white matter tracts underlying the motor regions for face and larynx in the persistent stuttering group. Contrary to previous findings in adults who stutter, no increases were found in the RH speech regions in stuttering or recovered children and no differences in right–left asymmetries. Based on these findings, Chang et al. [34] suggested that the anatomical increases in RH structures previously found in adults who stutter might have resulted from a lifetime of stuttering. In a subsequent study, Chang et al. [37] examined subtle differences in white matter development across the whole brain in a larger group of children, stutterers and controls, aged 3–10 years, and revealed that children who stutter exhibited significantly reduced fractional anisotropy in white matter tracts that interconnect auditory and motor structures, in tracts that interconnect cortical and subcortical regions and in the corpus callosum. The authors suggested that "the observed white matter changes indicate possible structural connectivity deficits in children who stutter, in interrelated neural circuits that enable skilled movement control through efficient sensorimotor integration and timing of movements" [37, p. 694].

In another study with a larger sample of children who stutter, aged 3–9 years, Chang and Zhu [35] found decreased white matter connectivity in white matter tracts that interconnected the frontal motor areas with the auditory regions and tracts that interconnected supplementary motor areas and deeper structures, which led them to the conclusion that auditory–motor and basal ganglia–thalamocortical networks have different developmental trajectories in DS, which may in turn disturb speech planning and execution processes related to fluent speech motor control.

In a VBM study conducted by Choo et al. [38], no differences were detected in the corpus callosum area and white matter volume between the groups of children with persistent stuttering, children who recovered from stuttering and typically developing children aged 9–12 years. These findings led authors to the assumption that the changes in the corpus callosum volume observed in their previous study of adults who stutter might be the result of a long-term adaptation to persistent stuttering.

Beal et al. [14] also compared grey matter volume of stuttering and non-stuttering children, aged 6 and 12 years, using the VBM and found decreased grey matter volume in the bilateral inferior frontal gyri and left putamen, but increased grey matter volume in the right Rolandic operculum and superior temporal gyrus. Also, a decreased white matter volume bilaterally in the forceps minor of the corpus callosum was found.

To sum up, the results of previous anatomical studies using functional neuroimaging techniques provide strong evidence of anomalous anatomy in perisylvian speech and language areas, as well as in prefrontal and sensorimotor areas in both adults and children who stutter. These anatomical changes suggest the existence of some kind of hemispheric imbalance which could prompt deficits in the speech-language system processing, and in particular, enhance its vulnerability to speech dysfluencies.

Although insufficient, these studies provide the first strong evidence that the brain of stutterers differs from the brain of non-stutterers on a micro-anatomical level. As Janke et al. [76] note, the different "hardware" composition in subjects who stutter logically implies morphological predisposition towards stuttering.

Neurophysiological evidence

Results obtained from neurophysiological studies of DS complete the data from neuroanatomical studies, providing additional support for the position that the brains of people who stutter differ from the brains of normally fluent speakers in functional activation patterns of language and motor areas.

The majority of EEG studies of adults and children who stutter reveal atypical patterns of EEG asymmetries both at rest [111, 159, 169] and during hyperventilation [28, 111], but mostly during linguistic task performance [28, 44, 53, 81, 98, 101, 121, 171].

Some studies have observed epileptiform EEG activities in part of stutterers, leading to the assumption of a possible organic etiopathogenesis of this neurodevelopmental condition [81, 109].

Studies using event-related potentials (ERPs) also found an aberrant pattern of interhemispheric activity in the majority of adults who stutter [20, 58, 98, 102]. Recently, Weber-Fox and co-authors [154, 155] conducted two ERP studies of children who stutter in order to examine neural indices of aspects of language processing. The first one aimed to examine aspects of phonological/rhyme processing using visually presented words in 9- to 12-year old stutterers [154]. Results indicated that the neural processes related to phonological rehearsal and target word anticipation were atypical for the group of stutterers. Additionally, the relative contributions of the LH and RH in the linguistic integration stage of processing differed for the stuttering group compared to the non-stuttering group.

The second study examined ERP indices of language processing in 4- to 5-year old children who stutter and fluent controls matched for age, non-verbal IQ, working memory and language skills [153]. The results revealed between-group differences in the ERP measures of peak latencies, mean amplitudes and hemispheric distribution, suggesting potentially important distinctions in neural activations that implicated less efficient semantic processing, less mature neural functions for prosodic/syntactic process and atypical hemispheric involvement for processing phrase structure constraints. The authors interpreted these findings as strong evidence that early in the development of stuttering, the neural networks underlying language processing have evolved sufficiently atypically [154, 155].

Introduction of functional neuroimaging techniques that allow the measurement of the subtle changes in regional cerebral blood flow or metabolic rate has opened up new possibilities for the study of the possible neural correlates of stuttering, and in particular, of the specifics of stutterers' brain laterality [75].

In a review of functional neuroimaging studies conducted with adults with DS, Ingham [75] summarized that the findings, both in the resting state and during the execution of different linguistic tasks, have strongly confirmed that stutterers show different cerebral dominance from non-stutterers, as supplemental motor area, inferior lateral premotor area, auditory association area A2, anterior insula and cerebellum, especially in the RH, have been the main regions incorporated in the abnormal nervous system. The biggest differences between stutterers and non-stutterers have been recorded during tasks that invoke dysfluent speech, such as spontaneous speech and reading aloud, as stutterers showed unusual regional cerebral activations and deactivations which can be summarized as follows:

- hypoactivity in left-hemispheric cortical areas associated with language – Broca's area [30, 32, 63, 163] and Wernicke's area [30, 63, 153, 163];
- hyperactivity in motor areas, including diffuse over-activity in cerebral and cerebellar motor systems, and right-sided lateralization of cerebral motor systems [63]; and
- inadequate increased RH neural activation during speech production but not for speech perception [162].

Some researchers reported that part of these differences have modified under conditions that produce fluent speech [48, 63, 162, 163], but others reported persistence of these differences not only under conditions of fluent speech production but also during the implementation of non-linguistic tasks [32].

Localization of these activations and deactivations, not only in motor areas but also in premotor areas, auditory areas and some subcortical structures, indicates that stutterers and non-stutterers differ in the lateralization of various cortical processes, supporting the assumption that stuttering is associated not only with the motor system but also with the phase of pre-planning of speech production [32, 63, 75, 163].

The few neuroimaging studies examining differences in the brain function of children who stutter have also received evidence for aberrant timing of activity between the two hemispheres for speech processing and an inefficient integration between motor and auditory areas and between cortical and subcortical structures related to self-initiated speech [36].

In a magnetoencephalography (MEG) study, Beal et al. [14] examined vocalization-induced suppression, a phenomenon that is considered to reflect the interaction between speech motor and auditory regions in children who stutter and in fluently speaking children, all aged 6–12 years. The researchers measured the brain's evoked responses to listening to a tone, listening to a vowel and producing a vowel and found that there were no differences between stutterers and non-stutterers in their evoked response when simply listening to the tone, but there were clear differences in their response to vowel perception and production. Children who stutter had a delayed latency of the evoked responses in both hemispheres, indicating that timely and synchronized interactions between auditory and motor areas are affected in stutterers.

In a subsequent MEG study of picture naming, Sowman et al. [141] failed to observe differences in the lateralization of the brain activity in language-related regions in preschool-aged children soon after the onset of stuttering. The results revealed significantly lateralized activation in the LH in both groups, leading the authors to the conclusion that these findings support the idea that anomalous functional lateralization in stutterers may be the result of neuroplastic adaptation rather than a causal factor.

In a functional near infrared spectroscopy (fNIRS) study, Sato et al. [133] examined the extent of left–right hemispheric asymmetries for phonological and prosodic contrast tasks in adults, school-aged children and preschool-aged children who stutter, comparing their results to those of age-matched controls. The authors found that while non-stuttering individuals, both adults and children, consistently exhibited left-hemispheric asymmetry for the phonemic contrasts compared to the prosodic contrasts, none of the studied stutterers showed a left advantage in the phonemic contrast over the prosodic contrast condition. These findings clearly indicate an abnormal functional lateralization for auditory speech processing in stutterers, even at preschool age.

In summary, the above data provide clear evidence that the functional organization of brain speech processing in stutterers differs from that of non-stutterers.

Evidence from lateralized task performance

The conception of atypical language lateralization in subjects who stutter has not received consistent support from studies using perceptual tasks such as dichotic listening and divided visual field measures.

In the dichotic listening task, two different stimuli are presented simultaneously, one arriving at each ear. In the divided visual field task, a stimulus is presented briefly in either the left or the right visual field. In such presentation, information in left ear/visual field is initially projected to the RH and that in the right ear/field is initially projected to the LH. A right ear/visual field advantage is found for recognizing verbal information and a left ear/visual field advantage is found with non-verbal material information [83, 84].

Dichotic listening studies in DS are far from clear in regard to laterality and the auditory processing abilities of people who stutter. Curry and Gregory [43] used a dichotic word test consisting of high familiar consonant-vowel (CV)-consonant words and found that a majority (75 percent) of the non-stuttering group and fewer than half (45 percent) of the stuttering group showed the typical right-ear advantage (REA). Moreover, stutterers had smaller between-ear differences on the test than did non-stutterers, indicating a hemispheric asymmetry reduction in stutterers.

Brady and Berson [29] examined fully right-sided stutterers and non-stutterers and revealed a reversal left-ear preference in 17 percent of the stuttering group and none in the non-stutterers, suggesting that a subset of stutterers may have an anomaly in the lateralization of speech functions. Also, the authors reported that a non-significant tendency emerged for stutterers to show smaller between-ear differences on the test, concluding that this finding was consistent with the hypothesis that stutterers have less or incomplete lateralization of speech function.

Sommers et al. [140] used a single response mode for both dichotic words and digits to study dichotic ear preferences of stuttering children and adults. Stutterers showed significantly reduced right-ear advantage for dichotic words and digits and significantly lower frequency of right-ear preference for dichotic words than non-stutterers.

Cimmorell-Strong et al. [40] applied a stop CV dichotic listening task to forty-five right-handed boys who stutter, 5–9 years old, and forty-five matched controls, and found that two and a half times as many stutterers as non-stutterers displayed either a left-ear advantage (LEA) or no-ear advantage (NEA). This suggests a greater tendency on the part of stutterers, as opposed to non-stutterers, for reversed or bilateral representation of the auditory speech areas of the brain.

Blood and colleagues conducted a series of comparative studies of dichotic listening performance of stutterers and non-stutterers [19, 21, 22]. For example, Blood [19] found that almost half of studied children with DS did not show the typical REA for dichotic listening of CV stimuli: 17 percent of stutterers had LEA and 22 percent of stutterers had no significant ear advantage. In a subsequent study aiming to determine the differences among adult stutterers and non-stutterers on a dichotic word test, Blood and Blood [21] found significant difference between stuttering and non-stuttering subjects in the magnitude of the ear preference. Blood et al. [22] compared the performance of nine adults who stutter and nine controls on a dichotic digits test under conditions of free recall and directed attention. Both groups demonstrated REA on the free recall condition, but while the control group showed significantly better right ear scores, the group of stutterers showed no significant difference between the right and left ears. No differences between the free recall and directed listening conditions were found for both groups.

Morozov et al. [103] compared the performance of adults who stutter and fluently speaking adults on a dichotic word test and revealed lower frequency of left-hemispheric advantage (LHA): 43 percent of stutterers and 11 percent of non-stutterers demonstrated LEA for dichotic verbal perception. In another study with the same test, the authors examined 7- to 14-year old children who stutter and matched controls. The results found reduced hemispheric asymmetry and poorer perceptive performance in children who stutter in comparison with fluently speaking children [103].

Foundas et al. [62] recently investigated dichotic listening performance of CV stimuli in three attention conditions in adults with persistent DS and matched controls as a function of gender and handedness. Results indicated that for the control group, sex and handedness had no effects on performance of any of the dichotic listening conditions. Among the stutterers, the male left-handed group had a LEA in the non-directed attention condition, but was able to shift attention to the left and right ear better than any other group. The female right-handed group demonstrated a lack of lateral ear bias in the non-directed attention condition, which was relatively unable to selectively direct attention left or right and had the greatest tendency to hear a sound that was not presented to either ear. A female left-handed group was not examined in this study. No differences between the male right-handed group and control group were found. Also, for the stutter group, degree of handedness was significantly related to the percentage of left and right ear responses and to the lateralization shift magnitude. Based on these findings, Foundas and co-workers suggested that left-handed men who stutter and right-handed women who stutter had atypical auditory processing, but while left-handed men who stutter could have mixed dominance, right-handed women who stutter might have attentional deficits. The lack of differences between right-handed men who stutter and controls led the authors to conclude that aberrant hemispheric dominance cannot fully account for all cases of stuttering.

More recently, Robb et al. [125] studied seven adult stutterers and matched controls using CV stimuli in both undirected and directed attention tasks. The undirected attention task involved manipulating the interaural intensity difference of the CV stimuli presented to each ear. There were no between-group differences in the results obtained for the directed attention task, but obvious differences in the undirected attention results, indicating that stutterers showed a less robust REA for processing CV stimuli compared to non-stutterers, with a primary between-group difference in regard to the interaural intensity difference point at which a REA shifts to a LEA. This crossing-over point occurred earlier for stutterers. This finding was interpreted by the researchers as indicating a stronger RH involvement for the processing of speech in stutterers compared to non-stutterers.

In contrast to the above-mentioned studies, Quinn [118], Dorman and Porter [49] and Shklovskiy [135] failed to find significant differences between adult stutterers and non-stutterers, and Slorach and Noehr [136] and Gruber and Powell [69] obtained similar negative results with children who stutter and controls. Based on their findings, all these researchers concluded that cerebral dominance is not a significant factor in the aetiology of stuttering.

In an interesting study by Liebetrau and Daly [89], dichotic listening and masking level difference tasks were applied to 11- to 18-year old boys who stutter and matched, non-stuttering, controls. Stuttering children were differentiated into "organic" and "functional" subgroups on the basis of neuropsychological test performances. No statistically significant between-group differences on the dichotic listening task were found: the three groups exhibited a slight REA. Because organic stutterers performed significantly poorer than did controls on one masking level difference task and functional stutterers performed more like controls, the researchers suggested that these findings supported the idea "that stuttering is not a unitary disorder, but rather a generic label for a wide range of related disorders" [89, p. 229].

Rosenfield and Goodglass [128] conducted a study where the aim was to investigate dichotic listening performance for both speech (CV syllables) and non-speech (melodies) stimuli in adults who stutter and controls. In order to determine stability of performance, the same speech and non-speech tasks were carried out one week later. Results found no between-group differences for the verbal task (both groups showed a clear REA), but significant between-group differences for the non-verbal task. While the controls demonstrated a significant LEA for the music perception, the group of stutterers showed no clear ear advantage. Based on these findings, the researchers suggested the existence of unusual cerebral lateralization for auditory processing in people who stutter.

Also, two studies of the perception of emotional component of dichotic listening verbal stimuli found an atypical pattern of hemispheric asymmetries in stutterers [85, 103].

A smaller number of studies that used divided visual field presentation of verbal stimuli also found atypical patterns of functional asymmetries in stutterers as reflected in a stronger RH involvement, or reduced LH involvement, for the processing of speech in stutterers in comparison to non-stutterers, especially during the processing of meaningful linguistic stimuli [99, 120, 148].

To summarize, the deviations in language lateralization in stutterers established by studies using dichotic listening and divided visual field paradigms consist in lower frequency of LHA, reduced hemispheric asymmetry and poorer perceptive performance in stutterers in comparison to non-stutterers [19, 40, 43, 98, 103, 118, 135, 140]. High inter-individual variability of dichotic listening scores in studied samples of stutterers observed by some researchers led to the assumption that the atypical language lateralization is a factor contributing to the emergence and persistence of DS in a subset of stutterers [9, 40, 61, 89].

Theoretical models of stuttering as a result of atypical cerebral lateralization of speech and language functions

After the appearance of Orton-Travis's Cerebral Dominance Theory of stuttering, many different hypotheses about the observed lateralization-related differences between stutterers and non-stutterers have been proposed over the years.

One of the first models trying to explain the role of the atypical brain asymmetry in the genesis of DS belongs to Rosenfield [126]. Its main postulate is that, probably due to a genetically determined abnormality of the dominant mechanisms, most of the stutterers fail to master the control of laryngeal reflex mechanisms. As a result of the failure to alter the reflex mechanisms in an appropriate way, they change sublaryngeal air pressure, causing reflexively induced laryngeal-oral spasms.

The segmentation dysfunction hypothesis, proposed by Moore [100], is based on a differential specialization of the two cerebral hemispheres: the RH is specialized for the processing of holistic, non-segmental, time-independent information, while the LH is better in the processing of segmental, time-dependent auditory information. According to this model, stutterers tend to use the less efficient RH for language processing, resulting in less fluent speech. In other words, stuttering may be a linguistic segmentation dysfunction due to an increased use of the RH for linguistic-motor planning.

A similar explanation is offered by the model of Rastatter and Dell [120]. According to its main postulate, the LH of stutterers relies on some linguistic functions of the RH. Because of the LH's inability to completely integrate with the RH, it is possible that the motor programming system for speech receives conflicting information from the LH and the RH, or identical, but out-of-phase, information. Probably, the different signals or signals out-of-phase from both hemispheres towards motor-neural units are (at least in part) the cause for abnormal input.

Boberg et al. [25] proposes an alternative hypothesis based on their own study of the distribution of EEG alpha power in stutterers during the processing of verbal and visuospatial information, according to which stutterers are not able to maintain stable inhibitory control over homologic right-hemispheric cortical and subcortical regions during linguistic processing.

Webster and Poulos [157] formulate a model of DS based on their hypothesis of attentional lability. This model postulates that both the stutterers and the non-stutterers rely on LH processing for language and speech formulation, but stutterers inappropriately and ineffectively engage the RH during this processing, resulting in interference with LH processes, especially those implemented by the supplemental motor area.

Lokhov [90] creates a model of stuttering, postulating that the disorder is due to a disturbance of hemispheric interactions induced by the overcharge of the LH caused by the ineffective processing of the RH. This occurs when the LH, due to some deficits in RH processing (a negative emotional experience, pharmacological influences, traumatic injury, etc.) takes over the functions of primary processing of incoming verbal stimuli (normally performed by the RH) which are added to its relevant functions related to final semantic processing, analysis and verbal-motor execution.

Sommer et al. [139] proposed a hypothesis based mainly on the findings from DTI studies. There are existing signs of cortical disconnection in adults with persistent DS immediately below the laryngeal and tongue representation in the left sensorimotor cortex. As researchers point out, the immediate surrounding region is composed of the sensorimotor representation of tongue, larynx and pharynx, as well as the inferior arcuate fasciculus linking temporal and frontal language areas, which together form the temporo-frontal language system included in language perception and expression. Taking into account the fact that fibre tracts in this area connect sensorimotor representation of the oropharynx with the frontal operculum, involved in articulation, and the ventral motor cortex, related to the planning of motor aspects of speech, Sommer et al. concluded that disturbed signal transmission through the left rolandic operculum could impair sensorimotor integration necessary for fluent speech production. Observed alteration of the normal temporal pattern of activation in premotor and motor cortex leads to the assumption that persistent DS results from disturbed timing of activation in speech-relevant brain areas and, as a consequence, RH language areas compensate for this deficit, similar to recovery from aphasia [139].

Morozov et al. [103] offer a model of DS based on the data received in a series of experiments with dichotic verbal listening. According to this model, the sequential segmental analysis performed by the LH is disturbed in all stutterers. In some stutterers (those with a REA for verbal dichotic listening), there is a discoordination between the two simultaneously operating modes of processing – the LH sequential segmental mode and the RH holistic mode. For the rest of stutterers (those with LEA), an effective use of the RH holistic mode of processing for a broad class of signals is typical. Disturbed LH segmental analysis causes a slower speed of verbal information processing. During the process of acoustic feedback in speech expression, this delay of verbal information processing results in disturbance of the impulses to articulatory muscles and to the emergence of stuttering.

Current perspectives on the defining and studying of developmental stuttering

As a scientific, personal and psychosocial phenomenon, stuttering has attracted the attention of researchers from various fields, which explains the impressive amount of definitions, etiological hypotheses and classifications in this regard. Lately, more and more researchers are uniting around the opinion that it is considered a systemic disorder, for example, a symptom reflecting a defect in the system of fluent speech generation, a system that is diffusely represented in the central nervous system, including motor, linguistic and cognitive processing [27, 87, 88, 112, 114, 116, 152].

Within this perspective, functional models of DS that explain dysfluency with a failure of effective integration between motor, linguistic and cognitive processes are most popular [27, 88, 112, 114, 118, 152]. According to their basic postulates, normal fluency depends on successful and efficient implementation of operations in each component of the processing system. For this reason, the damage in each of the system's components or disturbance of their interactions may be a potential source of dysfluency. The possibility of existence of different specific loci of the functional deficit in the process of generating speech fluency presupposes the existence of different types of stuttering. In fact, the idea that DS is a complex multidimensional disorder which is characterized by a variety of pathological manifestations (emotional, behavioral and cognitive), and is caused by the complex interactions of genetic and environmental factors (physiological, psychosocial and/or psycholinguistic), finds increasing acceptance [4, 28, 41, 81, 124].

The application of the multidimensional approach for studying aetiology and pathogenetic mechanisms of DS established the concept of neurotic (psychogenic) and neurotiform (organic) subtypes of DS in the early 70s of the last century in the former USSR (for details, see [8]). This concept was well accepted only by the East European researchers [8, 15, 16, 28, 67, 119, 130, 151] and became the basis for creating various diagnostic and therapeutic methods. Among Western researchers, the concept remained unpopular. Nevertheless, a number of researchers, who did not accept the idea for a unitary causation of DS as well as homogeneity of people who stutter, have attempted to differentiate subgroups of stutterers. For example, based on the data obtained in a series of experiments, Daly and co-workers (cited in [89]) differentiated stutterers as "functional" and "organic" stutterers according to their performance on the Michigan Neuropsychological Test Battery. Questioning the unitary theory of stuttering and assuming its multidimensional nature, Riley and Riley [124] developed the component model of stuttering for diagnosing and treating children who stutter [124]. Also, Zimmermman et al. [172] offered a conceptual framework of multiple risk factors of stuttering, and later Smith and Kelly [137] reviewed it as related to the aetiology of stuttering.

Furthermore, the widely accepted view of the important role of hereditary factors in the genesis of DS [5, 6, 46, 82, 97, 117, 165, 166] gave the general direction of the research of Boyanova for more than two decades. Based on the data from anamnestic examination, neuropsychological assessments and electrophysiological studies of brain activation of a representative sample of children who stutter, obtained in a series of studies, Boyanova [28] found that the hereditary stuttering has emerged as an independent subtype of DS, other than the known and well-described psychogenic (neurotic) and organic (neurotiform) subtypes. In this new subtype of DS, hereditary factors may be considered in two aspects: regarding the speech-language functional system in general and regarding the functional specialization of cerebral hemispheres. This subgroup of children who stutter showed a statistically significant higher incidence of both positive family history of stuttering, or other speech and language disorders, and positive family history of left-handedness, as well as less expressed right-hand preference. These findings led Boyanova to suggest that the hereditary subtype of DS may be due to abnormal hemispheric control of some brain functions including speech, and that it could be a hereditary feature of the organization of brain function. Also, the researcher elaborated on a set of criteria for differential diagnostics of these three subtypes, giving preference for the titles to psychogenic subtype of stuttering (PSS), organic subtype of stuttering (OSS) and hereditary subtype of stuttering (HSS). The purpose of its formation is to serve for the easy differentiation of the main subtypes of DS based on their supposedly different aetiology and pathogenesis.

To sum up, all these assumptions, as well as the previous research findings, have influenced and directed my own subsequent studies towards the relationship between functional brain asymmetry and DS. First, the recognition of the multidimensional and multicausal nature of DS will be crucial to improving research methodology and enhancing the chance to understand the very complex problem of stuttering.

Second, stuttering has been viewed in different theoretical perspectives (for an overview, see [41, 67, 70]), but throughout the whole period of its systematic study, the most popular of these have remained neurogenic theories, considering it the result of discrete brain lesions or dysfunctions of the central nervous system, probably genetically determined. One of these theories is the Orton-Travis' model of atypical cerebral dominance [110, 149]. The strength and vitality of this model are reflected in findings from many recent neuropsychological studies leading to the progressive re-increase of its influence.

Third, almost all studies of cerebral laterality in subjects with DS have found some deviations in the pattern of hemispheric asymmetries in stutterers compared to non-stutterers, but only in part of them the revealed between-group differences have reached statistical significance. Also, almost all studies on laterality have reported a greater inter-individual variability of the results in the stutterers' groups in comparison with the control groups.

Precisely, these results have provoked the assumption that stutterers are a heterogeneous group regarding the status of brain lateralization and atypical cerebral dominance could cause stuttering only in part of the population of stutterers [29, 40, 61, 88, 103, 115, 128]. That is why it is surprising that despite the broader acceptance of the concept of DS as a multidimensional and multicausal disorder, most studies on cerebral lateralization continue to examine stutterers as a homogeneous group and to holistically analyze data and interpret the outcomes.

Overcoming this disadvantage of the research strategy, the present study aimed to determine whether significant differences in hemispheric asymmetry for dichotic speech perception and manual preference exist between these stuttering subgroups (with PSS, OSS and HSS) when separately compared with fluently speaking controls.

Personal research data

Taking into account the currently available empirical data and its theoretical interpretation, this study was conducted to verify the hypothesis that atypical cerebral lateralization is a key neuropsychological factor only for the appearance and persistence of HSS, and is irrelevant to PSS and OSS.

As mentioned above, this hypothesis is based on the findings of Boyanova [28], namely that the HSS emerges as a separate subtype, different from PSS and OSS. Thus, the present study is a logical extension of Boyanova's research with a shift in emphasis on the comparison of the pattern of functional brain asymmetries for dichotic verbal perception of each of the three subgroups of stutterers with the pattern of fluently speaking matched controls.

Based on the theory of language as a system, the perceptive and expressive sides of which are interrelated and interdependent parts of a whole, I assume that it is possible that all three subgroups of stutterers have some deviations in the patterns of hemispheric asymmetries for speech perception, but only in stutterers with HSS will these deviations be primary regarding the main pathological process. For PSS and OSS, these deviations will be secondary and will have no connection with the basic pathological process.

Subjects

The study sample included eighty-seven children with DS (sixty-eight boys and nineteen girls, their ages ranging from 7.1 to 11.4 years; *Mean* age = 9.1, *SD* = 1.3), and seventy-eight non-stuttering children (sixty-one boys and seventeen girls, their ages ranging from 6.9 to 11.3 years; *Mean* age = 9.2, *SD* = 1.5).

According to the information obtained by anamnesis, speech and language assessment and additional studies, all participating children had normal hearing and intelligence, normal neurological status and Bulgarian as their native language. Also, all controls had normal spoken and written language.

All children participated voluntarily and with their parents' and the schools' administration consent.

Differential diagnosis of subtypes of developmental stuttering

Differential diagnosis of PSS, OSS and HSS was made by means of the above-mentioned set of criteria for differential diagnosis, proposed by Boyanova [28], consisting of the following five criteria:

1. Presence/absence of psychotrauma as a factor that triggers the emergence of stuttering. In order to obtain the most reliable information possible, only one examiner talks with the parents and their stuttering child. The questions are versatile and aiming to extract comprehensive information on the child's micro- and macro-environmental interactions. The presence of psychotrauma is coded as 0 and the absence as 1.

2. Presence/absence of positive familial history of stuttering or other speech or language disorders. The presence of positive familial history is coded as 1 and the absence as 0.
3. Presence/absence of concomitant speech disorders in addition to dysfluencies – such as articulation disorders (misarticulation of 'r' due to short frenulum and misarticulation of 's, z, ts, sh, zh, ch', due to tooth and jaw malformations are not recorded as pathology), disarthric speech, functional rhinolalia, tahilalia and bradilalia. Encoding: presence as 1 and absence as 0.
4. Presence/absence of complications during pregnancy and childbirth. Information is collected from the mother through an interview. Encoding: presence as 1 and absence as 0.
5. Psychomotor reactivity: this factor relates to the eye-movement coordination and movement precision. It is examined through the test of Piorkowski. The task with the Piorkowski-type machine is expressed through following a field of vision with ten stochastically switched-on lamps presented on a rectangular plan. The subject must switch on the lamp in the appropriate time using the buttons located under the lamps. The device records the number of correct reactions per minute. In our case, any stuttering child performed the test twice: once with a rate of switching on the lamps 60/min and once 75/min. Performance evaluation is done according to age-related normative values. If the child's scores are lower than the relevant normative values, the assessment is "a disordered psychomotor reactivity", which is coded as 1, and conversely, if the child's scores are higher than the relevant normative values, the assessment is "a normal psychomotor reactivity", which is coded as 0.

An Index of Differential Diagnosis was calculated individually for each stuttering child. Children who scored between 0 and 0.35 were classified as having PSS, those who scored between 0.35 and 0.55 were classified as having HSS and those who scored between 0.55 and 1 were classified as having OSS. These cut-off points have been established by Boyanova [28], depending on statistical criteria.

Resulting from the implementation of differential diagnosis, all eighty-seven stutterers were divided into three subgroups with an unequal number of participants and random gender distribution:

- a subgroup with PSS – thirty-eight children or 43.68 percent of the total group, thirty-one boys and seven girls;
- a subgroup with OSS – twenty-two children or 25.29 percent of the total group, seventeen boys and five girls; and
- a subgroup with HSS – twenty-seven children or 31.03 percent of the total group, twenty boys and seven girls.

Assessment of handedness

Handedness is a controlled factor in the studies of hemispheric asymmetries and right-handedness is usually one of the criteria for the selection of participants.

In view of the objectives and hypotheses of this study, such a selection was deliberately not done.

Handedness of participants was assessed by a performance test including ten manual activities that usually are not target of purposeful education and most probably have not been put to social pressure for switching of left-hand preference: striking a match, throwing a ball, combing, taking an object, waving goodbye, zipping/unzipping, putting glasses in a spectacle, threading a needle, picking up a glass of water, unscrewing a lid. Each activity was scored as left = −1 and right = +1.

A Quotient of manual asymmetry (QMA) was calculated individually of each child, using the formula: $[(R - L) / (R + L)] \times 100$, where R is the number of actions performed with the right hand and L is the number of actions performed with the left hand. Children who scored between −70 and +70 were classified as mixed-handed, those who scored between +71 and +100 were classified as right-handed and those who scored between −71 and −100 were classified as left-handed. These cut-off points have been established by Dragovic [51] depending on statistical criteria.

In addition, detailed pedigrees, including first- and second-degree relatives, were obtained for all participants from both of their biological parents.

Dichotic listening: stimuli and procedure

Dichotic listening is a non-invasive technique widely used in studies of speech and language lateralization. In this study, it was used as a main research method.

A personally modified version of the classic dichotic test with CV syllables was used in this study [9]. The modification consisted of monaurally presented instruction "attention", that is only to one ear (in an appropriate random mode, but equal times to both ears), 1 second before playing each dichotic pair. This modification was made in order to reduce the influences of conscious or unconscious bias of attention towards any of the ears on the dichotic test performance. The test consisted of thirty-six dichotic trials with pairs of CV syllables with the six-stop consonants /b/, /d/, /g/, /p/, /t/, /k/ followed by a vowel /a/. The recall was made in writing, in free condition, after playing each dichotic trial. Written reproduction was preferred to spoken, since it was unlikely for the written response to arouse negative emotions as a result of spoken speech.

The participants were instructed to attend to both ears and to report both syllables if possible, but to report only one if not or to respond "pass" if neither syllable on a trial could be reported. Children were free to decide which syllables to report first on each trial. Responses were noted on a sheet of paper by the experimenter.

Before the test, each child was individually instructed as to what is expected of him/her and what the task is about. This was followed by a practice session of six pairs, so the child could get acquainted with the procedure.

In order to compensate for any imbalances in the equipment, the dichotic test was listened over twice changing the places of the earphones during the second listening (it was done 24 hours after the first listening). Dichotic listening performance of each participant was calculated on the basis of the scores from both listening test. The output from the cassette player was calibrated to 70 dB.

The dichotic test used was technically prepared in the sound-recording studio of the Bulgarian National Radio. It is a digital audio-compilation produced on CD-media of 700MB. The text is being read by a professional narrator.

Data analysis and statistics

The following main indicators for hemispheric asymmetries in the performance of lateralized perceptive tasks were used for the individual and group analysis of dichotic listening scores:

(1) Laterality Quotient (LQ) and (2) Perceptive performance.

A dichotic listening LQ was calculated for each of the participants, using the formula: [(Right-ear correct responses − Left-ear correct responses) / (Right-ear correct responses + Left-ear correct responses) × 100]. It reflects the difference between right- and left-ear performances in the dichotic listening test and provides a measure for both the direction and the magnitude of interaural asymmetry. The sign of the LQ indicates the direction of interaural asymmetry: positive (+) for REA/LHA and negative (−) for LEA/right-hemispheric advantage (RHA). The value of the LQ indicates the magnitude of interaural asymmetry.

Perceptive performance was assessed on the basis of the percentage of correctly identified syllables.

For statistical evaluation, the Crosstab chi-square test and Independent Sample t-tests in the SPSS 16.0 were applied. Also, effect size was calculated.

Results from the assessment of handedness

An overview of the results from the handedness measurements of the whole group of stutterers, the three stuttering subgroups and the control group is presented in Table 2.1.

The received results revealed that a significantly higher percentage of the control group (82.1%) exhibited right-handedness in comparison to the stutterers as a homogeneous group (66.7%) ($p < .05$), and in contrast, a significantly higher percentage of the whole group of stutterers showed mixed-handedness (31.0%) in comparison to the control group (17.9%) ($p < .05$). No significant between-group differences were found with respect to left-handedness ($p > .05$). For type of handedness, there were significant differences between the control group and the whole group of stutterers ($\chi^2_{[2]} = 5.944$, $p = .013$, Cramer's $V = 0.190$).

Chi-square comparisons of the results of each of the stuttering subgroups with those of the control group revealed slight and insignificant differences between the controls and both the subgroup with PSS ($\chi^2_{[2]} = 4.099$, $p = .129$, Cramer's

TABLE 2.1 Distribution of participants in study groups according to the demonstrated type of handedness and the presence of familial sinistrality (in %)

	Left-handedness		Mixed-handedness		Right-handedness		Familial sinistrality	
	n	%	n	%	n	%	n	%
Control group	0	0.0	14	17.9	64	82.1	17	21.8
Whole stuttering group	2	2.3	27	31.0	58	66.7	43	49.4
Subgroup with PSS	1	2.6	11	28.9	26	68.4	13	34.2
Subgroup with HSS	0	0.0	11	40.7	16	59.3	19	70.4
Subgroup with OSS	1	4.5	5	22.7	16	72.7	11	50.0

$V = 0.188$) and the subgroup with OSS ($\chi^2_{|2|} = 3.938$, $p = .140$, Cramer's $V = 0.198$), but statistically significant differences between the control group and the subgroup with HSS ($\chi^2_{|1|} = 5.744$, $p = .017$, $\varphi = 0.234$), consisting of greater frequency of mixed-handedness in HSS (40.7%) compared to the controls (17.9%).

Chi-square comparisons revealed significantly different frequencies of familial sinistrality in studied groups and subgroups. According to the results (Table 2.1), almost two and a half times more children from the whole stuttering group (49.4%) compared to the control group (21.8%) reported the presence of left-handed relative/s of the first and second degree ($\chi^2_{|1|} = 13.569$, $p < .000$, $\varphi = 0.287$). Although the frequency of familial sinistrality was higher in all stuttering subgroups compared to the control group, the differences between the control group (21.8%) and the subgroup with PSS (34.2%) were slight and insignificant ($\chi^2_{|1|} = 2.054$, $p = .152$, $\varphi = 0.133$), but statistically significant with both the subgroup with OSS (50.0%; $\chi^2_{|1|} = 6.771$, $p = .009$, $\varphi = 0.260$) and especially the subgroup with HSS (70.4%; $\chi^2_{|1|} = 21.005$, $p < .000$, $\varphi = 0.447$).

To sum up, the data analysis shows that the established statistically higher frequency of mixed-handedness among stuttering children as a homogeneous group compared to controls is mainly a result of a very high percentage of mixed-handers in the subgroup with HSS. Also, the finding of highest frequency of familial sinistrality in the subgroup with HSS compared to both the control group and the other stuttering subgroups brings the assumption that the atypical cerebral organization of the manual dominance in the HSS could be a hereditary feature.

Dichotic listening results

The analysis of dichotic test results showed specific differences between the control group and each of the stuttering subgroups, supporting the assumption that the population of stutterers is not homogeneous with respect to the functional brain asymmetries for language perception.

Between-group comparisons of the mean values of LQ (M, SD; %) found no differences between the control group (*Mean* LQ = +7.06, $SD = 11.57$) and both

Developmental stuttering 61

the whole stuttering group (*Mean* LQ = +6.39, *SD* = 15.38, *t* = 0.315, *p* = .753, Hedges' *g* = 0.050) and the subgroup with PSS (*Mean* LQ = +7.49, *SD* = 13.07, *t* = 0.180, *p* = .858, Hedges' *g* = 0.036), but obvious differences, although insignificant, between the control group and the other two stuttering subgroups: with OSS (*Mean* LQ = +10.55, *SD* = 15.94, *t* = 1.143, *p* = .256, Hedges' *g* = 0.276) and especially with HSS (*Mean* LQ = +1.44, *SD* = 17.10, *t* = 1.906, *p* = .059, Hedges' *g* = 0.426). Therefore, at a group level, all studied groups/subgroups showed the typical REA/LHA for dichotic speech perception, but it is important that the interaural asymmetry was the smallest in the subgroup with HSS and the biggest in the subgroup with OSS.

Figure 2.1 presents the comparative histograms of the distribution of individual LQs in the control group and the whole stuttering group.

As shown, the lack of differences between the mean group values of LQ masks the actual status of hemispheric asymmetries in stuttering subgroups due to diverging trends accounted for each of them: reduced hemispheric asymmetry in the group with HSS, increased in the group with OSS, and in the subgroup with PSS – identical to that of the non-stuttering group.

Was this lack of significant between-group differences in the mean values of LQ simply due to averaging, where the scores of REA and LEA cancel each other out within the studied groups? The performed chi-square comparisons of the frequency of REA in studied groups and subgroups (Table 2.2) revealed that similar to the control group, the majority of the whole stuttering group and the three stuttering subgroups demonstrated REA, that is the typical LHA for speech perception.

Nevertheless, while the percentages of children showing REA in the whole stuttering group (73.6%; $\chi^2_{|2|}$ = 0.990, *p* = .609, Cramer's *V* = 0.077), the subgroup with PSS (76.3%; $\chi^2_{|1|}$ = 0.529, *p* = .467, φ =0.068) and the subgroup with OSS

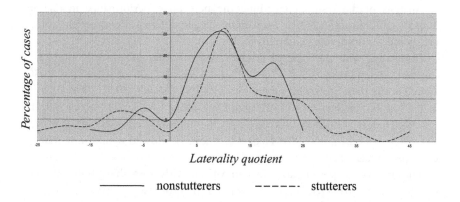

FIGURE 2.1 Comparative histograms of the distribution of individual LQs for dichotic listening in the control group and the whole stuttering group

TABLE 2.2 Percentage presentation of participants with REA, LEA and NEA in studied groups and subgroups

	REA		LEA		NEA	
	n	%	n	%	n	%
Control group	64	82.1	10	12.8	4	5.1
Whole stuttering group	64	73.6	22	25.3	1	1.1
Subgroup with PSS	29	76.3	9	23.7	0	0.0
Subgroup with HSS	17	63.0	9	33.3	1	3.7
Subgroup with OSS	18	81.8	4	18.2	0	0.0

(81.8%; $\chi^2_{|1|}$ = 0.001, p = .980, φ = 0.003) were very close to that in the control group (82.1%), the percentage of children showing REA was the lowest in the subgroup with HSS (63.0%) compared to all other groups/subgroups, as the difference with the control group had statistical significance ($\chi^2_{|2|}$ = 8.031, p = .018, Cramer's V = 0.277).

The mean absolute values of LQ (M, SD; %) of the studied groups and subgroups were compared because of the established significant between-group differences in the incidence of the typical REA. The results revealed slight and insignificant differences between the control group (*Mean absolute* LQ = 10.96, SD = 7.93) and the whole stuttering group (*Mean absolute* LQ = 12.53, SD = 10.90, t = 1.351, p = .179, Hedges' g = 0.165), as well as the subgroup with PSS (*Mean absolute* LQ = 12.34, SD = 8.43, t = 0.873, p = .385, Hedges' g = 0.173) and the subgroup with HSS (*Mean absolute* LQ = 10.88, SD = 13.10, t = 0.031, p = .975, Hedges' g = 0.006). Significant differences however were seen between the controls and the subgroup with OSS, reflected in a greater hemispheric asymmetry in this stuttering subgroup (*Mean absolute* LQ = 16.10, SD = 11.97, t = 2.381, p = .019, Hedges' g = 0.443).

Analysis of the results concerning the perceptive performance in dichotic listening conditions (M, SD; %) revealed the biggest differences between the control group and the stuttering subgroups (Table 2.3).

Compared with the control group (*Mean* = 59.7, SD = 8.1), the whole stuttering group (*Mean* = 50.1, SD = 9.9, t = 6.857, p < .001, Hedges' g = 1.056), as well as the three stuttering subgroups: with PSS (*Mean* = 52.7, SD = 10.2, t = 3.703, p < .05, Hedges' g = 0.792), with HSS (*Mean* = 52.3, SD = 8.6, t = 3.915, p < .05, Hedges' g = 0.899), and especially the subgroup with OSS (*Mean* = 43.0, SD = 8.5, t = 8.226, p < .001, Hedges' g = 2.039), showed significantly reduced mean percentage of correct responses. Furthermore, the group with OSS exhibited significantly worse performance in comparison with both the group with PSS (t = 8.71; p < .001, Hedges' g = 1.008) and the group with HSS (t = 3.82; p < .001, Hedges' g = 1.087).

An interesting finding emerged from the comparisons of the perceptive performances of subgroups with REA/LHA and those with LEA/RHA (Table 2.3).

TABLE 2.3 Mean percentage of correct identified syllables (*M*, *SD*; %) of studied groups and subgroups

	Whole groups/ subgroups		Subgroups with REA		Subgroups with LEA	
	M	SD	M	SD	M	SD
Control group	59.7	8.1	58.3	7.5	65.8	9.5
Whole stuttering group	50.1	9.9	50.7	10.0	47.9	10.5
Group with PSS	52.7	10.2	54.8	10.3	46.1	6.8
Group with HSS	52.3	8.6	51.1	8.1	56.2	9.9
Group with OSS	43.0	8.5	44.2	8.1	37.9	9.8

All stuttering subgroups with LEA displayed significantly worse performance in comparison to the control subgroup with LEA ($p < .001$) and all stuttering subgroups with REA, except that belonging to the subgroup with PSS, also displayed significantly worse performance in comparison to the control subgroup with REA ($p < .001$).

The finding that the performance of the REA subgroup of the PSS group was similar to that of the corresponding control subgroup led to the conclusion that the reduction of the perceptive effectiveness found for the whole PSS group was mainly due to its LEA subgroup.

Discussion

This study aimed to investigate and compare both the handedness and language lateralization of children with PSS, OSS and HSS with a control group of fluently speaking children of the same chronological age.

Comparison of the controls' data with stutterers' data as a homogeneous group, and then with those of each stuttering subgroups confirmed that DS is not a unitary disorder regarding the functional cerebral laterality and auditory processing, and clearly showed how the examination of stutterers as a homogeneous group could mask the real status of studied processes and lead to incorrect analysis and theoretical interpretations of findings. Furthermore, the observed specific differences between the patterns of results of each of stuttering subgroups compared separately with the control group support my initial assumption that both the causes for the deviations in the organization of hemispheric processes and interhemispheric relationships in speech perception, as well as their underlying mechanisms, could be different for the PSS, OSS and HSS.

My attempt to make an interpretation of observed deviations in hemispheric asymmetries in speech processing, particularly in speech perception in stuttering subgroups, is based on the model of hemispheric interactions in auditory verbal processing proposed by Morozov et al. [103], and some major postulates of the models of stuttering proposed by Orton [110], Travis [149], Moore [100], Morozov et al. [103], Rastatter and Dell [120] and Webster [156], which in my opinion explain to the fullest the relation between stuttering and anomalous cerebral lateralization.

According to the Morozov et al. model of hemispheric interactions in auditory verbal processing [103], there is a module for information processing and a module for decision-making in each hemisphere. The LH module for information processing performs the segmental analysis of linguistic items (phonemes, syllables), determines their characteristics (breaks, spectral peaks, characteristics of the phoneme transitions, etc.) and identifies the segments. The RH block of information processing compares the patterns of the incoming signals with the holistic engrams stored in the memory. Based on the obtained results, the module for decision-making of each hemisphere makes a decision. In the process of information processing, there is an exchange of information between the identical processing modules of both hemispheres as well as between the module for information processing and the module for decision-making of each hemisphere. This ensures for intermediate decision-making.

According to this model, each hemisphere is able to achieve independent signal identification, but for the RH, there are some restrictions associated with the limitations in the volume of its holistic engrams dictionary. In the real process of speech perception, both processing modes (left-hemispheric and right-hemispheric) operate in parallel, providing high speed and reliability of the stimulus identification.

A hypothetical model of mechanisms underlying the observed deviations in hemispheric asymmetry and interhemispheric interaction in psychogenic subtype of developmental stuttering

The pattern of results of the subgroup with PSS differed from those of the controls only with regard to the perceptive effectiveness in dichotic listening condition. This stuttering subgroup demonstrated significantly worse perceptive performance compared to controls, which was mainly due to its reduction in that part of the subgroup which showed LEA/RHA. There were no significant differences between this stuttering subgroup and the non-stuttering group regarding handedness.

According to the above-mentioned model of Morozov et al. [103], and based on the complex analysis of dichotic listening data, anamnesis information and handedness assessment, I could assume that the observed slight deficiency in auditory perceptive processing in this stuttering subgroup results from a RH dysfunction. The extent of manifestation of RH dysfunction, and hence the manifestation of the whole system deficit, depends on the status of hemispheric speech dominance. In cases of mature and stable LH dominance of speech processing (as Morozov et al. [103] have suggested, probably this is the case with children who demonstrated LHA for dichotic speech perception), there is a slight expression of the RH dysfunction. The control of the dominant and effectively functioning LH over the subdominant dysfunctional RH has a bidirectional effect:

reducing the expression of RH deficit and its partial compensation, leading to a weak expression of the speech perception system's deficit. And oppositely, when the LH dominance of speech processing is immature or unstable (probably, this is the case with children who demonstrated RHA for dichotic speech perception), the lack of restrictive and suppressive effects of the LH encourages the full expression of the RH deficit, resulting in a deepening of interhemispheric disintegration.

Probably, the RH dysfunction occurs mainly in the case of increasing its excitability caused by negative emotional experiences related to stressful life events and the child's fear and anxiety of stuttering, which are considered as RH function [66, 71, 85, 92, 143]. I assume that the subdominant RH has an unstable level of excitability. In emotionally neutral situations, when the level of activation of, the RH is low, the whole functional system works normally and efficiently, and speech dysfluencies reduce and even disappear. Any emotional experience increases the level of RH activation which triggers its dysfunction.

Such interpretation allows the assumption that the weak anomalies in the hemispheric interaction of the cortical speech system in children with PSS are functional in nature and depend on the emotional status of the subject.

Aforementioned findings and their interpretation fit well into the Belyakova's theory of pathophysiological mechanisms of this subtype of DS, according to which an increased emotionality dominates in the afferent synthesis of speech functional system and plays the role of a factor that triggers and maintains the pathological process [16].

A hypothetical model of mechanisms underlying the observed deviations in hemispheric asymmetry and interhemispheric interaction in organic subtype of developmental stuttering

The pattern of the abnormalities of dichotic listening performance registered in studied children suffering from OSS indicates a pronounced deficit in auditory perceptive processing. Compared with both the non-stuttering group and the other two stuttering subgroups, the subgroup with OSS showed the most pronounced and stable hemispheric asymmetry for dichotic speech perception, and a critical reduction of the perceptive performance. Furthermore, the frequency of children with strong right-handedness was the highest in this stuttering subgroup compared to the other stuttering subgroups.

These results could be interpreted as suggesting a deficit in auditory perceptive functions of both hemispheres, but a typical LH dominance for speech and manual functions. I can suppose that the segmental analysis performed by the LH is impaired, but this LH perceptive deficit is not compensated by the active involvement of the RH in auditory verbal processing, probably due to delayed or abnormal development of bilateral integration, or deficits in RH participation in auditory verbal processing activities comprising an impairment of the correct and timely retrieval of memory engrams.

If we accept the assumption of Morozov et al. [103] that the holistic, non-segmental (right-hemispheric) mode of information processing is especially effective in the early stages of auditory verbal processing, because it narrows the field of searching both the holistic engrams (stored in the RH) and the segment engrams (stored in the LH), I can suppose that in the case of RH function impairment, the manifestation of speech system's deficit would be greater.

I presume that early organic changes in the brain of children with OSS have caused a delayed morphological or functional maturation of the brain structures that underlie speech processing, thus resulting in less effective processing capacity of both cerebral hemispheres and insufficient interhemispheric cooperation, but normal LH speech dominance. The functional deficits of both hemispheres and their inability to completely integrate led to low speed and weak reliability of the speech perception, which in the process of acoustic feedback during the speech generation distorts synchronization of the impulses to speech muscles [103]. The combination of disturbances of afferent synthesis performed by speech functional system with disturbances of efferent synthesis caused by developmental delays of the general motor skills leads to the appearance of a pathologically shaped speech-motor stereotype, one of whose manifestations are the speech dysfluencies [16]. Thus, the observed deviations of interhemispheric interactions in children with OSS are some kind of expressions of a discrete pathology of brain functions and are not etiopathogenetically related to emergence of speech dysfluencies.

A hypothetical model of mechanisms underlying the link between hereditary subtype of developmental stuttering and atypical cerebral lateralization

The pattern of results from the complex research outcomes of children with HSS confirmed my initial hypothesis that in this subtype of stuttering, the emergence and persistence of speech dysfluencies are probably etiopathogenetically associated with a disturbance of hemispheric dominance due to aberrant functional lateralization of speech processing.

Since the dichotic listening test used in this study is informative primarily for hemispheric asymmetry of auditory verbal perception, my assumptions are well founded for the lateralization of speech perception rather than for speech expression.

I found that in the subgroup with HSS, compared to the controls and the other stuttering subgroups, the degree of hemisphere asymmetry for dichotic speech perception was the least pronounced and the percentage of children who showed REA/LHA was significantly lowest. Also, this stuttering subgroup demonstrated significantly worse perceptive performance compared to controls.

These results allow the assumption that children with HSS are characterized by disrupted auditory verbal processing due to weak and incomplete or reversed lateralization of speech perception. Moreover, the finding that only this stuttering subgroup exhibited significantly greater frequency of mixed-handedness compared to the controls supports the suggestion for more variable and insufficient lateralization of cerebral function in this subtype of DS.

The results from the additional examinations, indicating highest frequency of familial history of stuttering and familial sinistrality in HSS subgroup compared to all studied groups/subgroups, motivate the assumption that the atypical brain organization, including weak or reversed lateralization of hemisphere functions, could be a hereditable feature. The finding about the highest incidence of familial history of both stuttering and sinistrality only in the subgroup with HSS, which is also the only subgroup demonstrating insufficient or atypical lateralization, supports the assumption that genetic risk factors for atypical cerebral laterality are not separate from genetic risk factors for language impairment (for a review of the genetic models of the association between weak cerebral lateralization for language and language/literacy disorders, see [18]).

Perhaps the child was born with a genetically determined predisposition to a more bilateral representation of language organization. Duplication of the LH function of language perception in the RH (not excluded, the "RH segmental analysis" of linguistic items to rely on a system of characteristics different from that in the LH) may impede hemispheric specialization which, in turn, can cause a lower speed and accuracy of perceptive processing. "The competition" between the two cerebral hemispheres leads to the formation of an atypical pattern of functioning of the speech-language system, which normally works on the principle of the dominance. Similar to Morozov et al. [103], Rastatter and Dell [120] and Webster [156], I hypothesized that the left and right hemispheres' inability to integrate makes it possible for the motor speech programmers to receive conflicting or time uncoordinated information, which, during the speech generation, disturbs the timing of the neural impulses to the bilateral articulatory musculatory and provokes speech dysfluencies.

Duplication of the verbal perceptive functions of both hemispheres in the majority of subjects with HSS could provoke the formation of a second control centre regulating the verbal expression only in part of them. For the others, the duplication may remain only on the perceptive level and, if this is the case, some differences with regard to development and persistence of stuttering, outcome of therapy and characteristics of stuttering might exist.

My findings support an assumption suggested a long time ago about the role of impaired hemispheric asymmetries and interactions in the genesis of DS, but the most important finding is that this could, most probably, be a cause for the emergence only of the HSS.

Finally, I can summarize that this study gave satisfactory answers to some of the issues about DS. Though some new questions emerged, the received results generally confirmed the correctness of the approach to examine the complex relationships between functional brain asymmetries and speech and language disorders in the different types of neurodevelopmental conditions considering their non-unitary nature. In order to enhance the understanding of the mechanisms underlying different types of neurodevelopmental disorders, researchers must intensify their efforts to identify the different subtypes and study them separately.

References and further reading

1. Ambrose, N. G., Yairi, E. & Cox, N. (1993). Genetic aspects of early childhood stuttering. *JSHR, 36*(4), 701–706.
2. Andreou, G. & Karapetsas, A. (2002). Accuracy and speed of processing verbal stimuli among subjects with low and high ability in mathematics. *Educ. Psychol., 22*(5), 613–619.
3. Andrews, G., Craig, A., Feyer, A. M., Hoddinott, S., Howie, P. & Neilson, M. (1983). Stuttering: A review of research findings and theories circa 1982. *JSHD, 48*(3), 226–246.
4. Andrews, G. & Harris, M. (1964). *The syndrome of stuttering*. London: Heinemann Medical Books.
5. Andrews, G., Morris-Yates, A., Howie, P. & Martin, N. (1991). Genetic factors in stuttering confirmed. *Arch. Gen. Psychiatry, 48*(11), 1034–1035.
6. Andrews, O., Quinn, P. & Sorby, W. (1972). Stuttering: An investigation into cerebral dominance for speech. *J. Neurol. Neurosurg. Psychiatry, 35*(3), 414–418.
7. Annett, M. (1993). Handedness and educational success: The hypothesis of a genetic balanced polymorphism with heterozigote advantage for laterality and ability. *Br. J. Dev. Psychol., 11*, 359–370.
8. Asatiani, N., Kazakov, V. & Freydin, Y. (1988). Some questions about the clinical classification of stuttering [in Russian]. *Defektology, 1*, 28–32.
9. Asenova, I. (1997). *Study of hemispheric specialization in different types of stuttering by means of dichotic phonemic perception* [in Bulgarian]. PhD thesis. Blagoevgrad, Bulgaria: South-West University "Neofit Rilski" Publishing House.
10. Asenova, I. (2011). Professional training and language lateralization: A comparative study of mathematicians and artists [in Russian]. *Voprosy Psikhologii, 3*, 113–120.
11. Ashburner, J. & Friston, K. (2001). Why voxel-based morphometry should be used. *Neuroimage, 14*(6), 21–36.
12. Beal, D. S., Gracco, V. L., Brettschneider, J., Kroll, R. M. & De Nil, L. F. (2013). A voxel-based morphometry (VBM) analysis of regional grey and white matter volume abnormalities within the speech production network of children who stutter. *Cortex, 49*(8), 2151–2161.
13. Beal, D. S., Gracco, V. L., Lafaille, S. J. & Nil, L. F. (2007). Voxel-based morphometry of auditory and speech related cortex in stutterers. *Neuroreport, 18*(12), 1257–1260.
14. Beal, D. S., Quraan, M. A., Cheyne, D. O., Taylor, M. J., Gracco, V. L. & De Nil, L. F. (2011). Speech-induced suppression of evoked auditory fields in children who stutter. *Neuroimage, 54*(4), 2994–3003.
15. Bekker, K. & Sovak, M. (1981). *Logopedics* [in Russian]. Moscow, Russia: Prosveshcheniye.
16. Belyakova, L. (1981). *Clinical and physiological analysis of the central pathogenetic mechanisms of stuttering* [in Russian]. Dissertation for the Degree of Doctor of Sciences. Leningrad, Russian Federation: University Publishing House.
17. Bishop, D. V. M. (1990). *Handedness and developmental disorder*. Oxford: Blackwell.
18. Bishop, D. V. M. (2013). Cerebral asymmetry and language development: cause, correlate or consequence? *Science, 340*(6138), 1230531.
19. Blood, G. (1985). Laterality differences in child stutterers: Heterogeneity, severity levels, and statistical treatments. *JSHD, 50*(1), 66–72.
20. Blood, I. & Blood, G. (1984). Relationship between stuttering severity and brainstem-evoked response testing. *Percept. Mot. Skills, 59*(3), 935–938.

21 Blood, G. & Blood, I. (1989). Laterality preferences in adult female and male stutterers. *J. Fluency Dis.*, *14*(1), 1–10.
22 Blood, G., Blood, I. & Newton, K. (1986). Effect of directed attention on cerebral asymmetries in stuttering adults. *Percept. Mot. Skills*, *62*(2), 351–355.
23 Bloodstein, O. (1977). Stuttering. *JSHD*, *42*(2), 211–215.
24 Bloodstein, O. (1995). *A handbook of stuttering*. San Diego, CA: Singular Publishing Group.
25 Boberg, E., Yeudall, L., Schopflocher, D. & Bo-Lassen, P. (1983). The effect of an intensive behavioral program on the distribution of EEG alpha power in stutterers during the processing of verbal and visiospatial information. *J. Fluency Dis.*, *8*(3), 245–263.
26 Borden, G., Baer, T. & Kenney, M. (1985). Onset of voicing in stuttered and fluent utterances. *JSHD*, *28*(3), 363–372.
27 Borden, G. & Harris, K. (1990). *Speech science primer: Physiology, acoustics, and perception of speech*. Baltimore, MD: Williams & Wilkins.
28 Boyanova, V. (1990). *Anatomic-physiological peculiarities of children who stutter* [in Bulgarian]. Blagoevgrad, Bulgaria: South-West University "Neofit Rilski" Publishing House.
29 Brady, J. P. & Berson, J. (1975). Stuttering, dichotic listening, and cerebral dominance. *Arch. Gen. Psychiatry*, *32*(11), 1449–1452.
30 Brakus, R. & Golubovic, S. (1995). Bihemispheric confusion and stuttering. In W. Starkweather & H. Peters (Eds.), *Stuttering: proceedings of the first word congress on fluency disorders*, August 8–11 (Vol. 1, pp. 125–128). Nijmegen, Netherlands: Nijmegen University Press.
31 Branch, C., Milner, B. & Rasmussen, T. (1964). Intracarotid sodium amytal for lateralization of cerebral speech dominance. Observation in 123 patients. *J. Neurosurg.*, *21*, 399–405.
32 Braun, A., Varga, M., Stager, S., Schulz, G., Selbie, S., Maisog, J. & Ludlow, C. L. (1997). Altered patterns of cerebral activity during speech and language production in developmental stuttering: An H2 (15) O positron emission tomography study. *Brain*, *120*(Pt 5), 761–784.
33 Bryden, M. (1982). *Laterality: Functional asymmetry in the intact brain*. New York: Academic Press.
34 Chang, S. E., Erickson, K. I., Ambrose, N. G., Hasegawa-Johnson, M. A. & Ludlow, C. L. (2008). Brain anatomy differences in childhood stuttering. *Neuroimage*, *39*(3), 1333–1344.
35 Chang, S. E. & Zhu, D. C. (2013). Neural network connectivity differences in children who stutter. *Brain*, *136*(Pt 12), 3709–3726.
36 Chang, S. E. & Zhu, D. C. (2014). Research updates in neuroimaging studies of children who stutter. *Semin. Speech Lang.*, *35*(2), 67–79.
37 Chang, S. E., Zhu, D. C., Choo, A. L. & Angstadt, M. (2015). White matter neuroanatomical differences in young children who stutter. *Brain*, *138*(3), 694–711.
38 Choo, A. L., Chang, S. E., Zengin-Bolatkale, H., Ambrose, N. G. & Loucks, T. M. (2012). Corpus callosum morphology in children who stutter. *J. Commun. Disord.*, *45*(4), 279–289.
39 Choo, A. L., Kraft, S. J., Olivero, W., Ambrose, N. G., Sharma, H., Chang, S. E. & Loucks, T. M. (2011). Corpus callosum differences associated with persistent stuttering in adults. *J. Commun. Disord.*, *44*(4), 470–477.
40 Cimmorell-Strong, J., Gilbert, H. & Frick, J. (1983). Dichotic speech perception: A comparison between stuttering and non-stuttering children. *J. Fluency Disord.*, *81*(1), 77–91.

41 Cooper, E. (1990). *Understanding stuttering. Information for parents*. Chicago, IL: NESS.
42 Cornish, K. (1996). The Geschwind and Galaburda theory of cerebral lateralization: An empirical evaluation of its assumptions. *Curr. Psychol.*, 15(1), 68–76.
43 Curry, F. & Gregory, H. (1969). The performance of stutterers on dichotic listening. *JSHD*, 12(1), 73–82.
44 Danilov, V. & Cherepanov, I. (1970). *Pathophysiology of neuroses* [in Russian]. Leningrad, Russian Federation: Meditsina
45 Daskalov, D. (1982). *Speech disorders in children* [in Bulgarian]. Sofia, Bulgaria: Med. & Fizk.
46 Dellatolas, G., Annesi, I., Jallon, P., Chavances, M. & Lellouch, J. (1990). An epidemiological reconsideration of the Geschwind-Galaburda theory of cerebral lateralization. *Arch. Neurol.*, 47(7), 778–782.
47 Demonet, J. & Puel, M. (1994). Aphasie et correlate cerebraux des functions linguistiques. In X. Seron & M. Jeannerod (Eds.), *Neuropsychologie humaine* (pp. 336–359). Liege, Belgium: Mardaga.
48 De Nil, L., Kroll, R., Kapur, S. & Houle, S. (2000). A positron emission tomography study of silent and oral single word reading in stuttering and nonstuttering adults. *JSLHR*, 43(4), 1038–1053.
49 Dorman, M. F. & Porter, R. J. (1975). Hemispheric lateralization for phonemic perception in stutterers. *Cortex*, 11, 181–185.
50 Draganski, B., Gaser, C., Busch, V., Schuierer, G., Bogdahn, U. & May, A. (2004). Neuroplasticity: Changes in grey matter induced by training. *Nature*, 427, 311–312.
51 Dragovic, M. (2004). Categorization and validation of handedness using latent class analysis. *Acta Neuropsych.*, 16(4), 212–218.
52 Dworzynski, K., Remington, A., Rijksdijk, F., Howell, P. & Plomin, R. (2007). Genetic etiology in cases of recovered and persistent stuttering in an unselected, longitudinal sample of young twins. *Am. J. Speech Lang. Pathol.*, 16(2), 169–178.
53 Efimov, O. & Tsitseroshin, M. (1988). Peculiarities of the bilateral associations of fluctuations in the biopotentials of the brain hemispheres' cortex in children who stutter [in Russian]. *Fiziol Cheloveka*, 14(6), 892–903.
54 Ellis, A. & Young, A. (1988). *Human cognitive neuropsychology*. Hove, UK: Lawrence Erlbaum Associates.
55 Felsenfeld, S. (2002). Finding susceptibility genes for developmental disorders of speech: the long and winding road. *J. Commun. Disord.*, 35(4), 329–345.
56 Felsenfeld, S., Kirk, K., Zhu, G., Statham, D., Neale, M. & Martin, N. (2000). A study of the genetic and environmental etiology of stuttering in a selected twin simple. *Behav. Genet.*, 30(5), 359–366.
57 Filicheva, T. & Chevelyova, I. (1987). *Logopedic therapy in the special kindergarten* [in Russian]. Moscow, Russia: Prosveshcheniye.
58 Finitzo, T., Pool, K., Freeman, F., Devous, S. & Watson, B. (1991). Cortical dysfunction in developmental stutterers. In H. Peters, W. Hulstijn & C. Starkweather (Eds.), *Speech motor control and stuttering* (pp. 251–261). New York: Elsevier.
59 Florenskaya, Y. (1949). *Clinics and therapy of speech disorders* [in Russian]. Moscow, Russia: Medgiz.
60 Foundas, A., Bollich, A., Corey, D., Hurley, M. & Heilman, K. (2001). Anomalous anatomy of speech-language areas in adults with persistent developmental stuttering. *Neurology*, 57, 207–215.
61 Foundas, A., Corey, D., Angeles, V., Bolich, A., Crabtree-Hartman, E. & Heilman, K. (2003). Atypical cerebral laterality in adults with persistent developmental stuttering. *Neurology*, 61(10), 1378–1385.

62 Foundas, A. L., Corey, D. M., Hurley, M. M. & Heilman, K. M. (2004). Verbal dichotic listening in developmental stuttering: Subgroups with atypical auditory processing. *Cogn. Behav. Neurol.*, *17*(4), 224–232.
63 Fox, P., Ingham, R., Ingham, J., Hirsch, T., Downs, J., Martin, C. . . . & Lacaster, J. L. (1996). A PET study of the neural systems of stuttering. *Nature*, *382*(6587), 158–161.
64 Friederici, A., Meyer, D. & von Cramon, D. (2000). Auditory language comprehension: An event-related fMRI study on the processing of syntactic and lexical information. *Brain Lang.*, *74*(2), 289–300.
65 Fukawa, I., Yoshioka, H., Ozama, E. & Yoshida, S. (1988). Difference of susceptibility to delayed auditory feedback between stutterers and nonstutterers. *J. Speech Lang. Hear. Res.*, *31*(3), 475–479.
66 Gainotti, G. (1994). Bases neurobiologiques et controle des emotions. In X. Seron & M. Jeannerod (Eds.), *Neuropsychologie humaine* (pp. 471–486). Liege, Belgium: Mardaga.
67 Georgieva, D. (2000). *Speech fluency disorders* [in Bulgarian]. Sofia, Bulgaria: Sofia University "St. Kliment Ohridski" Publishing House.
68 Geschwind, N. & Galaburda, A. (1987). *Cerebral lateralization*. Cambridge, MA: MIT Press.
69 Gruber, L. & Powell, R. L. (1974). Responses of stuttering and non-stuttering children to a dichotic listening task. *Percept. Mot. Skills*, *38*(1), 263–264.
70 Hartman, B. (1994). *The neuropsychology of developmental stuttering*. London: Whurr Publishers.
71 Heilman, K. (1994). Emotion and the brain: A distributed modular network mediating emotional experience. In D. Zaidel (Ed.), *Neuropsychology* (pp. 139–158). San Diego, CA: Academic Press.
72 Hirnstein, M., Hugdahl, K. & Hausmann, M. (2014). How brain asymmetry relates to performance – A large scale dichotic listening study. *Front Psychol.*, *4*, 997.
73 Howie, P. (1981). Intrapair similarity in frequency of disfluency in monozygotic and dizygotic twin pairs containing stutterers. *Behav. Genet.*, *11*(3), 227–238.
74 Howie, P. (1981). Concordance for stuttering in monozygotic and dizygotic twin pairs. *JSHD*, *24*(3), 317–321.
75 Ingham, R. J. (2001). Brain imaging studies of developmental stuttering. *J. Commun. Disord.*, *34*(6), 493–516.
76 Janke, L., Hanggi, J. & Steinmetz, H. (2004). Morphological brain differences between adult stutterers and non-stutterers. *BMC Neurol.*, *4*, 23.
77 Janke, L., Kaiser, P., Bauer, A. & Kalveram, K. (1995). Upper lip, lower lip, and jaw peak velocity sequence during bilabial closures: No differences between stutterers and nonstutterers. *J. Acoust. Soc. Am.*, *97*, 3900–3903.
78 Janssen, P., Kloth, S. A. M., Kraaimaat, F. W. & Brutten, G. J. (1996). Genetic factors in stuttering: A replication of Ambrose, Yiari, and Cox's (1993) study with adult probands. *J. Fluency Disord.*, *21*(2), 105–108.
79 Jones, R. (1966). Observations on stammering after localized cerebral injury. *J. Neurol. Neurosurg. Psychiatry*, *29*(3), 192–195.
80 Kalinowski, J. (2003). Choral speech: The amelioration of stuttering via imitation and the mirror neuronal system. *Neurosci. Biobehav. Rev.*, *27*(4), 339–347.
81 Khedr, E., El-Nasser, W., Abdel Haleem, E., Bakr, M. & Trakhan, M. (2000). Evoked potentials and electroencephalography in stuttering. *Folia Phoniatrica et Logopaedica*, *52*(4), 178–186.
82 Kidd, K. (1980). Genetic models of stuttering. *J. Fluency Disord.*, *5*(3), 187–201.
83 Kimura, D. (1966). Dual function asymmetry of the brain in visual perception. *Neuropsychologia*, *4*(3), 275–285.

72 Developmental stuttering

84 Kimura, D. (1967). Functional asymmetry of the brain in dichotic listening. *Cortex*, *3*(2), 163–172.
85 Kurshev, V. (1973). *Stuttering* [in Russian]. Moscow, Russia: Meditsina.
86 Kuz'min, Y., Dmitriyeva, E. & Zaytseva, K. (1989). Functional asymmetry of the brain for the perception of emotions in children who stutter [in Russian]. *Fiziol Cheloveka*, *15*(2), 96–101.
87 Leung, A. & Robson, W. L. (1990). Stuttering. *Clin. Pediatr. (Phila)*, *29*(9), 498–502.
88 Levelt, W. (1989). *Speaking: From intention to articulation*. Cambridge, MA: MIT Press.
89 Liebetrau, R. & Daly, D. (1981). Auditory processing and perceptual abilities of "organic" and "functional" stuttering. *J. Fluency Disord.*, *6*, 219–223.
90 Lokhov, M. (1988). Interhemispheric asymmetry in the mechanisms of non-aphasic disorders of speech functions [in Russian]. *Fiziol Cheloveka*, *14*(11), 38–45.
91 Luria, A. R. (1966). *Higher cortical functions in man*. New York: Basic Books.
92 Luria, A. R. (1973). *Foundations of neurophysiology* [in Russian]. Moscow, Russia: MGU.
93 Lussenhop, A., Boggs, J. S., Laborwit, L. J. & Walle, E. L. (1973). Cerebral dominance in stutterers determined by Wada testing. *Neurology*, *23*(11), 1190–1192.
94 MacKeever, W., Seitz, K., Krutsch, A. & VanEys, P. (1995). On language laterality in normal dextrals and sinistrals: Results from the bilateral object naming latency task. *Neuropsychologia*, *33*(12), 1627–1635.
95 Messerli, P., Pegna, A. & Sordet, N. (1995). Hemispheric dominance for melody recognition in musicians and non-musicians. *Neuropsychologia*, *33*(4), 395–405.
96 Mikeev, M., Mohr, C., Afanasiev, S., Landis, T. & Thut, G. (2002). Motor control and cerebral hemispheric specialization in highly qualified judo wrestlers. *Neuropsychologia*, *40*(8), 1209–1219.
97 Missulovin, L. (1988). *Treatment of stuttering* [in Russian]. Leningrad, Russian Federation: Meditsina.
98 Molt, L. & Brading, T. (1995). Hemispheric patterns of auditory event-related potentials to dichotic CV-syllables in stutterers and normal speakers. In W. Starkweather & H. Peters (Eds.), *Stuttering: Proceedings of the first world congress on fluency disorders* (Vol. 1, pp. 147–150). Nijmegen, Netherlands: Nijmegen University Press.
99 Moore, W. (1976). Bilateral tachistoscopic word perception of stutterers and normal subjects. *Brain Lang.*, *3*(3), 434–442.
100 Moore, W. (1984). Central nervous system characteristics of stutterers. In R. Curlee & W. Perkins (Eds.), *Nature and treatment of stuttering: New directions* (pp. 49–71). San Diego, CA: Hill Press.
101 Moore, W. & Haynes, W. (1980). Alpha hemispheric asymmetry and stuttering: Some support for a segmentation dysfunction hypothesis. *JSHD*, *23*, 229–247.
102 Morgan, M., Cranford, J. & Burk, K. (1997). P300 event-related potentials in stutterers and nonstutterers. *JSHR*, *40*(6), 1334–1340.
103 Morozov, V. P., Vartanyan, I. A., Galunov, V. I., Dmitriyeva, Y. E., Zaytseva, K., Koroleva, I. . . . Shurgaya, G. G. (1988). *Speech perception: Questions about functional asymmetry of the brain* [in Russian]. Leningrad, Russian Federation: Nauka.
104 Munte, T., Altenmuller, E. & Janke, L. (2002). The musician's brain as a model of neuroplasticity. *Nat. Rev. Neurosci.*, *3*(6), 473–478.
105 Natke, U., Donath, T. & Kalveram, K. (2003). Control of voice fundamental frequency in speaking versus singing. *J. Acoust. Soc. Am.*, *113*(3), 1587–1593.
106 Natke, U., Grosser, J., Sandrieser, P. & Kalveram, K. (2002). The duration component of the stress effect in stuttering. *J. Fluency Disord.*, *27*(4), 305–317.

107 Natke, U. & Kalveram, K. (2001). Effects of frequency-shifted auditory feedback on fundamental frequency of long stressed and unstressed syllables. *JSLHR, 44*(3), 577–584.
108 Nessell, W. (1989). Stuttering (letter). *JAMA, 261*(1), 46–48.
109 Nowack, W. (1986). Adult onset stuttering and seizures. *Clin. Electroencephalogr., 17*(3), 142–145.
110 Orton, S. (1928). A physiological theory of reading disability and stuttering in children. *N. Engl. J. Med., 198*, 1045–1052.
111 Ozge, A., Toros, F. & Comelekoglu, U. (2004). The role of hemispheral asymmetry and regional activity of quantitative EEG in children with stuttering. *Child Psychiat. Hum Dev., 34*(4), 269–280.
112 Perkins, W., Kent, R. & Curlee, R. (1991). A theory of neurolinguistic function in stuttering. *JSHR, 34*(4), 734–752.
113 Peters, T. & Guitar, B. (1991). *Stuttering: An integrated approach to its nature and treatment.* Baltimore, MD: Williams & Wilkins.
114 Peters, H., Hulstijn, W. & Starkweather, C. (1991). *Speech motor control and stuttering.* Amsterdam, The Netherlands: Exerpta Medica.
115 Ponsford, R., Brown, W., Marsh, J. & Travis, L. (1975). Proceedings: Evoked potential correlates of cerebral dominance for speech perception in stutterers and non-stutterers. *Electroencephalogr. Clin. Neurophysiol., 39*(4), 434–439.
116 Postma, A. & Kolk, H. (1993). The covert repair hypothesis: Prearticulatory repair processes in normal and stuttered disfluencies. *JSHR, 36*, 472–487.
117 Poulos, M. & Webster, W. (1991). Family history as a basis for subgrouping people who stutter. *JSHR, 34*, 5–10.
118 Quinn, P. (1972). Stuttering, cerebral dominance and the dichotic word test. *Med. J. Aust., 2*(12), 639–643.
119 Rakhmilevich, A. & Oganesyan, Y. (1987). Peculiarities of speech intonation and functional state of internal muscles of the larynx in stutterers during phonation [in Russian]. *Defektology, 6*, 28–31.
120 Rastatter, M. & Dell, C. (1987). Vocal reaction times of stuttering subjects to tachistoscopically presented concrete and abstract words: A closer look at cerebral dominance and language processing. *JSHR, 30*(3), 306–310.
121 Rastatter, M., Stuart, A. & Joseph, K. (1998). Quantitative electroencephalogram of posterior cortical areas of fluent and stuttering persons. *Percept. Mot. Skills, 87*(2), 623–634.
122 Riecker, A., Ackermann, H., Wildgruber, D., Meyer, J., Dogil, G., Haider, H., & Grodd, W. (2000). Articulatory/phonemic sequencing at the level of the anterior perisylvian cortex: A functional magnetic resonance imaging (fMRI) study. *Brain Lang., 75*(2), 259–276.
123 Riecker, A., Wildgruber, D., Dogil, G., Grodd, W. & Ackermann, H. (2002). Hemispheric lateralization effects of rhythm implementation during syllable repetitions: An fMRI study. *Neuroimage, 16*(1), 169–176.
124 Riley, J. & Riley, G. (2000). A revised component model for diagnosing and treating children who stutter. *CICSD, 27*, 188–199.
125 Robb, M., Lynn, W. E. & O' Beirne, G. A. (2013). An exploration of dichotic listening among adults who stutter. *Clin. Ling. Phonetics, 27*(9), 681–693.
126 Rosenfield, D. (1980). Cerebral dominance and stuttering. *J. Fluency Disord., 5*(3), 171–185.
127 Rosenfield, D. (1989). Stuttering (letter). *N. Engl. J. Med., 15, 320*(24), 1630–1631.
128 Rosenfield, D. & Goodglass, H. (1980). Dichotic testing of cerebral dominance in stutterers. *Brain Lang., 11*(1), 170–180.

129 Rosenfield, D. & Viswanath, N. (2002). Neuroscience of stuttering. *Science, 295*(5557), 973–974.
130 Rychkova, N. (1981). Status of voluntary motor activity and speech of preschool children with a neurotic and neurotiform types of stuttering [in Russian]. *Defektology, 6*, 73–77.
131 Salmelin, R., Schnitzler, A., Schmitz, F. & Freund, H. (2000). Single word reading in developmental stutterers and fluent speakers. *Brain, 123*(Pt 6), 1184–1202.
132 Salmelin, R., Schnitzler, A., Schmitz, F., Jancke, L., Witte, O. & Freund, H. (1998). Functional organization of the auditory cortex is different in stutterers and fluent speakers. *Neuroreport, 9*(10), 2225–2229.
133 Sato, Y., Mori, K., Koizumi, T., Minagawa-Kawai, Y., Tanaka, A., Ozawa, E. . . . & Mazuka, R. (2011). Functional lateralization of speech processing in adults and children who stutter. *Front Psychol., 2*, 70.
134 Seery, C. H., Watkins, R. V., Mangelsdorf, S. C. & Shigeto, A. (2007). Subtyping stuttering II: Contributions from language and temperament. *J. Fluency Disord., 32*(3), 197–217.
135 Shklovskiy, V. (1976). Importance of the cerebral hemispheric dominance for speech in stuttering [in Russian]. *Defektology, 1*, 20–31.
136 Slorach, N. & Noehr, B. (1973). Dichotic listening in stuttering and dyslalic children. *Cortex, 9*(3), 295–300.
137 Smith, A. & Kelly, E. (1997). Stuttering: A dynamic, multifactorial model. In R. F. Curlee & G. M. Siegel (Eds.), *Nature and treatment of stuttering* (pp. 97–127). Boston, MA: Allyn & Bacon.
138 Snyder, P., Bilder, R., Wu, H., Bogerts, B. & Lieberman, J. (1995). Cerebellar volume asymmetries are related to handedness: A quantitative MRI study. *Neuropsychologia, 33*(4), 407–419.
139 Sommer, M., Koch, M., Walter, P., Weiller, C. & Buchel, C. (2002). Disconnection of speech-relevant brain areas in persistent developmental stuttering. *Lancet, 360*(3), 380–383.
140 Sommers, R., Brady, W. & Moore, W. (1975). Dichotic ear preference of stuttering children and adults. *Percept. Mot. Skills, 41*(3), 931–938.
141 Sowman, P. F., Crain, S., Harrison, E. & Johnson, B. W. (2014). Lateralization of brain activation in fluent and non-fluent preschool children: A magnetoencephalographic study of picture-naming. *Front Hum. Neurosci., 8*, 354.
142 Spajdel, M., Jariabkova, K. & Riecansky, I. (2007). The influence of musical experience on lateralization of auditory processing. *Laterality, 12*(6), 487–499.
143 Springer, S. & Deutsch, G. (1990). *Left brain, right brain* (3rd ed.). San Francisco, CA: W. H. Freeman.
144 Stamov, V. (1985). *To the issue of the functional specialization of the brain (some psychological-pedagogical problems)* [in Bulgarian]. Blagoevgrad, Bulgaria: South-West University "Neofit Rilski" Publishing House.
145 Stamov, V. (1989). *Logopedics* [in Bulgarian]. Blagoevgrad, Bulgaria: South-West University "Neofit Rilski" Publishing House.
146 Steinmetz, H., Volkman, J., Janke, L. & Freud, H. (1991). Anatomical left-right asymmetry of language-related temporal cortex is different in left- and right-handers. *Ann. Neurol., 29*(3), 315–319.
147 Strub, R., Black, F. & Naeser, M. (1987). Anomalous dominance in sibling stutterers: evidence from CT scan asymmetries, dichotic listening, neuropsychological testing, and handedness. *Brain Lang., 30*(2), 338–350.

148 Suvorova, V., Motova, M. & Turovskaya, Z. (1984). Reproductive images of binocular vision in atypical interhemispheric relations (in stutterers) [in Russian]. *Voprosy Psikhologii*, *1*, 105–111.
149 Travis, L. (1978). The cerebral dominance theory of stuttering 1931–1978. *JSHD*, *43*(3), 278–281.
150 Van Borsel, J., Achten, E., Santens, P., Lahorte, P. & Voet, T. (2003). fMRI of developmental stuttering: A pilot study. *Brain Lang.*, *85*(3), 369–376.
151 Volkova, L. (1989). *Logopedics* [in Russian]. Moscow, Russia: Prosveshcheniye.
152 Watson, B. & Freeman, F. (1994). Linguistic performance and regional blood flow in persons who stutter. *JSHR*, *37*(6), 1221–1228.
153 Watson, B., Pool, K., Devous, M. & Freeman, F. (1992). Brain blood flow related to acoustic laryngeal reaction time in adult developmental stutterers. *JSHR*, *35*, 555–561.
154 Weber-Fox, C. & Hampton, A. (2008). Stuttering and natural speech processing of semantic and syntactic constraints on verbs. *JSLHR*, *51*(5), 1058–1071.
155 Weber-Fox, C. M., Wray, A. H. & Arnold, H. (2013). Early childhood stuttering and electrophysiological indices of language processing. *J. Fluency Disord.*, *38*(2), 206–221.
156 Webster, W. G. (1997). Principles of human brain organization related to lateralization of language and speech motor functions in normal speakers and stutterers. In W. Hulstijn, H. Peters & P. Van Lieshout (Eds.), *Speech motor production: Motor control, brain research and fluency disorders* (pp. 119–139). Amsterdam, The Netherlands: Elsevier.
157 Webster, W. & Poulos, M. (1987). Handedness distribution among adults who stutter. *Cortex*, *24*(4), 705–708.
158 Wells, B. & Moore, W. (1990). EEG alpha asymmetries in stutterers and nonstutterers: Effects of linguistic variables on hemispheric processing and fluency. *Neuropsychologia*, *28*(12), 1295–1305.
159 Whitaker, H. & Kahn, H. (1994). Brain and language. In D. Zaidel (Ed.), *Neuropsychology* (pp. 126–138). San Diego, CA: Academic Press.
160 Wingate, M. (2002). *Foundations of stuttering*. San Diego, CA: Academic Press.
161 Wittke-Thompson, J. K., Ambrose, N. G., Yairi, E., Roe, C., Ober, C. & Cox, N. J. (2007). Genetic studies of stuttering in a founder population. *J. Fluency Disord.*, *32*(1), 33–50.
162 Wood, F., Stump, D., McKeehan, A., Sheldon, S., & Proctor, J. (1980). Patterns of regional cerebral blood flow during attempted reading aloud by stutterers both on and off haloperidol medication: Evidence for inadequate left frontal activation during stuttering. *Brain Lang.*, *9*(1), 141–144.
163 Wu, J., Maguire, G., Riley, G., Fallon, J., La Casse, L., Chin, S. . . . & Lottenberg, (1995). A positron emission tomography {18F} deoxiglucose study of developmental stuttering. *Neuroreport*, *6*(3), 501–505.
164 Yairi, E. (2007). Subtyping stuttering I: A review. *J. Fluency Disord.*, *32*(3), 165–196.
165 Yairi, E. & Ambrose, N. (1992). Onset of stuttering in preschool children: Selected factors. *JSHR*, *35*(4), 782–788.
166 Yairi, E. & Ambrose, N. (1996). Genetic of stuttering: A critical review. *JSHR*, *39*(4), 771–785.
167 Yairi, E. & Ambrose, N. (2013). Epidemiology of stuttering: 21st century advances. *J. Fluency Disord.*, *38*(2), 66–87.
168 Yairi, E., Ambrose, N., Paden, E. & Throneburg, R. (1996). Predictive factors of persistence and recovery: Pathways of childhood stuttering. *J. Commun. Disord.*, *29*(1), 53–77.

169 Yeudall, L., Manz, L., Ridehour, C., Tani, A., Lind, J. & Fedora, O. (1993). Variability in the central nervous system of stutterers. In E. Boberg (Ed.), *Neuropsychology of stuttering* (pp. 129–163). Edmonton, Canada: The University of Alberta Press.
170 Zaidel, E. & Schweiger, A. (1984). On wrong hypothesis about the right hemisphere. *Cogn. Neuropsychol.*, *1*(4), 215–222.
171 Zimmerman, G. & Knott, J. (1974). Slow potentials of the brain related to speech processing in normal speakers and stutterers. *Electroencephalogr. Clin. Neurophysiol.*, *37*(6), 599–607.
172 Zimmermman, G. N., Smith, A. & Hanley, J. M. (1981). Stuttering: In need of a unifying conceptual framework. *JSHR, 24*(1), 25–31.

3
DEVELOPMENTAL DYSLEXIA

Introduction

"Learning disabilities" (LD) represent a broad class of specific peculiarities of the cognitive development, when a child cannot master certain academic skills in the conditions of school education due to a variety of causes [140].

Specific learning disabilities (SLD) are a subcategory of the broad syndrome of LD. Children who suffer from SLD show significant deficits in acquisition of specific academic skills including reading, writing and/or mathematics, despite normal intelligence, perception, motivation, and adequate educational and socio-economic opportunities [140, 169, 176]. Developmental dyslexia (DD) is the most frequently found SLD in childhood. Currently this term designates the specific inability, or serious delays, in acquisition or automation of reading and spelling, caused by difficulties in decoding written words and seeking their pronounceable analogues [20, 97, 121, 140, 194, 196]. DD may overlap with related conditions such as dyspraxia, dysphasia and attention deficit hyperactive disorder (ADHD) [84].

Although numerous studies have led to the accumulation of a significant amount of data differentiating in many aspects subjects with dyslexia from normal readers, some issues concerning the neurological and neurolinguistic basis of DD remain discussed.

At present, there is a wide consensus that DD is a neurologically based learning-specific deficit with a genetic origin [194]. Nevertheless, researchers still have fundamental disagreements over the neurological and cognitive basis of the disorder [171].

Atypical cerebral dominance as an etiological factor of developmental dyslexia

Presently, it is widely assumed that the brain organization of language and speech as its instrumental realization is presented mainly in the left hemisphere (LH), and that reading, being one of the two main forms of receptive speech, is also realized by the collaboration between the two cerebral hemispheres, but under the leading and crucial role of the LH [10, 160, 231].

Among the existing models explaining hemispheric differences in visual-perceptive language processing, the dual route model of reading appears to be one of the most popular. According to this model, there are two reading mechanisms called lexical (orthographical) and non-lexical (sublexical or phonological) routes. Both routes are hemispheric-specialized, as the LH possesses both lexical and non-lexical (phonological) routes, while the right hemisphere (RH) possesses only a lexical route [37, 52]. During visual-perceptual processing of written material, the RH has access to the meaning of the words "directly" from their orthography, without the mediation of phonological decoding (lexical route) because it reads "ideographically", recognizing words as visual gestalts, while the LH reaches their semantics through the processes of grapheme to phoneme conversion (sublexical route).

Despite extensive empirical support for this hemispheric dual route model, some recent data conflict with it, suggesting that the RH may also have access to the non-lexical route, and that hemispheric specialization of both routes demonstrates individual differences depending on factors such as biological sex, menstrual stage (i.e. fluctuations in oestrogen), self-rated degree of masculinity (i.e. sexual attribution) and others (for a literature overview, see [223]).

One aspect of the debate concerning normal lateralization of reading mechanisms is the issue of the causal role of disturbed brain lateralization in the genesis of developmental reading disorders.

The original idea that reading disability is due to insufficiency of hemispheric dominance belongs to Orton (1928) [157]. In his own practice, he noticed that children with difficulties in reading and writing often wrote letters in reverse and demonstrated instability of hand preference.

Based on the postulate that the two hemispheres are symmetrical with regard to the medial line and considering these evidences as signs of incomplete hemisphere dominance, Orton suggested that visual information presented to the dominant hemisphere is oriented correctly and the one presented to the subdominant hemisphere is its mirror reflection. Therefore, in the absence of a well-developed hemispheric dominance, the presence of the two reflections – normal and inverted – may cause disturbance in reading and writing.

Orton's hypothesis has induced undying research interest until nowadays. Research has been traditionally focused in two directions: (1) studying the relationship between reading disorders and hand preference and (2) studying the relationship between reading disorders and hemispheric language lateralization.

Data accumulated over the years has caused the revision of some of Orton's concepts (e.g. the idea of mirror reflection has been discredited), but his main assumption that reading difficulties are associated with lateralized neurological deficits have received empirical support, leading to the emergence of the most popular etiological theories of DD – the neurobiological theories. These theories are built mostly on data from both autopsy and structural neuroimaging studies indicating the existence of structural abnormalities in the dyslexic brain (see below). Their underlying postulate is that DD is a result of perinatal brain injury causing microstructural abnormalities which, in turn, influence normal development of anatomical and functional cerebral asymmetries [72, 97, 121, 230].

Three basic hypotheses have been formulated within this group of theories: left, right- and inter-hemispheric hypotheses. The LH hypothesis connects DD with damage in the LH, in particular in the area of the left gyrus angularis or left planum temporale [48, 66, 163, 187, 193, 213]. The RH hypothesis links DD with abnormalities in the RH [64, 85], and inter-hemisphere hypothesis explains the emergence of DD with interhemispheric integration deficits or information transfer deficits due to structural abnormalities of the corpus callosum [19, 99, 182].

Among the most popular attempts for explaining Orton's hypothesis are the well-known Right Shift Theory of handedness and brain asymmetry of Annett [4, 5] and the Hormonal Theory of Cerebral Lateralization of Geschwind and Galaburda [72].

According to the basic assumption of the Right Shift Theory [4, 5], there is a gene (RS+) that induces right-handedness and gives advantage of language development in humans to the LH. The most likely disadvantage for people who lack RS+ would be a risk of developmental disorders of speech and related language functions. The key hypothesis with respect to reading is that reading skills reflect the heterozygote advantage (RS+ −) and relative homozygote disadvantage, as both homozygote genotypes (the RS + + and the RS − −) increase the risk for dyslexia. In support of this hypothesis is the data indicating that both the extreme left-handers and the extreme right-handers are worse readers than subjects with average or weak right-/left-handedness [7].

The Geschwind and Galaburda's theory [72] postulates an association between learning disorders and anomalous brain anatomy, with speculation that foetal testosterone could modify cerebral lateralization and immune functioning. Geschwind and Galaburda proposed that testosterone delays the maturation of parts of the LH resulting in faster development of both the corresponding regions in the RH and unaffected regions in the LH. As a result of depressed LH growth, verbal skills will be reduced and the risk of developmental learning disorders, a broad category including dyslexia, stuttering, delayed speech, autism and hyperactivity, will be increased. In all of these conditions, there will be an excess of males, a rather similar pattern of inheritance and increased incidence of personal and familial left-handedness [72, pp. 83–84].

What brings together the above-mentioned theories is that they can potentially account for the neurological bases of DD and are built on the notion that typical anatomical asymmetry (leftward asymmetry of language-related cortex) is related to typical functional lateralization (LH dominance for language). Therefore, atypical brain anatomy may be associated with atypical cerebral laterality, which in turn may increase susceptibility to developmental language disorders such as dyslexia. This conception is empirically supported by evidence that atypical anatomy is associated with atypical function [48, 83, 93, 100, 230] and that anatomical asymmetries of some language areas are correlated with language dominance [60].

Empirical evidences for atypical structural and functional asymmetries in developmental dyslexia

Neuroanatomic data for lateralized structural brain abnormalities

Historically, neuropathological studies of dyslexic brains gave the first evidence for a neurological basis of DD, turning attention towards a possible abnormality in specific stages of prenatal maturation of the cerebral cortex and suggesting a role of atypical development of brain asymmetries (for a literature review, see [78]).

Findings from autopsy studies of dyslexic brains have revealed foci of cerebrocortical microdysgenesis, such as neuronal ectopias, cerebrocortical scars, focal microgyria and architectonic dysplasias, located mainly in perisylvian regions and affecting predominantly the LH [64, 66, 97]. These neuropathological abnormalities are caused by brain injury and while ectopias are small aggregates of neurons and glia which form on the surface of the neocortex and are caused by disturbed neuronal migration occurring during embryonic and foetal development, cortical scars may occur at any time after completion of neuronal migration [121]. An essential finding was that the ectopias were abnormally connected to the thalamus, ipsilateral cortex and contralateral cortex, which creates the possibility for these anomalies to affect the development of other brain areas to which they are connected (for a literature overview, see [63]). It was found that some thalamic nuclei, such as lateral geniculate nucleus (which connects to the retina and the primary visual cortex) and medial geniculate nucleus (which connects to the primary auditory cortex and to auditory brainstem nuclei) exhibited changes in the size of neurons [65, 128]. These nuclei either had smaller-sized neurons, or the ratio between large and small neurons was changed with a prevalence of the small neurons. In addition, the primary visual cortex also showed changes both in neuronal sizes and in the normal pattern of cellular asymmetry [106]. Since smaller neurons are likely to have thinner axons with slower conduction velocities [128], these findings were interpreted as a possible anatomical substrate underlying the slower or abnormal visual and auditory temporal processing in DD [65, 128]. In addition, since it was considered that development of the neocortex depends on thalamic-derived trophic support, it was suggested that damage to any structure of the thalamus could lead to the development of abnormal patterns of cortical asymmetry [121].

An important finding is the presence of observed gender differences in the pattern and type of these cortical malformations. Cerebrocortical microdysgenesis was found in the dyslexic male brains, consisting of neuronal ectopias and architectonic dysplasias located mainly in perisylvian regions and affecting predominantly the LH. Overall, the dyslexic female brains showed fewer, and differently located, cortical malformations [97]. Ectopias were observed in a small part of studied dyslexic female brains, were typically located in the orbital frontal cortex and presented mainly symmetrically. In addition, there were more cortical scars in female dyslexic brains than in male dyslexic brains [97]. It was suggested that all these gender-related differences were due to the faster maturation of the female foetuses compared to male foetuses, leading to different outcomes of a cortical injury occurring during the second trimester of pregnancy on the structural brain development – ectopias in men and cortical scars in women [97].

Dyslexic brains apparently showed macroscopic peculiarities besides these microscopic anomalies, mainly consisting of the absence of normal lobar asymmetries.

One of the most consistent human brain asymmetries are the right > left asymmetry of the frontal lobes and the left > right asymmetry of the occipital lobes. Since approximately 70 percent of all healthy people have showed this pattern of brain asymmetry [74, 224] and its reduction or reversal have been found in subjects with neurodevelopmental disorders such as developmental stuttering (DS) [33, 59, 103], specific language impairment (SLI) [45, 222], attention deficit hyperactivity disorder (ADHD) [100], autism spectrum disorder (ASD) [91, 107, 180], etc., it has been considered that the rightward prefrontal and leftward occipital asymmetries are the typical patterns and all deviations from these patterns are atypical or anomalous.

The planum temporale in the LH is part of the area of Wernicke that is related to language comprehension and in the majority of healthy right-handed adults, its size is greater than the size of the corresponding structure in the RH. For this reason, the left planum temporale is seen as an anatomical marker of LH specialization for language comprehension and its left > right asymmetry is believed to parallel the functional linguistic preponderance of the LH [78].

Post-mortem studies of brain morphometry revealed symmetrical planum temporale in the dyslexic brains due to increased size of this structure in the RH (normal brains have left-sided asymmetrical planum temporale) [62, 66, 97]. However, subsequent magnetic resonance imaging (MRI) studies comparing left–right asymmetry of planum temporale in dyslexic and in normal readers got inconsistent results. Some of them [48, 100, 119, 123] replicated the findings of symmetrical planum temporale from autopsy studies, whereas others did not find symmetrical planum temporale in subjects suffering from DD [21, 125, 167, 177].

Studies of anatomical left–right asymmetries of other cerebral regions in dyslexic subjects also found deviations from patterns typically demonstrated by the controls. Examining the computerized brain tomograms of subjects with DD for brain asymmetry, Haslam et al. [83] revealed proportionately more symmetric occipital widths in dyslexics than in controls, and Hier et al. [93] found that as opposed to regularly observed in normal subjects pattern of parieto-occipital widths, a big part of the studied dyslexic sample (ten out of a total of twenty-four dyslexics) had a reversal asymmetry of parieto-occipital regions so that the right parieto-occipital region was wider than the left. This subgroup also had lower mean verbal IQ scores compared to the remaining fourteen dyslexics with typical leftward occipital asymmetry.

Using MRI methodologies, Hynd et al. [100] established a lack of asymmetry or anomalous anterior frontal asymmetry in dyslexic children compared to normal readers at the same age, but no differences regarding the occipital asymmetries. In a subsequent MRI study of dyslexic and control adults, Duara et al. [48] received the opposite pattern of results consisting of an atypical right > left asymmetry in the occipital region in dyslexics, but no group differences in the frontal lobe asymmetry. Using a voxel-based analysis of magnetic resonance images of dyslexic men and matched controls, Brown et al. [28] revealed widely distributed morphologic differences between studied groups affecting several brain regions. The researchers found evidence of decreases in grey matter in dyslexics, especially in the left temporal lobe and bilaterally in the temporo-parieto-occipital juncture, but also in the frontal lobe, caudate, thalamus and cerebellum.

The assumption that the inconsistency of data from structural brain studies was due to heterogeneity of DD provoked a number of studies aiming to compare patterns of anatomical asymmetry in different subtypes of DD. Such a study was conducted by Zadina et al. [230]. Researchers compared dyslexics and controls (college students, aged 18–25 years) on cognitive/behavioral tests and a volumetric MRI scan. Reading tests revealed five clinical subgroups: two subgroups of controls and three subgroups of dyslexics, which were statistically different on all applied cognitive/behavioral measures. No significant differences in both the total brain volume and total LH and RH volumes were found, but lobar volumes of dyslexics and controls were significantly different. As a total group, dyslexics had a larger percentage of total prefrontal brain volume and superior prefrontal volume compared to the total control group. The comparative analyses performed to investigate lobar volumes in diagnostic subgroups, however, revealed that the subgroups differed in their pattern of asymmetry. The subgroup of the phonological deficit dyslexics showed greater reversal in the total prefrontal volume than other subgroups, and also had atypically reversed occipital asymmetries. Zadina et al. [230] concluded that the results of this study support the concepts that DD is a heterogeneous disorder comprised of subtypes and that anomalous anatomy may reflect anomalous functional cerebral laterality.

In summary, neuroanatomical research gives evidence that the central nervous system in dyslexic subjects is affected at multiple levels and pathways. Findings from autopsy and neuroimaging studies showed that brain areas involved in perceptual, cognitive and metacognitive processing, as well as visual and auditory pathways, are affected by anatomical anomalies, which underlies the view that DD has multiple natures and is caused by the complex interaction of both low- and high-level processing deficits (for an overview, see [63]).

Neurophysiological evidence of lateralized functional abnormalities

Although inconsistent, the results of most studies of electroencephalography (EEG) brain activity in DD during resting condition established deviations in delta, theta and alpha activities in dyslexic children and (specific) learning disabled children, with a total increase of slow activities (delta and theta) and decrease in alpha activity mainly in parieto-occipital and frontotemporal regions (for literature overview, see [39, 81]). As it is well known that absolute and relative delta and theta powers decrease with age while alpha relative power increases, the increase in delta and theta powers with a concomitant decrease in alpha power was considered to be related to an immature EEG pattern. For this reason, above-mentioned findings have been interpreted as supporting the hypothesis that dyslexic children have a maturational lag [203] (see [81, 161] for a review).

EEG studies of dyslexics during the performance of different tasks (especially tasks including linguistic, perceptual and attentive processes associated with cognitive mechanisms considered to be impaired in DD) also have revealed functional differences in beta, alpha and theta rhythms between dyslexic and normal readers, notably in areas related to phonological processing [67, 116, 200]. For example, Galin et al. [67] compared EEG activity of dyslexics and normal readers while reading easy and difficult texts and during two other verbal tasks without a reading component, namely narrative speaking and listening to a story. Researchers found that in the theta and low beta bands, the difference between oral and silent reading was greater for controls than for dyslexics, as the between-group difference in theta was found only in the reading tasks, and low beta was found in the change from listening to speaking. Based on these results, Galin et al. [67] suggested that the groups differ in reading strategies they use and hypothesized that these cognitive differences are reflected in the theta activity of the temporal lobe.

Aiming to investigate whether dyslexics show deficits in attentional control and/or semantic encoding, Klimesch et al. [116] analyzed alpha and beta band power changes while normal and dyslexic children were reading numbers, words and pseudowords and found that dyslexics had a lack of attentional control during words encoding at left occipital sites and a lack of a selective topographic activation pattern during the semantic encoding of words.

A group of researchers investigated language-related lateralization of theta and beta rhythms [200], and delta rhythm [161] during various phases of word processing in dyslexic and control children using a word-pair paradigm (the same words were contrasted in three different tasks: phonological, semantic and orthographic). Dyslexics showed a delay in behavioral responses paralleled by sustained theta EEG peak activity, a dysfunctional pattern of right-lateralized theta and beta activation at left frontal sites in all tasks (controls showed greater left-sided theta and beta activations specifically during the phonological task), as well as a dysfunctional pattern of greater left lateralization of EEG responses at posterior locations during both phonological and orthographic tasks (controls showed the opposed pattern) [200]. With regard to the pattern of delta activation, while controls showed left activation (reduced delta) during the phonological task and bilateral activation in the other two tasks, dyslexics showed greater overall delta amplitude, indicating a cerebral maturation delay and an altered language laterality pattern [161]. Researchers concluded that these findings indicate a deficit in recruitment of LH structures for encoding and integrating the phonological components of words and suggest disruption of the fundamental hierarchy within the linguistic network [200].

In two subsequent studies, Heim and co-workers [86, 87] applied high temporal resolution magnetoencephalography (MEG) in order to investigate hemispheric laterality in the organization of the perisylvian region in DD. In the first one, researchers [87] used a passive oddball paradigm with pure tones and consonant-vowel (CV) syllables to explore functional aspects of the LH auditory cortex in dyslexics and matched typically developing children and revealed deviations in the organization of the LH auditory cortex in children with DD. In the second study, Heim et al. [86] examined interhemispheric source differences of magnetic responses to the synthetic syllable [ba:] in the auditory cortex of dyslexic and typically developing children and adolescents and found altered hemispheric asymmetry, reflecting an atypical organization of the RH in dyslexics. Heim et al. [86] pointed out that "the findings of LH and RH deviances by no means contradict each other but characterize the temporal dynamic of the relevant brain processes in individuals with dyslexia, which is not surprising in the context of the notion of the brain as a highly dynamic system" (p. 1721).

Also, in a study using magnetic source imaging, Simos et al. [197] found that while dyslexic childrens' activation profiles consistently featured activation of the left basal temporal cortices followed by activation of the right temporoparietal areas (including the angular gyrus), that of non-dyslexic children showed predominant activation of left basal followed by left temporoparietal activation.

Brunswick and Rippon [30] recorded auditory evoked potentials (Eps) during dichotic verbal listening in a group of dyslexic children and a group of matched normal readers and found that while normal readers produced significantly greater N100 amplitudes in the left temporal region during dichotic listening, dyslexics displayed approximately equivalent levels of amplitude bilaterally.

In a recent study conducted by Moll et al. [143], event-related potentials (ERPs) were used in order to assess discrimination accuracy and automaticity in letter-sound processing in children with and without DD using a crossmodal (visual-auditory) passive oddball paradigm. Children with DD showed delayed and less left-lateralized responses over frontotemporal electrodes to the deviant speech sound in the early time window, and higher amplitudes extending more over right frontal electrodes in the late time window. Also, the researchers found that longer latencies in the early time window and stronger RH activation in the late time window were associated with slower reading and naming speed, and stronger RH activation in the late time window correlated with poorer phonological awareness skills. Based on this pattern of the results, Moll et al. [143] suggested that children with DD show delayed letter-sound processing in the early phase, which influence later processing stages that involve phonological processing, visual-verbal mapping and memory processes.

Studies using modern high-resolution techniques of neuroimaging confirmed the presence of abnormalities in functional asymmetry of cortical activity in dyslexic subjects. For example, in a series of Positron Emission Tomography (PET) studies, Rumsey and co-workers [183, 185] found that compared to normal readers, dyslexic subjects showed reduced activation, or unusual deactivation, in mid- to posterior temporal cortex bilaterally and in inferior parietal cortex, predominantly in the LH when performing tasks of phonological processing and lexical decision [185], as well as an aberrant pattern of activation in right frontotemporal regions during a tonal memory task [183].

Gross-Glenn et al. [76] reported their PET scan data revealing more symmetric bilateral activation in prefrontal and inferior occipital regions during oral reading in dyslexics in contrast to the asymmetry observed in normal readers. In a subsequent PET study conducted by Brunswick et al. [29], reduced activation in dyslexic readers than in control subjects was found in the Wernicke's area (37 area of Brodmann), left cerebellum, left thalamus and medial extrastriate cortex during explicit reading, and reduced activation in the Wernicke's area during implicit reading. Researchers suggested that the reduced activation in Wernicke's area may indicate a specific impairment in lexical retrieval [29]. Using the same sets of stimuli in tasks requiring repetition of real words and pseudowords, these researchers received PET scan data revealing less activation in dyslexic adults than the controls in the right superior temporal and right post-central gyri and also in the left cerebellum [133].

Shaywitz et al. [195] used functional MRI (fMRI) to compare brain activation patterns in dyslexic and non-dyslexic subjects while performing different reading tasks and found large between-group differences, as dyslexics showed relative underactivation in posterior regions (Wernicke's area, the angular gyrus and striate cortex) and relative overactivation in an anterior region (inferior frontal gyrus).

Georgiewa et al. [68] conducted an interesting study combining fMRI and ERPs during non-oral reading of words and non-words and found significant differences between the studied groups of dyslexic and control children. The fMRI detected a hyperactivation in the left inferior frontal gyrus in dyslexics, and the ERP showed a significant between-group distinction concerning the topographic difference for left frontal electrodes in a time window 250–600ms after stimulus onset for non-word reading. Researchers concluded that the results obtained by both techniques indicated obvious differences in phonological processing between dyslexic and normal-reading children.

Applying functional transcranial doppler sonography (fTCD) with the aim to compare functional asymmetry during a word generation task between dyslexic and non-dyslexic adults, Illingworth and Bishop [101] found a reduced leftward asymmetry in subjects with dyslexia.

In summary, the results received by neurophysiological and neuroimaging techniques support the conclusion that the observed aberrant patterns of brain activation in dyslexic subjects may provide a neural signature for the basic impairment in DD that most probably is phonological [195].

The issue concerning DD that still remains controversial is whether its neural manifestation is functional or structural in nature and, if structural, whether it presents the neural substrate of DD or rather appears to be an epiphenomenon of other processes such as delayed cortical maturation [133].

Evidence from lateralized task performance for atypical lateralization

Taking into account the understandable interference from structure to function, the Cerebral Dominance Theory of DD has received consistent support by studies using perceptual tasks such as dichotic listening and divided visual field measures, which have found an atypical pattern of hemispheric dominance in the performance of various cognitive tasks.

Studies using tachistoscopic paradigm found that both dyslexic and non-dyslexic children demonstrated greater left visual field advantage for face perception but only non-dyslexic children demonstrated greater right visual field advantage for word perception (dyslexic children did not) [136, 164], suggesting partial disturbance of cerebral dominance in DD only for language [136]. Using the same paradigm, Waldie [221] conducted an interesting study aiming to investigate hemispheric specialization for reading in children with different types of DD (dysphonetic, dyseidetic and mixed type) and matched controls as reflected by performance on lexical decision task and dual-task procedure consisting of oral and silent reading during speeded finger taping. The results revealed different patterns of asymmetry in each dyslexic subgroup, with each showing an atypical pattern of hemispheric processing relative to the non-dyslexic group. Moreover, based on the performance of both tasks, Waldie established the existence of two distinct dysphonetic dyslexic subgroups: one with the normal pattern of asymmetry (right visual/right-hand response advantage) and the other with the reversed (left visual/ left-hand response advantage). This led him to hypothesize that children with dysphonetic dyslexia represent two distinct groups with heterogeneous hemispheric specialization for reading and different underlying impairment [221].

Witelson [226, 227] examined differences in hemispheric specialization for spatial and language functions between good and poor readers using a dichotic listening test for investigating linguistic functioning and combined visual-half field and dichaptic procedures for investigating spatial form perception. Based on the received data, Witelson concluded that poor readers had the typical LH specialization for language functions and lack of RH specialization or bilateral presentation of spatial processing, and suggested that the existence of spatial functions in both hemispheres in dyslexics was the probable cause of impairments of the LH reading functions.

Studies of language laterality in DD which have used dichotic listening paradigm are most numerous. Received results, although inconsistent, outlined two patterns of altered performance in dyslexic subjects depending on the linguistic task demands [144]. The first, mainly observed in studies using dichotic listening of digits [144, 146, 214], words [144, 214] and free-recall procedure, consists in more pronounced right-ear advantage (REA)/ left-hemispheric advantage (LHA) for the perception of this type of verbal stimuli in dyslexic subjects than in matched controls, due to significantly worse left-ear performance accompanied by relatively preserved right-ear performance [144]. It was suggested that the atypical pattern of the performance in some children with DD indicated a binaural integration deficit, most probably caused by poor information transfer between the two cerebral hemispheres [144] – an assumption well supported by the reports for similar patterns of dichotic listening performance in patients with congenital callosal agenesis or callosotomy (for a review, see [167]). In addition, it was pointed out that the preserved performance of the right ear did not support the hypothesis of LH deficit in DD [144].

The second pattern of altered performance in DD has been observed in dichotic listening of CV syllables. In this case, dyslexic subjects (children, youth and adults) showed reduced REA/LHA or no-ear advantage (NEA)/lack of hemispheric asymmetry compared to non-dyslexic controls, usually accompanied by worse perception of both ears, but more pronounced on the right ear [9, 89, 96, 144, 214].

A modified version of Orton's original hypothesis of the significant relationship between maladaptive cerebral lateralization and DD [109, 154] has emerged from the attempts to analyze the data received by studies using directed attention modification of the classic dichotic listening test [11, 109–113, 144, 153–156]. In the directed attention dichotic listening paradigm, the attention of the subject is manipulated through the examiner's instruction requiring exclusive surveillance and report from each ear in a predetermined sequence. It was found that the size and/or the direction of the ear advantage could be altered based on the focus of the subjects' attention in the forced attention conditions. Normally, in healthy subjects, focused attention to the right ear increased the expected REA for dichotic verbal perception and focused attention to the left ear led to a reversal of the ear advantage from a REA to a left-ear advantage (LEA) [155]. However, it was found that dyslexic subjects did not show the changes typically observed in healthy subjects in the ear advantage in directed attention conditions. Studies' findings indicated significant group differences in the strength of hemispheric asymmetry and ability to switch attention [8, 95, 96, 153, 155]. For example, in a meta-analytical study comprising data from fifteen dichotic studies of dyslexic and non-dyslexic children (both left- and right-handed) that used CV syllables, free-recall and directed-attention conditions, an interaction among age, reading ability and handedness on dichotic listening outcome was found [155]. The statistical aggregation of research results indicated that "younger (6–9 years) and older (9–13 years) good readers and older poor readers shifted attention and thus overcame the REA bias, whereas younger poor readers shifted attention only in the directed-right condition" [155, p. 97]. Researchers concluded that between-group differences in patterns of ear report are indicative of a combination of varied functional lateralization and attentional strategies employed during dichotic listening of CV stimuli.

Thus, according to attentional-based modification of the Orton's conceptualization, DD may be produced by an interhemispheric attentional dysfunction interacting with age-invariant cerebral asymmetries [109, 111, 154]. It is hypothesized that dyslexics have a normal but weaker lateralization that is related specifically to phonological word decoding. "Dyslexics suffer from exuberant RH processing in response to spatial attentional demands that, in turn, interferes transcallosally with the development of the sound-symbol representations that are required for the fluent reading" [111, p. 395]. Therefore, lateralization, per se, is unaffected by the disorder, and the differences in ear advantages are underlined by an attentional deficit.

Current perspectives in defining the deficit underlying developmental dyslexia

Reading is a higher order cognitive ability and like others, such as writing, speech and mathematics, develops during a relatively short period, building on previously acquired, basic perceptual-motor skills [37, 52, 82]. Reading is a complex and hierarchical process including numerous cognitive operations [10, 102, 140], which largely explains the existing difficulties in detecting the basic neuropsychological deficit underlying DD.

In general, the debates have focused on the following key issues:

- First, whether DD is due to fundamental sensory/perceptual deficits or to cognitive/metacognitive deficits.
- Second, if the deficit underlying DD is cognitive in nature, whether it affects a function other than language (e.g. the higher visual processing)?
- Third, if a sensory or perceptual deficit is the underlying cause of DD, then which is the affected modality: the visual, auditory or motor one.
- Fourth, how many types of processing have been affected, which stages of these types of processing have been affected and to what extent they have been impaired (for an overview, see [48]).

Various theories have been proposed for the explanation of the neurological and cognitive mechanisms underlying DD. Currently, four major theories, each of which is supported by a whole body of empirical evidence, dominate the dyslexia scene. As Ramus et al. [174] points out, these theories can be grouped within two antagonistic frameworks: the first is represented by the phonological theory and the second by the sensorimotor dysfunction theories.

Developmental dyslexia as a result of specific phonological deficit (Phonological Theory)

The predominant theory is that DD is due to a fundamental phonological deficit, that is a deficit in the processing of phonological information [68, 171, 173, 190, 193, 194, 213, 225]. It is based on numerous studies confirming that although in part of dyslexics there are sensory/perceptual or attentional abnormalities, all dyslexic subjects demonstrate phonological deficits reflected in a worse performance on tasks requiring phonological awareness (i.e. conscious segmentation and manipulation of speech sounds) [55, 173, 208, 210]. According to the Phonological Theory, dyslexic subjects suffer from a specific impairment in the representation, storage and/or retrieval of speech sounds that impedes the learning of grapheme-phoneme correspondences – a key condition for learning to read alphabetic systems [26, 27, 101, 173, 218].

There is no consensus among researchers about the nature of the phonological deficit, but there is a wide agreement that the specific phonological deficit is the most revealing sign of this neurodevelopmental disorder, although it often co-occurs within a more general sensorimotor syndrome [171–173, 190]. Therefore, the existence of lower sensory/perceptual deficits is not denied, but it is suggested that these deficits may be irrelevant to the process of learning to read and their presence could not explain the specific difficulties in phonological processing. Moreover, there is an empirically supported assumption that the sensory/perceptual deficits in both visual and auditory modalities observed in dyslexics may be a consequence of (and not a cause for) cognitive deficits, which emerge first and are caused by earlier developmental changes occurring in the high-level cortex (for details, see [63]).

Phonological processing is defined as the ability to manipulate speech sounds in spoken and written language [10, 29, 37, 52, 108, 145, 232]. In reading, this type of processing includes the following linguistic processes [37]:

1. Graphemic parsing – This is the process by which a letter string is converted to the grapheme string ("grapheme" means a letter or a letter group that corresponds to a single phoneme, as in the concrete context the grapheme is the written equivalent of the phoneme).
2. Grapheme-phoneme conversion – This is the process in which the grapheme string is converted to the phoneme string by a set of grapheme-phoneme conversion rules which are valid for the concrete language (piecemeal phonology).
3. Phoneme integration – This is the process by which the phonemes are integrated into a unitary phonological representation. In the case of oral reading, this phonological representation is introduced into the phonological buffer (a type of working memory), where it is stored and retains an active form during the subsequent processing phase of its transformation (element-by-element) into a format appropriate for articulation.

According to the phonological deficit hypothesis, in cases of DD, the existence of a specific problem at each of the processing stages may impede the acquiring of phonological awareness, that is ability to understand the relationships between the graphemes of the written word and the corresponding phonemes of the spoken word. Therefore, the primary deficit in DD is a deficit of phonological awareness, and a secondary deficit could be a difficulty in the manipulation of sublexical units in verbal working memory (the phonological buffer) [51]. A direct consequence of these deficits is the impairment of all subprocesses involved in the grapheme-phonemic conversion, resulting in reading disturbances, as well as in disturbances of others linguistic processes such as spelling, spoken language and writing [171, 172].

It is suggested that at the brain level, this cognitive deficit would arise from a congenital dysfunction of left perisylvian cortical regions which are responsible for phonological representations and grapheme-phoneme conversion [66, 212]. This view is based on an impressive amount of evidence of structural and functional abnormalities in a widespread cortical network, mainly distributed in the LH and usually involved in phonological processing, namely, Broca's area, planum temporale, superior and middle temporal gyri, angular, fusiform and supramarginal gyri [29, 46, 55, 66, 70–72, 133, 168, 195, 213].

Brain activation patterns observed in dyslexics, consisting of relative underactivation in the posterior brain regions contrasted with relative overactivation in the frontal areas, are viewed as a neurological support for phonological deficits in dyslexia and evidence for destruction of neural systems involved in linking visual representations of letters with the corresponding phonological representations [68, 195].

Despite the traditional view that phonological abilities are specifically related to the LH, there are research findings provoking the assumption that phonological reading is mediated, to some extent, by interhemispheric transfer functions of corpus callosum [131]. Indeed, the hypothesis that poor communication between the two hemispheres may underlie some cases of developmental reading disorders, has been well supported by studies using different behavioural methods. Interhemispheric transfer deficits in reading have been suggested by the results of these studies received through dichotic listening tasks [110], through lateralized visual and tactile tasks [75] or tasks assessing the manual reaction time [42]; by results indicating a failure of interhemispheric integration between auditory verbal and visual-verbal processing received through a dichotic listening task and a parallel divided visual field task [19], as well as by findings indicating deficits in bimanual motor coordination in dyslexic adults [144]. In favour of the hypothesis are also the reports for similarity of the patterns of reading of subjects with congenital callosal agenesis and subjects with phonological type of DD [212].

As the biggest weakness of the phonological theory has been pointed out, its inability to account for the presence of sensory and motor deficits in subjects with DD, typically, these deficits are not considered by the proponents of the theory as key features of DD with causal role in its aetiology (for a critical look, see [173]).

Developmental dyslexia as a result of impaired automaticity of the reading process (Automaticity/Cerebellar Theory)

Automaticity Theory of Dyslexia, or currently better known as Cerebellar Theory of Dyslexia [53, 149–152], postulates that the cause for reading disorders at the biological level is a weak dysfunction of the cerebellum leading to the emergence of some cognitive difficulties. Given the role of the cerebellum in motor control and, therefore, in speech articulation, this theory postulates that retarded or dysfunctional articulation would lead to deficient phonological representations. On the other hand, the cerebellum plays a significant role in the automatization of activities, and it is logical that a weak capacity for automatization would affect the learning of grapheme-phoneme correspondences. Moreover, recent neuroimaging studies, especially those in which fMRI has been combined with hierarchically organized reading tasks, have shown some new aspects of cerebellar function, emphasizing mostly on the importance of cerebro-cerebellar relations for various cognitive functions, including language. With regard to the processes involved in reading, it has been found that the cerebellum participates in cognitive processes that are an essential and integral part of the identification of words in reading (for literature overview, see [152, 173]).

To summarize, the core hypothesis of the Automaticity/Cerebellar Theory of DD concludes that cerebellar abnormalities cause the impaired automatization of articulatory skills and auditory processes, as the cerebellum is probably involved in DD by two mechanisms: the first suggesting that a cerebellar dysfunction causes mild motor problems that lead to articulation deficits, impaired sensitivity to the phonemic language structure and to the phonological deficit, and the other mechanism suggesting that a cerebellar dysfunction leads to reduced processing speed, which in turn could affect a variety of cognitive functions [152].

Cerebellar Theory of DD has been supported by evidence of impaired performance of dyslexics on a range of cerebellar tasks [56], in dual tasks demonstrating poorly automatized skill of motor balance [149], in non-motor cerebellar task indicating obvious time estimation deficits [151], as well as by clinical evidence of a variety of linguistic difficulties including disprosodia, agrammatism, mild anomia and reduced verbal fluency arising from damage to the cerebellum [189]. Results from brain imaging studies have also established that dyslexic subjects demonstrate anatomical, metabolic and activation changes in the cerebellum in comparison to non-dyslexic subjects [28, 57, 125, 150, 170].

In a critical overview of the disadvantages of the Cerebellar Theory of DD, Ramus et al. [173, 174] has indicated the following weak points of this theory: its inability to explain the sensory disorders; reliance on outdated view of motor theory of speech postulating a causal relationship between the development of phonological representations and speech articulation (this concept has been abandoned because of the existence of cases of normal phonological development despite severe dysarthria or speech apraxia (for a discussion, see [174]); and lack of clarity about the proportion of dyslexics affected by motor problems.

Developmental dyslexia as a result of impaired processing of sequential and rapidly varying perceptual information (Magnocellular Theory)

The Magnocellular Theory of Dyslexia [205, 208, 209] has been evaluated as a fair attempt to integrate multiple findings and theoretical assumptions about the nature of the observed in DD variety of deficits – visual, auditory, tactile, motor and phonological [63, 173, 208], as well as to account for all manifestations of DD through a single biological cause [173]. Precursors of this modern and unifying theory are the visual and the auditory theories of DD. Currently, their proponents agree that visual and auditory deficits in DD are part of a more general magnocellular dysfunction (for an overview, see [173]).

The Rapid Auditory Processing Theory

The main hypothesis of the Rapid Auditory Processing Theory of DD postulates that this developmental condition is due to an auditory deficit consisting of impaired perception of short or rapidly varying sounds [211]. This more basic auditory deficit, in turn, may cause the phonological deficit and subsequently the difficulties in learning to read. Therefore, this theory does not deny the existence of specific phonological deficit in DD, but considers it as secondary to a more basic auditory deficit [211].

There is evidence in support of this theory confirming that dyslexics have poor performance on auditory tasks, including frequency discrimination [2, 132] and temporal order judgement [148, 211], as well as evidence for abnormal neurophysiological responses to various auditory stimuli [118, 132, 148, 180] and worse categorical perception of phonemic contrasts [1, 142].

The Visual Theory

The Visual Theory of Dyslexia considers DD as being caused by a visual impairment that leads to difficulties when processing letters and words in a written text [128, 129, 209]. The theory does not exclude a phonological deficit, but emphasizes the crucial role of a visual disorder for reading difficulties, at least in part of dyslexics.

At the biological level, the cause of reading disorders is viewed in the division of the visual system into magnocellular and parvocellular pathways that have different roles and properties. Since the visual magnocellular system is responsible for timing visual events when reading, it is hypothesized that the magnocellular pathway is selectively disrupted in certain dyslexic individuals, which leads to deficiencies in visual processing, and, via the posterior parietal cortex, to abnormal binocular control and visuospatial attention (for details, see [206]).

The visual theory is empirically supported by evidence from anatomical studies establishing structural abnormalities of the magnocellular layers of the lateral geniculate nucleus [128]; from functional brain imaging studies finding an abnormal processing of visual motion [49] and psychophysical studies showing decreased sensitivity to low spatial frequencies and high temporal frequencies [129], reduced luminance contrast sensitivity and a weaker sensitivity to motion [41], and reduced flicker contrast sensitivity in dyslexics [138].

Magnocellular Theory

Magnocellular Theory of DD postulates that the magnocellular dysfunction is not restricted to the visual pathways but is generalized to all modalities – visual, auditory and tactile. In addition, since the cerebellum receives massive input from various magnocellular systems in the brain, it is also predicted to be affected by the general magnocellular defect [205–210].

Reading requires fast and accurate processing of transient visual and auditory stimuli and the largest cells in the brain, known as magnocellular neurons, are specialized in this type of processing. Magnocellular neurons are highly myelinated and transmit and process rapidly changing sensory and motor signals along the nervous system. Notably, the magnocellular visual system is responsible for timing events in the visual world and plays a particularly important role in motion perception and the control of eye movements (saccades, tracking, fixation) (for details, see [206, 208]).

Accumulation of evidence confirming that many dyslexic subjects have dysfunction of the visual magnocellular system, which correlates with their reading disorder (unlike good readers who have high magnocellular sensitivity) [40, 49, 128, 129, 138, 210, 211], led to the emergence of the magnocellular hypothesis of DD, which underwent significant changes over the years.

There is no such clearly defined system of magnocellular neurones in the auditory system as there is for the visual system. Nevertheless, anatomically, magnocellular differentiation of each of the subcortical auditory relay nuclei is well established [65]. Also, it is known that auditory magnocellular neurones are specialized in tracking rapid frequency and amplitude changes in acoustic signals [215]. Based on this, it has been suggested that auditory "magnocells" participate in the temporal analysis of sounds that is analogous to that in the visual system. The fact that the accurate tracking of acoustic amplitude and frequency transients is extremely important for identifying the phonological elements of speech suggests that the difficulties of dyslexic subjects with phonological analysis are fundamentally due to a defect in their auditory "magnocellular system". This assumption is supported by evidence for a disorganization of magnocellular division of the medial geniculate nucleus (the auditory relay in the thalamus), particularly left sided in dyslexic brains (studied post-mortem) [65]; evidence for reduced sensitivity to changes in amplitude and frequency of simple auditory tones in many dyslexics [132, 207], and evidence for high correlations between this sensitivity and phonological abilities for both dyslexic and normal readers [228].

There are findings that visual difficulties may preponderate in some dyslexics and phonological difficulties may prevail in others, but actually, the majority of the dyslexic population has both types of abnormalities. This finding, together with the established significant correlations between sensitivity to auditory transient signals and performance in visual motion tests [228], supports the hypothesis that childrens' reading skills may be dependent on the development degree of their auditory and visual magnocellular systems. Moreover, since many dyslexics also have slightly disturbed motor skills, it has been hypothesized that DD may be caused by mild generalized damage of all magnocellular neurons – visual, auditory and motor. "The variability in the involvement of visual, auditory and motor systems indicates that this damage is patchy and individually idiosyncratic" [208, p. 71].

In summary, the magnocellular hypothesis postulates that DD may result from abnormal development of magnocellular neurons throughout the whole brain, due to damage occurring (most likely) during prenatal development. The visual magnocellular system and its auditory and motor equivalents can all be impaired in subjects with DD [63, 170, 209], which in turn may cause visual instability, reduced phonological skills and motor problems typically observed in dyslexics (for a detailed overview of the relevant literature, see [206, 208]).

Summarizing the evidence supporting the magnocellular theory and analyzing them in the context of the evidence for the genetic basis of DD [31, 57], Stein and Talcott [208] enriched this theory with the hypothesis that "fundamentally dyslexia results from some kind of adverse immunological influence on the development of magnocells in the nervous system" (p. 72). However, the authors themselves have noted that although hopeful, and with the potential to integrate all the main findings about DD, at this stage, this hypothesis remains highly speculative.

In a detailed overview of the criticism of the magnocellular theory of DD, Ramus et al. [173] summarized that its major weakness is the inability to explain the absence of sensory and motor disorders in a significant proportion of dyslexic subjects.

Developmental dyslexia as a result of interhemispheric dysfunction of attention (Attentional Theory)

The emergence of the hypothesis that DD is caused by an interhemispheric dysfunction of attention [109, 113, 154] is provoked by evidence divided in three different groups: first, that cerebral asymmetries of cognitive processing are independent and different from lateralized activation of the attention [115]; second, that the LH language lateralization emerges early in ontogenesis and remains unchanged throughout childhood [94]; and third, that lateralization of attention develops actively during the first school years [3]. Hence, the main hypothesis underlying this dyslexia model is that academic deficits in DD are due to interhemispheric dysfunction of attention, interacting with cognitive cerebral asymmetries which remain unchangeable across the lifespan (for details, see [113]). Therefore, what distinguishes children with DD from normal readers is the deviation from normal development of lateralization of attention (not of language lateralization) [109, 113], which causes their learning difficulties [109, 113, 154].

According to the main assumption of the attentional model of DD, demands on attention and cognitive processing related to the performance of academic tasks which are specific to each hemisphere, may induce situation-specific patterns of maladaptive lateralization. Attention dysfunction (activation dysfunction) creates conditions for cognitive interference during the performance of tasks or components of tasks (e.g. reading, writing, arithmetic). Reading-related specific linguistic processes that are lateralized in modular subsystems in the LH [90] may not develop because of their vulnerability to cognitive interference, especially in children with DD [113].

Current issues and perspectives in studying developmental dyslexia

A review of current literature dedicated to DD shows that despite the apparent progress in studying it, many additional issues with fundamental significance to understanding the nature of DD, such as its pathogenetic mechanisms and typology, remain unclear.

Confusing inter-individual variability of the patterns of reading disorders on the one hand, and the lack of unified criteria for differentiation of major subtypes of DD on the other, largely explain the existence of various typologies of DD.

There are three main approaches to look for to identify subgroups of DD. Under the first, more traditional approach, the main DD subtypes were identified according to the primary cognitive deficit, with emphasis on auditory/visual distinctions. It was considered that the impairment of each of the cognitive processes included in reading would lead to the emergence of particular types of reading errors. For this reason, the specificity of reading errors has been taken as a major differential diagnostic criterion.

Reading, however, is a complex and hierarchical cognitive process related to almost all mental activities. It includes multiple cognitive operations depending on a variety of skills, such as auditory and visual discrimination, decoding of graphic symbols into speech, sound blending, language proficiency, as well as short-term auditory and visual memory, attentional processes, etc. [10, 52, 140, 220]. For this reason, applying this approach created typologies with different numbers and designations of main subtypes. Nevertheless, in all these typologies, the visual (also called optical or visual-spatial) and auditory (also called phonematic or acoustic) types of DD are presented, and in some typologies mnestic type of DD is also presented [114, 140, 169, 220].

The second approach is based on learning to read models. Within this approach, two very similar typologies have become popular. The first one, proposed by Boder [25], includes three subtypes of DD: dysphonetic, dyseidetic and mixed (or dysphoneidetic). Children with dysphonetic dyslexia prefer to use global reading strategies and have difficulties with grapheme-phoneme integration, often add or drop letters or syllables and easily make semantic substitutions. Unlike them, children with dyseidetic dyslexia usually use phonetic strategies and have difficulties with whole word recognition and spelling, which makes reading slow and painful. Children with mixed dyslexia have difficulties with both the phonetic analysis and the whole word recognition.

Bakker [12, 13, 15] extended the analyses of Boder and attempted to link reading errors with neuropsychological processes involved in reading. On this basis, the author created a typology of DD in which reading speed and accuracy were taken as the criteria for distinguishing the two subtypes: (1) linguistic dyslexia (L-type or also known as "guessing" type) in which reading is relatively fast, but inaccurate, with mistakes such as omissions, additions or reversal of letters, syllables, words; and (2) perceptual dyslexia (P-type, or "spelling" type) in which reading is sufficiently accurate, but slow and interrupted by pauses and repetitions. Some researchers also proposed an M (mixed)-type of dyslexia, which combines the features of the other two types, and is characterized by slow and inaccurate reading [139].

This typology is based on the Bakker's hemispheric model of learning to read, subsequently further developed by other investigators and empirically well-supported studies [12–15, 126, 127, 139, 159, 216, 217]. According to its main postulates, initial reading is predominantly mediated by the RH, but with the improvement of the reading process, reading gradually passes under primary control of the LH. Therefore, learning to read is associated with progressive disengagement of the RH (extrastriate and inferotemporal regions) reflected in decreasing reliance on non-lexical form recognition systems for word recognition, and gradual involvement of the LH in the reading process, with more frequent reliance on phonemic skills (inferior frontal areas) and lexical word recognition systems (middle temporal regions) (for details, see [216]). For this reason, the predominant RH involvement in initial reading is a prerequisite, but becomes an obstacle when reading enters the next (advanced) stage of development [13]. Based on evidence from ERP studies indicating age-related change in hemispheric mediation of word reading from the RH to the LH [15, 44, 126, 127], it has been suggested that if some young readers start to use LH strategies from an early stage of learning to read and somehow "skip", the RH phase before visual-spatial analysis of the written material has become automatized, they will develop L-type of DD, and, conversely, if some young readers persistently over-rely on early RH reading strategies, they will develop a P-type of DD [12–15].

The third approach to the distinction between dyslexic types is based on computational models designed to account for visual word recognition and reading aloud. Among the numerous models of word identification that have been proposed during the last three to four decades, two models have become the most popular and have given impetus for a lot of research: the Dual Route Cascaded (DRC) model [37, 38, 52] and triangle models [80, 165, 192].

According to the DRC model, reading words aloud uses two separate mechanisms: lexical (orthographical, semantic) and sublexical (non-lexical, phonological). The lexical route operates at whole-word level and words are recognized as holistic units. This mechanism converts written words directly into mental representations of word forms without the mediation of grapheme-to-phoneme translation. It is suggested that the lexical route can be used for reading aloud known real words, even exception words (i.e. words that do not follow grapheme-phoneme correspondence rules). In contrast, the sublexical (non-lexical) mechanism operates by converting sublexical units (letters) of the written word/pseudoword in their phonological correspondences based on grapheme-phoneme conversion rules. This reading mechanism is required in reading unfamiliar words, meaningless letter strings and non-words. The kind of reading task is what determines which of the two reading mechanisms will be used, as the skilled readers use mainly the lexical route. Skilled reading requires efficient development of both reading mechanisms and well-established control over intra- and interhemispheric communications in their selective and predominant inclusions. Also, it has been suggested that while the lexical and non-lexical routes may function independently in healthy adults, their development is likely to be intertwined over the course of reading acquisition [32, 102].

Although the DRC model has been developed to account for skilled adult reading, as well as acquired dyslexia, its proponents argue that it offers a coherent account of DD [32, 102]. According to the traditional dual route view, there are two main types of DD: phonological and surface (or orthographic). Phonological dyslexia emerges from damage to the phonological (sublexical) reading mechanism, while surface dyslexia emerges from damage to the lexical (semantic) reading mechanism [33, 134, 201, 204]. The main differentiating criterion is whether the difficulties are manifested mainly in reading unknown words and pseudowords (which is typical of phonological DD) or in reading familiar words, especially those with nonstandard spelling (which is typical of orthographic DD). Frequently occurring impairments of both reading mechanisms are interpreted by the supporters of the dual route model as cumulating the deficits of phonological and orthographic dyslexia, thus showing dysfunctions of both the sublexical and lexical reading routes (mixed dyslexia) [184, 205]. Proponents of the hypothesis that a phonological processing problem is the underlying neuropsychological deficit of all cases of DD consider also the two dyslexic groups corresponding to the profiles of surface and phonological dyslexia as the poles of a continuum, rather than dichotomous groups [34, 134, 204].

The triangle models have fundamental assumptions that are opposite to those of the DRC model and offer different accounts of phonological and surface subtypes of dyslexia [80, 165, 192]. According to these models, phonological dyslexia reflects deficits in the creation of stable phonological representations, and surface dyslexia is due to a shortage of resources or slowed learning of words mapping onto their spoken forms.

In the framework of the triangle model proposed by Seidenberg and McClelland [192], Harm and Seidenberg [80] offered a conceptualization of normal reading acquisition, as well as DD. Based on findings from simulating the phonological and surface subtypes of DD by causing different types of damage to the network before training, Harm and Seidenberg [80] advanced a severity hypothesis suggesting that all pure cases of phonological dyslexia should be mild cases, while cases of mixed or relative phonological dyslexia should result from a more severe phonological impairment. Based on empirical findings that the surface dyslexics' performance on a variety of reading-related tasks was very similar to that of younger, typically developing, readers [134, 201, 204], the authors conceptualized surface dyslexia as "reading delay dyslexia".

However, findings that are problematic for both models suggest the need for their improvement. For example, testing the predictions of the dual route and connectionist models of reading, Peterson et al. [163] received results that contradicted the strong version of the severity hypothesis, as well as the conceptualization of surface dyslexia as "reading delay dyslexia", and were also inconsistent with the dual route model.

All of the above-described typologies of DD comprise two main subtypes of dyslexia and one mixed (combined) subtype. Despite the differences, there is some overlapping of the profiles of reading difficulties of the visual (optical), dyseidetic, perceptual (P-type) and orthographic (surface) subtypes on the one hand, and auditory (phonematic, acoustic), dysphonetic, linguistic (L-type) and phonological subtype on the other.

The issue related to different subtypes of DD is further complicated by the typical comorbid pathology for this condition (for literature review, see [99, 178]). Dyslexics demonstrate a wide variety of additional symptoms apart from reading difficulty and specific language impairment is reported as the most frequent comorbidity with DD (for literature review, see [24, 124]).

Literature review shows that all deficits of higher cortical functions occur more often in dyslexics than in normal readers [73, 121, 208]. There are reports for deficits in visual and auditory perception, visual-auditory integration and motor coordination, as well as insufficient development of gnosis, praxis and lower level of speech development [114, 140, 220]. Also, it is noted that childhood "milestones" – crawling, walking, speaking and throwing are often delayed [114, 140, 220].

The issue of the role of atypical hemispheric asymmetries in the emergence and persistence of DD still remains debated and systematically studied.

Not all studies on handedness have found a higher incidence of left- and mixed-handedness among dyslexic children. A greater frequency of left- and mixed-handedness in dyslexic samples was revealed by Anett and Kilshaw [6], Eglinton and Anett [51], Geschwind and Behan [71], Helland [88] and Schachter et al. [188]; but Bishop [23] and Jariabkova et al. [104] failed to find such a difference between dyslexics and normal readers. Brunswick and Rippon [30] reported that dyslexic subjects had less pronounced right-handedness in comparison with non-dyslexic subjects.

Similarly, researchers experimentally studied the relationship between language lateralization and DD and also failed to reach consensus about the significance of atypical hemispheric asymmetries in the genesis of reading disorders (as discussed above).

Taken together, these evidences inevitably put forward questions about the causes for ambiguity of experimental data. Among the most commonly cited causes for data inconsistency is the failure to account for the heterogeneity of dyslexic populations, insufficiently strict matching of studied control and experimental groups, the use of different experimental tasks, as well as differences in theoretical frameworks underlying interpretation of the empirical data [92, 139, 144, 159, 230].

It is truly impressive that despite the awareness for the need and usefulness of distinguishing the different types of DD when investigating the relationship between hemispheric asymmetry and reading disorders, studies examining the functional hemispheric asymmetries in the subtypes of DD are still few in numbers and provide inconsistent results.

Although received results are not fully consistent, they rather support the claim that the dyslexic population is highly heterogeneous, with each subgroup exhibiting a distinct neuropsychological test profile and reading pattern, and different performances of lateralized verbal tasks [34, 89, 144, 159, 221], as well as different patterns of anatomical asymmetries [230].

Most of these studies have used dichotic listening of speech stimuli – a non-invasive and sufficiently reliable method for studying language lateralization. Studies that have used the Bakker's typology for differentiating dyslexic subgroups received consistent results, namely, REA for verbal stimuli in the linguistic dyslexic subgroup and mixed dyslexic subgroup (similar to controls), but no significant ear advantage or LEA in the perceptual dyslexic subgroup [14, 16–18, 139, 159].

Using Boder typology, Cohen et al. [36] found a strong REA in the dyseidetic dyslexic subgroup and moderate REA in the mixed dyslexic subgroup. With regard to the dysphonetic dyslexic subgroup, closer inspection of the individual performances revealed a bimodal distribution with the majority (twelve subjects) demonstrating a strong LEA and the others (eight subjects), exhibiting a strong REA. In contrast, using the same typology of DD, Obrzut [153] failed to discriminate the normal group from the dyslexic subgroups based on ear asymmetry, as measured by dichotic REA.

Results from two other dichotic listening studies [122, 137] which used the typology of DD based on the "dual route" model of reading with the phonological and surface dyslexic types were also inconsistent. In the first one, Lamm and Epstein [122] applied free recall tests of digits and words to 320 dyslexic children and their matched controls with the aim to examine dichotic listening performance in different subtypes of DD under high and low verbal workload conditions. Results revealed significant differences within dyslexic subgroups, as the surface dyslexic subgroup showed extreme ear neglect or total performance collapse but only under high verbal workload conditions, the phonological dyslexic subgroup demonstrated a poor total performance both under high and low workload levels, but visuomotor dyslexic subgroup did not differ in any measure from the controls. In the second study, carried out by Martinez and Sanchez [137], fifty boys with DD, divided in three dyslexic subgroups (with surface, phonological or mixed subtype), fifty controls of a similar age and twenty-five controls according to reading level were examined by dichotic listening test with CV syllables. As a whole group, dyslexics demonstrated lower lateralization index and reduced perceptive performance in comparison to both control groups, but the differences were only clearly significant when the most severe cases of phonological dyslexia were selected.

Inconsistency of results from studies with DD subtypes may be due to the use of different classification schemes and criteria for subgrouping the dyslexic samples studied, or due to the use of various types of verbal stimuli (words, digits, syllables) for which processing may be lateralized to a different extent. Also, controlling participants' handedness in some studies and lack of control in others could be such a factor.

Sharing the view that DD is a developmental disorder associated with heterogeneous populations with distinct cognitive deficits and independent reading achievements, I planned the present study as a consecutive attempt to investigate the link between the cerebral lateralization and different subtypes of DD.

Personal research data

The main aim of the present study is to investigate in a comparative perspective the handedness and functional cerebral asymmetry for speech sound perception in children with normally developed reading skills and in dyslexic children, in order to verify the hypothesis that dyslexic subjects represent a heterogeneous population in terms of phonological processing, language lateralization and manual preference.

Subjects

Diagnostics

All participants in this study were pupils in regular classes (with second grade completed or pupils in third or fourth grade), Bulgarian being their native language. The subjects of the dyslexic group and the control group of normal readers were selected in two stages. The primary selection of the potential participants in both groups was based on information provided by teachers of basic school disciplines (Bulgarian language and literature, mathematics), the class academic advisors and the school psychologist. They were asked to point out pupils with very good academic skills (having As and Bs in all courses of their previous academic year) and without speech and language disturbances (for the control group), as well as pupils who have good academic record (As, Bs, Cs in the courses of their previous academic year) but demonstrate obvious reading difficulties, though having no other speech disturbances (for the dyslexic group).

After the primary selection, the subjects of the so-formed groups went through a secondary selection made by a specialist (secondary selection was performed by the author of the book in her capacity of a certified speech therapist, neuropsychologist and doctor of psychology) under the most widely used criteria for diagnostics of the developmental reading difficulties and for differentiation of DD from the other types of SLD [20, 196].

1. Normal non-verbal intelligence (IQ > 75) – Measured by the Standard Progressive Matrices (SPM) of Raven.
2. Normal hearing and absence of neurological deficits – The estimation was based on data provided by the school doctor and from the anamnesis.
3. Normal spoken language, written language and arithmetic skills – Measured by a battery of tests including a test for assessment of the spoken language expression (articulation and verbal description of a series of subject pictures), a test for assessment of the written language expression (dictation and written reiterating of a heard text) and a test for assessment of the computational arithmetic skills (fundamental arithmetic operations). Tests used are part of a protocol of neuropsychological research of children, generated by the Laboratory of Neuropsychology at the Scholarly Institute of Neurology, Psychiatry and Neurosurgery of the Medical Academy, Sofia, Bulgaria, in 1985.

4. Reading abilities – Since Bulgarian orthography is a shallow orthography and the problem of "nonstandard orthography" does not exist in Bulgarian language, as well as in other Slavic languages using Cyrillic alphabet (e.g. Russian and Macedonian), reading words with atypical spelling was not included in the reading tasks. In this study, the evaluation of reading abilities was based on the performance of the following reading tasks:

   (a) oral reading of syllables (twenty patterns);
   (b) oral reading of familiar words (ten low-frequency words and ten high-frequency words with different syllabic structure and length);
   (c) oral reading of unfamiliar words (twenty patterns with different syllabic structure and length);
   (d) oral reading of non-words (twenty double syllabic patterns); and
   (e) oral reading of text (fifty high-frequency words).

Reading comprehension was assessed through tasks of reading familiar words and text. After reading each word, the child is required to either explain it or compose a sentence with it (at the child's choice), and after reading the text, to answer questions asked by the researcher (same for all children). Reading fluency was assessed through tasks of text reading. The evaluation in both variables was dichotomous – "good/bad".

Table 3.1 presents descriptive data from the study of the reading abilities of the dyslexic and control groups.

As a result of the entire assessment, two groups were formed: a group of sixty-six dyslexic children (twenty-one girls and forty-five boys, age ranging from 8.4 to 11.5 years, *Mean* age = 9.9, *SD* = 1.2), all having normal spoken language skills and no articulated difficulties with computational arithmetic and written language, and a control group of seventy-eight normal readers (twenty-four girls

TABLE 3.1 Details of reading abilities (average number of reading errors and *SD*) of the dyslexic and control groups

	Normal readers M (SD)	Dyslexics M (SD)	p
Syllable errors	0.03 (0.19)	2.85 (2.15)	< .000
Familiar word errors	0.15 (0.36)	4.12 (2.01)	< .000
Unfamiliar word errors	0.40 (0.57)	7.94 (4.49)	< .000
Non-word errors	0.24 (0.43)	4.61 (2.95)	< .000
Text errors	0.21 (0.44)	4.97 (2.97)	< .000
Errors in the reading comprehension of familiar words (% participants)	1.28	54.55	< .000
Errors in the reading comprehension of text (% participants)	2.56	40.91	< .000
Reading dysfluency (% participants)	0.00	56.06	< .000

and fifty-four boys, age ranging from 8.2 to 11.2 years, *Mean* age = 9.4, *SD* = 1.1), having normal spoken and written language skills and normal arithmetic skills.

Thus, children of both studied groups do not differ substantially with regard to age, sex, IQ and expressive (spoken and written) language and computational arithmetic skills.

Differential diagnostics

Within the context of findings of existence of heterogeneity at the level of symptoms in DD [141, 158], dyslexic subgroup division in this study was made on the base of the dual route model of reading [37, 52], despite certain limitations on its application due to the specificity of Bulgarian orthography, which is a regular orthography (belongs to the family of shallow orthographies). Three types of processes that underlie reading functions were used to define the dyslexic subgroups: phonological, orthographic and semantic functions. The localization of reading difficulties (errors) in decoding and/or comprehension was used as a criterion for dyslexic subgroup divisions: (1) in non-lexical reading (syllables, pseudowords, unfamiliar words), (2) in lexical reading (familiar words) or (3) in narrative reading (text). As a result, three dyslexic subgroups with uneven distribution regarding age and sex were formed, as in each of these subgroups, a weak inter-individual variability in the differentiating assessment scores was observed:

1. Subgroup fitting phonological dyslexia profile – Phonological Dyslexia Subtype (PDS). It represented 21 percent of all dyslexics (fourteen subjects). Reading errors occurred mainly in non-lexical reading (syllables and pseudowords) and in reading unfamiliar words. Children from this group made episodic mistakes (1 or 2) when reading familiar words and text, as in text reading mistakes were mostly grammatical (e.g. a noun with an indefinite article is read with a definite and vice versa). The reading comprehension is preserved.
2. Subgroup fitting surface dyslexia profile – Surface Dyslexia Subtype (SDS). This dyslexic subgroup represented 36.37 percent (twenty-four subjects) of all studied dyslexics. There were many reading errors reported in all reading tasks. Reading comprehension in text reading was preserved but episodic errors in reading comprehension of familiar words (most often of low frequency) still occurred, mostly as a result of wrong guessing.
3. Subgroup fitting mixed dyslexia profile – Mixed Dyslexia Subtype (MDS). It represented 42.42 percent (twenty-eight subjects) of the whole dyslexic group. Many reading errors in all reading tasks occurred. Reading comprehension of familiar words and text was problematic.

Table 3.2 represents the descriptive data from the assessment of the reading abilities of the three dyslexic subgroups.

TABLE 3.2 Details of the reading abilities (average number of reading errors and *SD*) of the three dyslexic subgroups

	PDS M (SD)	SDS M (SD)	MDS M (SD)
Syllable errors	1.71 (0.73)	3.04 (1.82)	3.25 (2.68)
Familiar word errors	1.28 (1.07)	5.25 (1.45)	4.57 (1.37)
Unfamiliar word errors	5.29 (2.40)	7.92 (3.72)	9.29 (5.34)
Non-word errors	2.86 (1.61)	4.58 (3.24)	5.50 (2.49)
Text errors	1.14 (0.66)	5.25 (2.13)	6.64 (2.57)
Errors in the reading comprehension of familiar words (% participants)	4.28	37.50	89.29
Errors in the reading comprehension of a text (% participants)	7.14	8.33	85.71
Reading dysfluency (% participants)	35.71	50.00	71.43

Assessment of handedness

Subjects' handedness is one of the factors controlled in the studies using dichotic listening paradigm. Right-handedness particularly is among the participants' selection criteria. That was not made in the present study for two reasons: first because left-handedness and mixed-handedness are among the factors connected to the occurrence of DD [6, 71, 72, 157], and second because it is possible that this factor is connected only to a particular type of DD.

The measurement of participants' handedness was made by the performance test described in Chapter 2 "Developmental stuttering", section "Assessment of Handedness". A Quotient of manual asymmetry (QMA) was calculated individually for each child. Children who scored between −70 and +70 were classified as mixed-handed, those who scored between +71 and +100 were classified as right-handed, and those who scored between −71 and −100 were classified as left-handed. These cut-off points have been established by Dragovic [47] depending on statistical criteria.

In addition, detailed pedigrees, including first- and second-degree relatives, were obtained for all participating children from both of their biological parents. This was done in order to make between-group comparisons regarding the frequencies of familial sinistrality.

Dichotic listening: stimuli and procedure

The dichotic test used with consonant-vowel syllables is described in detail in Chapter 2 "Developmental stuttering", section "Dichotic listening". In contrast to the study of stutterers, here the recall was made orally, in free condition, after playing each dichotic pair. Oral reproduction was preferred to written reproduction for two reasons: first, none of the examined children had a speaking disturbance which could influence the correct reproduction, and second, the spoken response disallowed the possibility of arousing negative emotions as a result of written speech use.

Data analysis and statistics

Laterality quotient (LQ) and Perceptive performance were the main variables used for the individual and group analysis of dichotic listening scores. Their calculations are described in Chapter 2 "Developmental stuttering", subchapter "Data analysis and statistics".

For statistical evaluation, the Crosstab chi-square test and Independent Sample *t*-tests in the SPSS 16.0 were applied. Also, effect size was calculated.

Results from the assessment of handedness

An overview of the results from handedness measurements of the total dyslexia group, the three dyslexic subgroups and the control group is presented in Table 3.3.

The obtained results revealed that a significantly higher percentage of the control group (82.1 percent) exhibited right-handedness in comparison to the total dyslexia group (47.0 percent) ($p < .05$), and in contrast, a significantly higher percentage of the total group of dyslexics showed mixed-handedness (50.0 percent) in comparison to the control group (17.9 percent) ($p < .05$). No significant between-group differences were found with respect to the left-handedness: 0.0 percent of the control group and only 3.0 percent of the total dyslexia group were left-handers ($p > .05$). For type of handedness, there were significant differences between the control group and the total dyslexia group ($x^2_{|2|} = 20.285$, $p < .000$, Cramer's $V = 0.375$).

Chi-square comparisons of the results of each dyslexic subgroup with those of the control group revealed slight and insignificant differences between the controls and PDS ($x^2_{|2|} = 2.331$, $p = .312$, Cramer's $V = 0.154$), but statistically significant differences between the control group and both the MDS ($x^2_{|2|} = 11.791$,

TABLE 3.3 Distribution of participants in study groups according to the demonstrated type of handedness and the presence of familial sinistrality (in %)

	Left-handedness		Mixed-handedness		Right-handedness		Familial sinistrality	
	n	%	n	%	n	%	n	%
Control group	0	0.0	14	17.9	64	82.1	16	20.5
Dyslexics (total group)	2	3.0	33	50.0	31	47.0	24	36.4
Subgroup with PDS	0	0.0	4	28.6	10	71.4	6	42.9
Subgroup with SDS	0	0.0	18	75.0	6	25.0	5	20.8
Subgroup with MDS	2	7.1	11	39.3	15	53.6	14	50.0

$p = .003$, Cramer's $V = 0.334$) and the SDS ($x^2_{|1|} = 27.745$, $p < .000$, $\varphi = 0.522$), consisting of greater frequency of mixed-handedness in these dyslexic subgroups compared to the controls, especially in the SDS.

Chi-square comparisons regarding the frequency of familial sinistrality in studied groups (Table 3.3) revealed statistically significant differences between the controls (20.5 percent) and both the total dyslexia group (36.4 percent) ($x^2_{|1|} = 4.477$, $p = .034$, $\varphi = 0.176$) and MDS ($x^2_{|1|} = 8.829$, $p = .003$, $\varphi = 0.289$), slight and insignificant differences between the controls and PDS ($x^2_{|1|} = 3.257$, $p = .071$, $\varphi = 0.188$), and no differences between the controls and the SDS subgroup ($x^2_{|1|} = 0.001$, $p = .973$, $\varphi = 0.003$).

Dichotic listening results

Comparison of the dichotic listening results of the control group and the total dyslexic group revealed slight and insignificant differences in the mean LQ scores (M, SD; %): control group – Mean LQ = +7.97, SD = 10.62; the total dyslexic group – Mean LQ = +11.69, SD = 20.23 ($t = 1.39$, $p > .05$, Hedges' $g = 0.268$). Therefore, at a group level, both groups demonstrated the typical REA for dichotic verbal perception and did not significantly differ in both direction and magnitude of interaural asymmetry.

The performed chi-square comparisons of the frequency of REA in the two groups also found no between-group differences: 82.05 percent of the control group and 78.79 percent of the total dyslexic group showed REA, that is the typical LHA for speech perception ($p > .05$).

Analysis of the results concerning the perceptive performance in dichotic listening conditions, as measured by the mean percentage of correctly reported syllables on both ears, and separately on the left and right ear (M, SD; %), revealed significant differences between the two groups (Table 3.4).

The total dyslexic group displayed significantly worse dichotic speech perception in comparison to the control group. As can be seen from the table, the decrease in the mean overall percentage of correctly identified syllables of the dyslexic group (Mean = 47.42, SD = 10.68 vs. Mean = 59.41, SD = 7.89 of the controls; $t = 7.545$, $p < .001$, Hedges' $g = 1.293$) was due to the equally worse perception of

TABLE 3.4 Mean percentage of correct identified syllables (M; SD) of the control group and the total dyslexic group

	Mean overall performance		Mean right-ear performance		Mean left-ear performance	
	M	SD	M	SD	M	SD
Control group	59.41	7.89	63.91	8.34	54.91	11.42
Total dyslexic group	47.42	10.68	52.61	13.92	42.26	14.66

patterns presented to the right ear (*Mean* = 52.61, *SD* = 13.92 vs. *Mean* = 63.91, *SD* = 8.34 of the control group, *t* = 5.777, *p* < .001, Hedges' *g* = 1.005) and to the left ear (*Mean* = 42.26, *SD* = 14.66 vs. *Mean* = 54.91, *SD* =11.42 of the controls; *t* = 5.701, *p* < .001, Hedges' *g* = 0.973).

Overall, the results received indicated that dyslexics as a homogeneous group did not differ significantly from the controls in direction and magnitude of interaural asymmetry but had considerably worse performance in dichotic speech perception.

These conclusions were completely discredited after a comparative analysis of the results of controls and those of dyslexic subgroups. Each one of the dyslexic subgroups showed specific differences from the control group, giving evidence for the heterogeneity of the dyslexic population with regard to the hemispheric asymmetry for speech sound perception (Tables 3.5 and 3.6).

Table 3.5 presents the mean LQ scores (*M*, *SD*; %) of the control group and the three dyslexic subgroups, as well as of their subgroups formed depending on the type of hemispheric advantage, RHA or LHA. Table 3.6 presents the mean percentage of the correct responses of the control group and the dyslexic subgroups on both ears, and separately on the left and right ears (*M*, *SD*; %).

Between-group comparisons of the mean LQ scores found significant differences between the control group (*Mean* LQ = +7.97, *SD* = 10.62) and both the SDS (*Mean* LQ = +1.17, *SD* = 15.54, *t* = 2.005, *p* < .05, Hedges' *g* = 0.569) and the PDS (*Mean* LQ = +25.60, *SD* = 13.57, *t* = 4.615, *p* < .001, Hedges' *g* = 1.589), and no differences between the control group and the MDS (*Mean* LQ = +13.75, *SD* = 21.62, *t* = 1.357, *p* > 0.05, Hedges' *g* = 0.403). Therefore, although at a group level, all dyslexic subgroups showed the typical REA/LHA for dichotic speech perception, the interaural asymmetry was significantly very small and close to 0 in the SDS and quite strong in the PDS.

It is very important that the typical REA/LHA, demonstrated by 82.1 percent of the control group, was founded in 100.0 percent of the PDS, 92.9 percent of the MDS and only in 50.0 percent of the SDS. The remaining 50.0 percent of the SDS and 7.2 percent of the MDS, as well as 17.9 percent of the control

TABLE 3.5 Values of LQ (*M*; *SD*) of the control group and dyslexic subgroups and of their subgroups with different type of hemispheric advantage

	Total groups		Subgroups with LHA/REA		Subgroups with RHA/LEA	
	M	SD	M	SD	M	SD
Control group	+7.97	10.62	+11.27	8.14	−11.78	9.10
SDS	+1.17	15.54	+14.80	8.83	−12.46	5.60
PDS	+25.60	13.57	+25.60	10.63	—	—
MDS	+13.75	21.62	+16.04	14.11	−50.92	3.28

group, showed LEA/RHA. These between-group differences were statistically significant ($\chi^2_{|3|}$ = 20.501, p < .000) and had a large effect size (Cramer's V = 0.377).

Because of the reported significant higher incidence of atypical LEA/RHA in the SDS (50.0 percent), the mean LQ scores (M, SD; %) of the subgroups with REA/LHA, and the subgroups with REA/LHA, were separately compared (Table 3.5). Regarding the results of subgroups demonstrating REA/LHA, there were significant between-group differences only between the controls and the PDS reflected in a stronger hemispheric asymmetry in the PDS subgroup (Mean LQ = +11.27, SD = 8.14 for the control subgroup; Mean LQ = +25.60, SD = 10.63 for the PDS subgroup; t = 4.76, p < .001, Hedges' g = 1.664). Regarding the results of subgroups with LEA/RHA, the differences between the MDS subgroup and both the control subgroup (Mean LQ = –50.92, SD = 3.28 for the MDS subgroup; Mean LQ = –11.78, SD = 9.10 for the control subgroup; t = 11.648, p < .000, Hedges' g = 4.441) and the SDS subgroup (Mean LQ = –12.46, SD = 5.60 for the SDS subgroup; t = 13.604, p < .000, Hedges' g = 7.064) were highly statistically significant and had a large effect size.

A very important finding was that although there was a lack of significant differences between the mean LQ scores of the control subgroup with REA/LHA and the MDS subgroup with REA/LHA (Mean LQ = +11.27, SD = 8.14 for the control subgroup; Mean LQ = +16.04, SD = 14.11 for the MDS subgroup; t = 1.69, p > .05), 46.2 percent of this dyslexic subgroup had very high values of their individual LQ, more than +30.0 percent, and 34.6 percent had LQ equal or very close to zero (from 0.0 percent to +3.7 percent).

Another interesting finding was observed, namely, a significantly higher instability of the sign of individual LQs, reflected in its change from first to second listening of the dichotic test, in the SDS compared to all other groups. A negative LQ score for one of the test listening and positive for the other demonstrated 62.5 percent of the SDS versus 24.4 percent of the control group, 28.6 percent of the MDS, and 0.00 percent of the PDS. The between-group differences had a statistical significance and an intermediate effect size ($\chi^2_{|3|}$ = 19.550, p < .000, Cramer's V = 0.368).

Also, important results emerged from the between-group comparisons of perceptive performance as measured by the mean percentage of correctly reported syllables on both ears (mean overall performance), and separately on the left and right ear, respectively (mean right-/left-ear performance) (Table 3.6).

As shown in the table, both the PDS and MDS demonstrated equally worse performance in comparison to the controls, but the SDS showed similar performance to the controls. However, while the decrease in mean overall performance of the MDS (Mean = 41.27, SD = 9.08 vs. Mean = 59.41, SD = 7.89 of the control group, t = 9.379, p < .000, Hedges' g = 2.261) resulted in equally worse perception of patterns presented both to the right ear (Mean = 47.12, SD = 14.33 vs. Mean = 63.91, SD = 8.34 of the controls; t = 5.856, p < .000, Hedges' g = 1.640) and to the left ear (Mean = 35.42, SD = 10.83 vs. Mean = 54.91, SD = 11.42 of the

TABLE 3.6 Percentage of correct responses (M; SD) of the control group and the dyslexic subgroups

	Mean overall performance M	Mean overall performance SD	Mean right-ear performance M	Mean right-ear performance SD	Mean left-ear performance M	Mean left-ear performance SD
Control group	59.41	7.89	63.91	8.34	54.91	11.42
SDS	57.00	5.36	57.64	10.62	56.25	10.53
PDS	43.46	9.20	54.96	14.64	31.95	7.55
MDS	41.27	9.08	47.12	14.33	35.42	10.83

control group, $t = 8.053$, $p < .000$, Hedges' $g = 1.729$), the worse mean overall performance of the PDS (Mean = 43.46, SD = 9.20, $t = 6.099$, $p < .000$, Hedges' $g = 1.971$) was mainly due to the much worse perception of syllables presented to the left ear (Mean = 31.95, SD = 7.55, $t = 9.582$, $p < .000$, Hedges' $g = 2.097$) than to the right ear (Mean = 54.96, SD = 14.64, $t = 2.229$, $p < .05$, Hedges' $g = 0.941$).

As mentioned above, the SDS did not differ significantly from the control group in their mean overall performance (Mean = 57.00, SD = 5.36 vs. Mean = 59.41, SD = 7.89 of the control group, $t = 1.706$, $p > .05$, Hedges' $g = 0.326$) and the mean left-ear performance (Mean = 56.25, SD = 10.53 vs. Mean = 54.91, SD = 11.42 of the control group, $t = 0.534$, $p > .05$, Hedges' $g = 0.119$), but differed significantly from the controls in the mean right-ear performance (Mean = 57.64, SD = 10.62 vs. Mean = 63.91, SD = 8.34 of the controls, $t = 2.652$, $p < .05$, Hedges' $g = 0.703$).

Another important finding was that a considerably high percentage of both the PDS (35.7 percent) and the MDS (42.9 percent) displayed an effect of extreme neglect of one of the ears in dichotic listening conditions that was manifested in an absolute inability to perceive both of the dichotically presented syllables. This effect was observed in none of the controls or children from the SDS. The between-group differences were statistically significant ($\chi^2_{[4]} = 47.270$, $p < .000$) and had a large effect size (Cramer's $V = 0.573$).

Discussion

The present study attempted to answer the following crucial issues concerning DD, namely, whether dyslexic children are a heterogeneous population with respect to the following: (1) handedness; (2) phonological processing; and (3) functional hemispheric asymmetries for language perception.

With regard to the first issue, the results showed that mixed handedness was significantly more common in dyslexic children than in normal readers, which is consistent with literature data for greater frequency of mixed handedness [6, 51, 71, 88, 188] and weak right-handedness [30] among dyslexic subjects. Comparison of handedness-related results of dyslexic subgroups, however, confirmed my prior assumption that an aberrant pattern of handedness will not be observed at all dyslexic subgroups, which would explain the inconsistency of the results of previous studies. Present findings clearly showed that mixed-handedness was significantly highly presented in the SDS and the MDS but not in the PDS.

Results concerning frequency of familial sinistrality revealed that only the whole dyslexic group and the MDS had significantly higher incidence of familial sinistrality.

With regard to the second issue – whether the phonological processing is impaired in all dyslexic children or only in some dyslexic subgroups – the present results found significantly worse overall performance of the PDS and MDS, but normal performance of the SDS (similar to that of the control group), which rather suggests that the phonological deficit is not common for all dyslexics [149, 209, 211, 229]. Taking into account the significantly reduced right-ear performance, however, it is not excluded that there is a slight LH deficit to compensate for the excessive involvement of the RH in auditory processing.

With regard to the third issue, the results clearly indicated that hemispheric asymmetry and interhemispheric interaction for speech sound perception in children with DD differed from that in normal readers at the same age, but this became clear only after comparisons of the results of each dyslexic subgroup with those of the controls. Each dyslexic subgroup showed a specific pattern of hemispheric asymmetry for dichotic listening, which was different both from the pattern of the controls and the patterns of the rest of the dyslexic subgroups – a finding consistent with the results of previous studies, which examined hemispheric asymmetries in DD subtypes using lateralized verbal tasks [34, 89, 144, 159, 221]. But, since the deviations in the patterns of hemispheric asymmetry of each dyslexic subgroup showed opposite tendencies, the analysis of the results of dyslexics as a homogeneous group levelled their importance and masked their existence. The same effect of masking between-group differences due to the heterogeneity of dyslexic population has been reported by other authors [125, 230].

Present results from the dichotic listening test generally coincide with the results of previous studies using the Bakker's classification scheme of subtypes of DD (including a P-type and a L-type) for subgrouping dyslexic subjects [14, 16, 17, 18, 139, 159], but differ from the results received in the study of Martinez, and Sanchez [137], in which the same CV syllables dichotic listening paradigm, as well as the same division of dyslexic children in subgroups with phonological, surface (orthographic) and mixed type of dyslexia, were used. Martinez and Sanchez found that although the dyslexic group showed a lower Laterality Index than did the control group, the differences were only clearly significant when the most severe cases of the phonological dyslexia subgroup were selected.

Some of the reasons for the inconsistency of present results and those of Martinez and Sanchez [137] could be seen in different characteristics of studied samples: while Martinez and Sanchez studied only right-handed boys, the sample in this study was heterogeneous with respect to the participants' gender and handedness, that is gender and handedness were uncontrolled factors in sample selection.

Analyzing the findings in the context of the hemispheric reading model, I take into account all data obtained for dyslexic subgroups and propose a conceptual model to account for the observed deviations in hemispheric asymmetry and interhemispheric interaction in each of the DD subtypes (surface, phonological and mixed subtype), which, at present, are hypothetical and need further investigation and verification.

A hypothetical model of mechanisms underlying the observed deviations in hemispheric asymmetry and interhemispheric interaction in phonological subtype of developmental dyslexia

Obvious deviations in the pattern of hemispheric asymmetry and interhemispheric interaction for speech sound perception in dichotic listening condition were found for the group with the phonological subtype of DD. Compared to the controls and the other two dyslexic subgroups, the PDS demonstrated the highest frequency of REA/LHA, the strongest and very stable LH asymmetry in dichotic listening and parallel with that, significantly worse overall performance, mainly due to the much worse perception of the patterns addressed to the left ear/RH. Also, more than a third of this dyslexic subgroup displayed an effect of extreme neglect of one of the ears in dichotic listening conditions – a phenomenon also observed in another study of dyslexic subjects [122].

These findings give evidence that PDS exhibit phonological processing deficit due to auditory dysfunction not only of the LH, but also of the RH, which is consistent with the results of a previous study suggesting a significant contribution of the RH in alterations of central auditory processing in children with DD [147]. Also, the observed normal but stronger LH asymmetry of language perception suggesting a poor interhemispheric communication and deficits in the transmission of information from the non-specialized, in these operations the RH, to the specialized LH [144]. Lack of differences with the control group regarding handedness rather supports the assumption that the deviations in inter-hemispheric interactions in PDS are related specifically to phonological processing.

In spite of the traditional presumption that phonological abilities are linked specifically to the LH, several studies have shown the significant mediating role of the corpus callosum for phonological reading [212], and the pattern of the PDS's results received in the present study support such an assumption. Furthermore, the results of PDS reaffirm the hypothesis that poor communication between the two cerebral hemispheres could underlie some type of developmental reading disturbances [19, 42, 43, 75, 110, 145, 212] and allows the suggestion that ineffective interactions between the hemispheres during reading-related phonological operations may contribute to the deficit in the accuracy of phonological processing in PDS.

In the framework of the Bakker's hemispheric model of learning to read, and based on evidence from ERP studies indicating age-related change in hemispheric mediation of word reading from the RH to the LH [15, 44, 126, 127], it has been suggested that if some novice readers start to use LH strategies from the very beginning of the learning-to-read process and skip the normal predominance of RH strategies in this initial stage, they will develop linguistic type of DD. As the profiles of reading difficulties of linguistic type of dyslexia from the Bakker's classification scheme of subtypes of DD [12, 13, 15] and phonological subtype of dyslexia based on the DRC model of reading [37, 38] largely overlap, results of PDS obtained from the present study allow the extension of this hypothesis with the assumption that the establishment of good intra-hemispheric, but poor inter-hemispheric interactions between reading-related domains may contribute to reading difficulties in the phonological subtype of DD without be causally linked to their emergence.

A hypothetical model of mechanisms underlying the link between surface subtype of developmental dyslexia and atypical cerebral lateralization

Results from the dichotic listening test showed that at a group level, the SDS exhibited a highly reduced left-hemispheric asymmetry for speech sound perception, and at an individual level, this dyslexic subgroup demonstrated significantly greater frequency of the atypical LEA/RHA, and higher instability of hemispheric dominance, reflected in the sign change of the individual LQs from first to second listening of the dichotic test.

Only in this dyslexic subgroup was normal overall performance observed, despite slightly reduced right ear performance, which rather supports the notion that non-phonological impairments underlie the surface dyslexia.

This pattern of results, which could be interpreted as evidence for reversed or bilateral representation of language perception and lack of stable hemispheric dominance, supports the suggestion that the failure to develop a dominant language hemisphere might impede the establishment of the fundamental hierarchy within the linguistic network involved in reading [200]. As for the reason about the reduced right-ear performance observed in SDS, the present findings could not give an answer as to whether the excessive involvement of the RH in reading processes causes a deficit in recruitment of the LH for encoding and integrating the phonological components of words, or if it is a consequence of a deficit in the LH phonological processing potentially reflecting compensatory mechanisms. Nevertheless, the results obtained allow the assumption that the lack of stable hemispheric dominance and exuberant RH language processing may be causally related to the emergence of the surface subtype of DD. Moreover, the finding that 75 percent of the SDS demonstrated mixed handedness, that is weakly expressed manual preference, may indicate a poor or insufficient lateralization of cerebral functions rather than a partial disturbance of cerebral dominance affecting only auditory speech processing.

In the framework of Bakker's hemispheric model of learning to read [12–15], it may be hypothesized that the lack of hemispheric dominance for language in the SDS could underlie the failure of normal change in hemispheric mediation of word reading from the RH to the LH (when reading comes out from the initial and enters the advanced stage of development) and the persistence of overreliance on early RH reading strategies, that in turn causes reading difficulties.

Such an assumption could account for the reported similarity of the performance on a variety of reading tasks between children with SDS and younger normal readers [80, 134, 201, 204], and also does not contradict the conceptualization of surface dyslexia as "reading delay dyslexia" in the Harm and Seidenberg model of DD [80].

A hypothetical model of mechanisms underlying the observed deviations in hemispheric asymmetry and interhemispheric interaction in mixed subtype of developmental dyslexia

Closer inspection of individual performances of the MDS revealed that this dyslexic subgroup is not a unitary group, as evidently two subgroups emerged. The first represented 42.9 percent (twelve subjects) of the whole MDS and demonstrated a pattern of dichotic listening performance identical to that of the PDS. All these dyslexics exhibited a very strong and stable LH asymmetry for dichotic perception of speech sounds, an effect of extreme neglect of one of the ears in dichotic listening conditions, and critically worse overall performance, especially of the patterns addressed to the left ear/RH. Also, no differences between this MDS' subgroup and controls were found with regard to the measurements of handedness and familial sinistrality.

Given the typical profile of reading errors in MDS (many errors in all reading tasks and impaired reading comprehension), this aberrant pattern of hemispheric asymmetry for speech perception suggests a normal but stronger LH dominance for language perception with both a pronounced deficit in the LH phonological processing and disturbance of interhemispheric integration during reading-related phonological operations.

Lack of difference between this MDS' subgroup and PDS in the patterns of dichotic listening performance, and the substantial difference in their reading errors profiles, supports the suggestion that the phonological deficit is common for this MDS' subgroup and PDS, but most probably to a different extent – mild in PDS and strong in the MDS, as in addition, the MDS' subgroup also has other underlying deficits in other domains. Furthermore, the pattern of the dichotic listening results, together with the specific profile of reading difficulties in the MDS, suggest that the establishment of both ineffective intra- and inter-hemispheric interactions between reading-related areas may contribute to reading difficulties in this subtype of the mixed type of DD without necessarily be causally linked to their emergence.

The other subgroup of the studied MDS, representing 32.1 percent (nine children) of the whole MDS, showed lack of asymmetry or highly reduced LH asymmetry (0.0 percent < LQ < +3.7 percent) and a critical decrease of the overall performance due to equally poor perception of the patterns of both ears. Furthermore, eight of these nine children were mixed-handed.

The results led to the suggestion that similar to SDS, this MDS' subgroup suffers from bilateral representation of language perception and the lack of dominant language hemisphere, which is most probably part of a weaker lateralization of the cerebral functions, may be causally related to reading difficulties in this subtype of the mixed type of DD.

The finding that all these nine children reported a familial sinistrality history allows the assumption that the weak cerebral lateralization, including more bilateral representation of language organization, could be a hereditable trait. It can be hypothesized that the lack of hemispheric dominance for language interferes with the establishment of appropriate and effective intra-hemispheric interactions within the reading-related networks in both hemispheres, which in turn led to strong deficits in integration of distinct domains of linguistic network involved in reading.

In summary, the present study provided evidence that DD is a heterogeneous disorder in terms of hemispheric specialization for speech sound perception and handedness. All three dyslexic subgroups exhibited some kind of deviations from the pattern of hemispheric asymmetry and interhemispheric interaction observed in the group of normal readers at the same age. The dyslexic subgroups' patterns of abnormal hemispheric asymmetry and interhemispheric interaction, however, outlined opposite tendencies, which in turn led to their masking at the whole group level.

Three major patterns of abnormalities in hemispheric lateralization were found in dyslexic subgroups. The first one was typical for the SDS: unstable hemispheric dominance or atypical right-hemispheric dominance for speech sound perception and slight auditory processing deficit paralleled by mixed-handedness. These findings allow the hypothesis that the lack of hemispheric dominance and exuberant RH phonological processing may be causally related to the emergence of the surface subtype of DD.

The second one was typical for the PDS and almost half of the MDS: excessively strong and stable left-hemispheric asymmetry and strong auditory processing deficit accompanied by right-handedness. These findings led to the suggestion that the lack of necessary interhemispheric cooperation during phonological processing could contribute to reading difficulties of the PDS and a considerable part of the MDS without being causally related to the emergence of these DD subtypes.

The third pattern of abnormal hemispheric asymmetry was observed in one-third of the MDS: lack of asymmetry, or very slight LH asymmetry, and strong perceptive deficit paralleled by mixed handedness and familial sinistrality. These findings allow the hypothesis that the weak lateralization of the cerebral functions, including bilateral representation of language organization and lack of hemispheric dominance, may be a hereditable feature which causes reading difficulties in this subset of the MDS.

In addition, the results obtained in the current study are relevant to some conceptions concerning phonological processing deficits in DD. First, present results support the view that phonological processing deficits are not common for all dyslexics [149, 209, 211, 229], rather than the idea that phonological deficit is common for all dyslexics but may vary in severity [80, 198]. Second, the present results seem to be consistent with the view that phonological deficits may co-exist with non-phonological deficits that contribute to the specific profile of reading difficulties in each of the DD subtypes [162, 171, 189]. Third, the results of this study seem to be consistent with the hypothesis of Ramus and Szenkovits [175] which suggests that multiple mechanisms may underlie the phonological processing deficits in DD.

In conclusion, this study highlighted the necessity and usefulness of investigating DD at the level of each dyslexic subtype rather than as a unitary disorder. Moreover, this study clearly demonstrated the real risk of obtaining false results and making wrong conclusions and interpretations if we treat people with DD as a homogeneous group.

References and further reading

1. Adlard, A. & Hazan, V. (1998). Speech perception in children with specific reading difficulties (dyslexia). *Q. J. Exp. Psychol.*, *51*(1), 153–157.
2. Ahissar, M., Protopapa, S. A., Reid, M. & Merzenich, M. (2000). Auditory processing parallels reading abilities in adults. *Proc. Natl. Acad. Sci. USA*, 97(12), 6832–6837.
3. Anderson, B. & Hugdahl, K. (1987). Effects of sex, age, and forced attention on dichotic listening in children: A longitudinal study. *Dev. Neuropsychol.*, *3*(3–4), 191–206.
4. Annett, M. (1985). *Left, right hand and brain: The right shift theory.* London: Erlbaum Associate.
5. Annett, M., Eglinton, E. & Smythe, P. (1996). Types of dyslexia and the shift to dextrality. *J. Child. Psychol. Psychiatry*, *37*(2), 167–180. DOI: 10.1111/j.1469-7610.1996.tb01388.
6. Annett, M. & Kilshaw, D. (1984). Lateral preference and skill in dyslexics: Implications of the right shift theory. *J. Child Psychol. Psychiatry*, *25*(3), 357–377.
7. Annett, M. & Manning, M. (1990). Reading and balanced polimorphism for laterality and ability. *Br. J. Child. Psychol. Psychiatry*, *31*(4), 511–552.
8. Asbjornsen, A. & Bryden, M. (1997). Auditory attentional shifts in reading-disabled students: Quantification of attentional effectiveness by the attentional shift index. *Neuropsychologia*, *36*(2), 143–148.
9. Asbjornsen, A., Helland, T., Obrzut, J. & Boliek, C. (2004). The role of dichotic listening performance and tasks of executive functions in reading impairment: A discriminant function analysis. *Child Neuropsychol.*, *9*(4), 277–288.
10. Asenova, I. (2009). *Neuropsychology* [in Bulgarian]. Blagoevgrad, Bulgaria: Publishing House "Sanin N & N".
11. Aylward, E. (1984). Lateral asymmetry in subgroups of dyslexic children. *Brain Lang.*, *22*(2), 221–231.
12. Bakker, D. (1979). Hemispheric differences and reading strategies? Two dyslexias? *Bull. Orton Soc.*, *29*(1), 84–100.
13. Bakker, D. J. (1990). *Neuropsychological treatment of dyslexia.* New York: Oxford University Press.
14. Bakker, D. & Kappers, E. (1988). Dichotic listening and reading (dis)ability. In K. Hugdahl (Ed.), *Handbook of dichotic listening: Theory, methods and research* (pp. 513–526). London: Wiley.

15 Bakker, D. & Licht, R. (1986). Learning to read: Changing horses in midstream. In G. Pavlidis & D. Fisher (Eds.), *Dyslexia: Neuropsychology and treatment* (pp. 87–95). London: Wiley & Sons.
16 Bakker, D., Licht, R., Kok, A. & Bouma, A. (1980). Cortical responses to word reading by right- and left-eared normal and reading disturbed children. *J. Clin. Neuropsychol.*, 2(1), 1–12.
17 Bakker, D., Smink, T. & Reitsma, P. (1973). Ear dominance and reading ability. *Cortex*, 9(3), 301–312.
18 Bakker, D. & Vinke, J. (1985). Effects of hemisphere-specific stimulation on brain activity and reading in dyslexics. *J. Clin. Exp. Neuropsychol.*, 7(5), 505–525.
19 Beaumont, J., Thompson, M. & Rugg, M. (1981). An intrahemispheric integration deficit in dyslexia. *Curr. Psychol. Res.*, 1(3–4), 185–198.
20 Bell, S., McCallum, S. & Cox, E. (2003). Toward a research-based assessment of dyslexia: Using cognitive measures to identify reading disabilities. *J. Learn. Disabil.*, 36(6), 505–516.
21 Best, M. & Demb, J. B. (1999). Normal planum temporale asymmetry in dyslexics with a magnocellular pathway deficit. *Neuroreport*, 10(3), 607–612.
22 Bigler, E., Mortensen, S., Neeley, S., Ozonoff, S., Krasny, L., Johnson, M. . . . & Lainhart, J. E. (2007). Superior temporal gyrus, language function, and autism. *Dev. Neuropsychol.*, 31(2), 217–238.
23 Bishop, D. V. M. (1990). *Handedness and developmental disorder*. Oxford: Blackwell Scientific Publication.
24 Bishop, D. V. M. (1997). *Uncommon understanding: Development and disorders of language comprehension in children*. Hove, UK: Psychology Press.
25 Boder, E. (1973). Developmental dyslexia: A diagnostic approach based on three atypical reading-spelling patterns. *Dev. Med. Child Neurol.*, 15(5), 663–687.
26 Bradley, L. & Bryant, P. (1978). Difficulties in auditory organization as a possible cause of reading backwardness. *Nature*, 271, 746–747.
27 Brady, S. & Shankweiler, D. (1991). *Phonological processes in literacy*. Hillsdale, NJ: Lawrence Erlbaum.
28 Brown, W., Eliez, S., Menon, V., Rumsey, J., White, C. & Reiss, A. (2001). Preliminary evidence of widespread morphological variations of the brain in dyslexia. *Neurology*, 56(6), 781–783.
29 Brunswick, N., McCrory, C., Price, C., Erith, C. & Frith, U. (1999). Explicit and implicit processing of words and pseudowords by adult development dyslexics. A search for Wernicke's Wortsschatz? *Brain*, 122(Pt 10), 1901–1917.
30 Brunswick, N. & Rippon, G. (1994). Auditory event-related potentials, dichotic listening performance and handedness as indices of lateralization in dyslexic and normal readers. *Int. J. Psychophysiol.*, 18(3), 265–275.
31 Cardon, L., Smith, S., Fulker, D., Kimberling, W., Pennington, B. & Defries, J. (1994). Quantitative trait locus for reading disability on chromosome 6. *Science*, 266(5183), 276–279.
32 Castles, A., Bates, T. C. & Coltheart, M. (2006). John Marshall and the developmental dyslexias. *Aphasiology*, 20(9–11), 871–892.
33 Castles, A. & Coltheart, M. (1993). Varieties of developmental dyslexia. *Cognition*, 47(2), 149–180.
34 Castles, A., Datta, H., Gayan, J. & Olson, R. (1999). Varieties of developmental reading disorder: Genetic and environmental influences. *J. Exp. Child Psychol.*, 72(2), 73–94.
35 Chang, S. E., Erickson, K. I., Ambrose, N. G., Hasegawa-Johnson, M. A. & Ludlow, C. L. (2008). Brain anatomy differences in childhood stuttering. *Neuroimage*, 39(3), 1333–1344.

36 Cohen, M., Hynd, G. & Hugdahl, K. (1992). Dichotic listening performance in subtypes of developmental dyslexia and a left temporal lobe brain tumor contrast group. *Brain Lang.*, *42*(2), 187–202.

37 Colheart, M., Curtis, B., Atkins, P. & Holler, M. (1993). Models of reading aloud: A dual-route and parallel-distributed-processing approach. *Psychol. Rev.*, *100*, 589–608.

38 Coltheart, M., Rastle, K., Perry, C., Langdon, R. & Ziegler, J. (2001). DRC: A dual route cascaded model of visual word recognition and reading aloud. *Psychol. Rev.*, *108*(1), 204–256.

39 Colon, E., Notermans, S., DeWeerd, J. & Kap, J. (1979). The discriminatory role of EEG power in dyslexic children. *J. Neurol.*, *221*, 257–262.

40 Cornelissen, P., Hancen, P., Hutton, J., Evangelinou, V. & Stein, J. (1998). Magnocellular visual function and children's single word reading. *Vision Res.*, *38*(3), 471–482.

41 Cornelissen, P., Richardson, A., Mason, A., Fowler, S. & Stein, J. (1995). Contrast sensitivity and coherent motion detection measured at photopic luminance levels in dyslexics and controls. *Vision Res.*, *35*(10), 1483–1494.

42 Davidson, R., Leslie, S. & Saron, C. (1990). Reaction time measures of interhemispheric transfer time in reading disabled and normal children. *Neuropsychologia*, *28*(5), 471–485.

43 Davidson, R. & Saron, C. (1992). Evoked potential measures of interhemispheric transfer time in reading disabled and normal boys. *Dev. Neuropsychol.*, *8*(2–3), 261–277.

44 De Graaff, M. (1995). *Hemispheric engagement during letter and word identification in beginning readers*. Doctoral dissertation. Amsterdam, The Netherlands: Vrije Universiteit.

45 de Guibert, C. Maumet, C., Jannin, P., Ferre, J.-C., Treguier, C., Barillot, C. . . . & Briaben, A. (2011). Abnormal functional lateralization and activity of language brain areas in typical specific language impairment (developmental dysphasia). *Brain*, *134*(10), 3044–3058.

46 Demonet, L., Taylor, M. & Chaix, Y. (2004). Developmental dyslexia. *Lancet*, *363*(9419), 1451–1460.

47 Dragovic, M. (2004). Categorization and validation of handedness using latent class analysis. *Acta Neuropsychiatr.*, *16*, 212–218.

48 Duara, R., Kushch, A. & Gross-Glenn, K. (1991). Neuroanatomic differences between dyslexic and abnormal readers on magnetic resonance imaging scans. *Arch. Neurol.*, *48*(4), 410–416.

49 Eden, G. & VanMeter, J. (1996). Abnormal processing of visual motion in dyslexia revealed by functional brain imaging. *Nature*, *382*, 66–69.

50 Edgar, C., Yeo, R., Gangeslad, S., Blake, M., Davis, J., Lewine, D. . . . & Cañive, J. M. (2006). Reduced auditory M-100 asymmetry in schizophrenia and dyslexia: An application of an approach of the developmental instability for assessment of the atypical brain asymmetry. *Neuropsychologia*, *44*(2), 289–299.

51 Eglinton, E. & Annett, M. (1994). Handedness and dyslexia: A meta-analysis. *Percept. Mot. Skills*, *79*(3), 1611–1616.

52 Ellis, A. & Young, A. (1988). *Human cognitive neuropsychology*. Hove, UK: Lawrence Erlbaum Associate.

53 Facoetti, A. & Molteni, M. (2001). The gradient of visual attention in developmental dyslexia. *Neuropsychologia*, *39*(4), 352–357.

54 Facoetti, A., Zorzi, M., Cestnick, L., Lorusso, M., Molteni, M., Umulta, C., . . . & Mascetti, G. G. (2006). The relationship between visio-spatial attention and nonword reading in developmental dyslexia. *Cogn. Neuropsychol.*, *23*(6), 841–855.

55 Farmer, M. & Klein, R. (1995). The evidence for a temporal processing deficit linked to dyslexia: A review. *Psychon. Bull. Rev.*, *2*(4), 460–493.

56 Fawcett, A., Nicolson, R. & Dean, P. (1996). Impaired performance of children with dyslexia on a range of cerebellar tasks. *Ann. Dyslexia, 46*(1), 259–283.
57 Finch, A., Nicolson, R. & Fawcett, A. (2002). Evidence for a neuroanatomical difference within the olivo-cerebellar pathway of adults with dyslexia. *Cortex, 38*(4), 529–539.
58 Fisher, S., Marlowe, A., Lamb, J., Maestrinin, E., Williams, D., Richardson, A. . . . & Monaco, A. P. (1999). A quantitative trait locus on chromosome 6p influences different aspects of development dyslexia. *Am. J. Hum. Genet., 64*(1), 146–156.
59 Foundas, A., Corey, D., Angeles, V., Bolich, A., Crabtree-Hartman, E. & Heilman, K. (2003). Atypical cerebral laterality in adults with persistent developmental stuttering. *Neurology, 61*(10), 1378–1385.
60 Foundas, A. L., Leonard, C. M. & Heilman, K. M. (1995). Morphologic cerebral asymmetries and handedness: The pars triangularis and planum temporale. *Arch. Neurol., 52*(5), 501–508.
61 Frith, U. (1985). Beneath the surface of developmental dyslexia. In K. Patterson, J. Marshall & M. Colheart (Eds.), *Surface dyslexia: Neuropsychological and cognitive studies of phonological reading* (pp. 301–330). London: Lawrence Erlbaum.
62 Galaburda, A. (1993). Neuroanatomical basis of developmental dyslexia. *Neurol. Clin., 11*(1), 161–173.
63 Galaburda, A. (1999). Developmental dyslexia: A multilevel syndrome. *Dyslexia, 5*(4), 183–191.
64 Galaburda, A. & Kemper, T. (1979). Citoarhitectonic abnormalities in developmental dyslexia: A case study. *Ann. Neurol., 6*(2), 94–100.
65 Galaburda, A., Menard, M. & Rosen, G. (1994). Evidence for aberrant auditory anatomy in developmental dyslexia. *Proc. Natl. Acad. Sci. USA, 91*(17), 8010–8013.
66 Galaburda, A., Sherman, G., Rosen, G., Aboatiz, F. & Geschwind, N. (1985). Developmental dyslexia: Four consecutive patients with cortical anomalies. *Ann. Neurol., 18*(2), 222–233.
67 Galin, D., Raz, J., Fein, G., Johnstone, H., Herron, J. & Yingling, C. (1992). EEG spectra in dyslexic and normal readers during oral and silent reading. *Electroencephalogr. Clin. Neurophysiol., 82*(2), 87–101.
68 Georgiewa, P., Popatanasov, A., Klapp, B. & Dimitrov, B. (2003). *Event related potential and fMRI differences in Phonological reading of dyslexic children* (pp. 289–296). 3rd FEPS Congress, France.
69 Georgiewa, P., Rzanny, R., Gaser, C., Gerhard, U. J., Vieweg, U., Freesmeyer, D. . . . & Blanz, B. (2002). Phonological processing in dyslexic children: A study combining functional imaging and event related potentials. *Neurosci. Lett., 318*(1), 5–8.
70 Georgiewa, P., Rzanny, R., Glauche, V., Knab, R., Kaiser, W. & Blanz, B. (1999). fMRI during word processing in dyslexic and normal reading children. *Neuroreport, 10*(16), 3459–3465.
71 Geschwind, N. & Behan, P. (1982). Left handedness: Association with immune disease, migraine and developmental learning disorder. *Proc. Natl. Acad. Sci. USA, 79*(16), 5097–5100.
72 Geschwind, N. & Galaburda, A. (1987). *Cerebral lateralization*. Cambridge, MA: MIT Press.
73 Glezerman, T. (1983). *Brain dysfunctions in children* [in Russian]. Moscow, Russia: Nauka.
74 Good, C. D., Johnsrude, I. S., Ashburner, J. Henson, R. N., Friston, K. J. & Frackowiak, R. S. (2001). A voxel-based morphometric study of aging in 465 normal adult human brains. *Neuroimage 14*(1), 21–36.

75 Grant, A., Zangaladze, A., Thiagarajah, M. & Sathian, K. (1999). Tactile perception in developmental dyslexia: A psychophysical study using gratings. *Neuropsychologia*, *37*(10), 1201–1211.
76 Gross-Glenn, K., Duara, R., Barker, W., Loewenstein, D., Chang, J. Y., Yoshii, F. ... & Lubs, H. A. (1991). Positron emission tomographic studies during serial word reading by normal and dyslexic adults. *J. Clin. Exp. Neuropsychol.*, *13*(4), 531–544.
77 Gross-Glenn, K. & Rothenberg, S. (1984). Evidence for deficit in interhemispheric transfer of information in dyslexic boys. *Int. J. Neurosci.*, *24*(1), 23–35.
78 Habib, M., Robichon, F., Levrier, O., Khalil, R. & Salamon, G. (1995). Diverging asymmetries of temporo-parietal cortical areas: A reappraisal of Geschwind/Galaburda theory. *Brain*, *48*(2), 238–258.
79 Hari, R. & Renvall, H. (2001). Impaired processing of rapid stimulus sequences in dyslexia. *Trends Cogn. Sci.*, *5*(12), 525–532.
80 Harm, M. W. & Seidenberg, M. S. (1999). Phonology, reading acquisition, and dyslexia: Insights from connectionist models. *Psychol. Rev.*, *106*(3), 491–528.
81 Harmony, T., Marosi, E., Diaz de Leon, A., Becker, J. & Fernandez, T. (1990). Effect of sex, psychosocial disadvantages and biological risk factors on EEG maturation. *Electroencephalogr. Clin. Neurophysiol.*, *75*(6), 482–491.
82 Hartman, B. (1994). *The neuropsychology of developmental stuttering*. London: Whurr Publishers.
83 Haslam, R., Dalby, J., Johns, R. & Rademaker, A. (1981). Cerebral asymmetry in developmental dyslexia. *Arch. Neurol.*, *38*(11), 679–682.
84 Hayes, C. B. (Ed.). (2006). *Dyslexia in children: New research*. New York: Nova Science Publisher.
85 Hecaen, H. (1962). Clinical symptomatology in right and left hemispheric lesions. In V. Mountcastle (Ed.), *Interhemispheric relations and cerebral dominance* (pp. 263–295). Baltimore, MD: Johns Hopkins Press.
86 Heim, S., Eulitz, C. & Elbert, T. (2003). Altered hemispheric asymmetry of auditory p100m in dyslexia. *Eur. J. Neurosci.*, *17*(8), 1715–1722.
87 Heim, S., Eulitz, C., Kaufmann, J., Fuchter, I., Pantev, C., Lamprecht-Dinnesen, A. ... & Elbert, T. (2000). Atypical organization of the auditory cortex in dyslexia as revealed by MEG. *Neuropsychologia*, *38*(13), 1749–1759.
88 Helland, T. (1995). Dyslexia, laterality and short term memory. *Scand. J. Logoped Phoniatr.*, *20*(4), 157–164.
89 Helland, T. & Asbjornsen, A. (2001). Brain asymmetry for language in dyslexic children. *Laterality*, *6*(4), 289–301.
90 Hellige, L. (1993). *Hemispheric asymmetry*. Cambridge, MA: Harvard University Press.
91 Herbert, M., Harris, G., Adrien, K., Ziegler, D., Makris, N. & Kenedy, D. (2002). Abnormal asymmetry in language association cortex in autism. *Ann. Neurol.*, *52*(5), 588–596.
92 Hernandez, S., Camacho-Rosales, J., Nieto, A. & Barroso, J. (1997). Cerebral asymmetry and reading performance: Effects of language lateralization and hand preference. *Child Neuropsychol.*, *3*(3), 206–225.
93 Hier, D., LeMay, M., Rosenberger, P. & Perlo, V. (1978). Developmental dyslexia: Evidence for a reversal of subgroup with a reversal of asymmetry. *Arch. Neurol.*, *35*(2), 90–92.
94 Hiscock, M. (1988). Behavioral asymmetries in normal children. In D. Molfese & S. Segalowitz (Eds.), *Brain lateralization in children* (pp. 84–169). New York: Guilford.
95 Hugdahl, K. & Heiervang, E. (1999). Brain markers of dyslexia: Planum temporale asymmetry and dichotic listening to CV-syllables. In I. Lundberg, F. Tonnesen & I. Austad (Eds.), *Dyslexia: Advances in theory and practice. Neuropsychology and Cognition* (Vol. 16, pp. 157–171). Dordrecht, The Netherlands: Kluwer Academic Publishers.

96 Hugdahl, K., Helland, T., Faerevaag, M., Lyssand, E. & Asbjornsen, A. (1995). Absence of ear advantage on the consonant-vowel dichotic listening test in adolescents adult dyslexics: Specific auditory-phonemic dysfunction. *J. Clin. Expl. Neuropsychol.*, *17*(6), 833–840.
97 Humphreys, P., Kaufmann, W. & Galaburda, A. (1990). Developmental dyslexia in women: Neuropathological findings in three patients. *Ann. Neurol.*, *28*(6), 727–738.
98 Hynd, G., Hall, J., Novey, E. & Eliopulos, D. (1995). Dyslexia and corpus callosum morphology. *Arch. Neurol.*, *48*, 539–545.
99 Hynd, G., Morgan, A., Edmonds, J., Black, K., Riccio, C. & Lombardino, L. (1995). Reading disabilities, comorbid psychopathology, and the specificity of neurolinguistic deficits. *Dev. Neuropsychol.*, *11*(3), 311–322.
100 Hynd, G. W., Semrud-Clikeman, M., Lorys, A., Novey, E. S. & Eliopulos, D. (1990). Brain morphology in developmental dyslexia and attention deficit disorder/hyperactivity. *Arch. Neurol.*, *47*(8), 919–926.
101 Illingworth, S. & Bishop, D. (2009). Atypical cerebral lateralisation in adults with compensated developmental dyslexia demonstrated using functional transcranial Doppler ultrasound. *Brain Lang.*, *111*(1), 61–65.
102 Jackson, N. E. & Coltheart, M. (2001). *Routes to reading success and failure: Toward an integrated cognitive psychology of atypical reading.* New York: Psychology Press.
103 Janke, L., Hanggi, J. & Steinmetz, H. (2004). Morphological brain differences between adult stutterers and non-stutterers. *BMC Neurol.*, *4*, 23.
104 Jariabkova, K., Hugdahl, K. & Glos, J. (1995). Immune disorders and handedness in dyslexic boys and their relatives. *Scand. J. Psychol.*, *36*(4), 355–362.
105 Jeeves, M. & Temple, C. (1987). Further study of language functioning in callosal agenesis. *Brain Lang.*, *21*, 105–122.
106 Jenner, A. R., Rosen, G. D. & Galaburda, A. M. (1999). Neuronal asymmetries in primary visual cortex of dyslexic and non-dyslexic brains. *Ann. Neurol.*, *46*(2), 189–196.
107 Jou, R., Minshew, N., Keshavan, M., Vitale, M. & Hardan, A. (2010). Enlarged right superior temporal gyrus in children and adolescents with autism. *Brain Res.*, *1360*, 205–212.
108 Joubert, S. & Lecours, A. (2000). The role of sublexical graphemic processing in reading. *Brain Lang.*, *72*(1), 1–13.
109 Kershner, J. (1988). Dual processing models of learning disability. In D. Molfese & S. Segalowitz (Eds.), *Brain lateralization in children* (pp. 527–546). New York: Guilford.
110 Kershner, J., Henninger, P. & Cooke, W. (1984). Written recall induces a right hemisphere linguistic advantage for digits in dyslexic children. *Brain Lang.*, *21*(1), 105–122.
111 Kershner, J. & Micallef, J. (1991). Cerebral laterality in dyslexic children: Implications for phonological word decoding deficits. *Reading and Writing: An Interdiscip. J.*, *3*(3–4), 395–411.
112 Kershner, J. & Morton, L. (1990). Directed attention dichotic listening in reading disabled children: A test of four models of maladaptive lateralization. *Neuropsychologia*, *28*(2), 181–198.
113 Kershner, J. & Stringer, R. (1991). Effects of reading and writing on cerebral laterality in good readers and children with dyslexia. *J. Learn Dis.*, *24*, 560–567.
114 Khvattsev, M. (1959). *Logopedics* [in Russian]. Moscow, Russia: Prosveshcheniye.
115 Kinsbourne, M. (1970). The cerebral basis of lateral asymmetries in attention. *Acta Psychologia*, *33*, 193–201.
116 Klimesch, W., Doppelmayr, M., Wimmer, H., Gruber, W., Rohm, D., Schwaiger, J. . . . & Hutzler, F. (2001). Alpha and beta band power changes in normal and dyslexic children. *Clin. Neurophysiol.*, *112*(7), 1186–1195.

117 Koff, E., Naeser, M. A., Pieniadz, J. M., Foundas, A. L. & Levine, H. L. (1986). Computerized tomographic scan hemispheric asymmetries in right- and left-handed male and female subjects. *Arch. Neurol. 43*(5), 487–491.
118 Kujala, T., Myllyviita, K., Tervaniemi, M., Alho, K., Kallio, J. & Näätänen, R. (2000). Basic auditory dysfunction in dyslexia as demonstrated by brain activity measurements. *Psychophysiology, 37*(2), 262–266.
119 Kushch, A., Gross-Glenn, K., Jallad, B., Lubs, H., Rabin, M., Feldman, E. . . . & Duara, R. (1993). Temporal lobe surface area measurements on MRI in normal and dyslexic readers. *Neuropsychologia, 31*(8), 811–821.
120 Laasonen, M., Tomma-Holme, J., Lahti-Nuuttila, P., Service, E. & Virsu, V. (2000). Rate of information segregation in developmentally dyslexic children. *Brain Lang., 75*(1), 66–81.
121 Lambe, E. (1999). Dyslexia, gender and brain imaging. *Neuropsychologia, 37*(5), 521–536.
122 Lamm, O. & Epstein, R. (1994). Dichotic listening performance under high and low lexical work load in subtypes of developmental dyslexia. *Neuropsychologia, 32*(7), 757–785.
123 Larsen, J., Hoien, T., Lundberg, I. & Odegaard, H. (1990). MRI evaluation of the size and symmetry of the planum temporale in adolescents with developmental dyslexia. *Brain Lang., 39*(2), 289–301.
124 Leonard, L. (1998). *Children with specific language impairment.* Cambridge, MA: MIT Press.
125 Leonard, C., Eckert, M., Lombardino, L., Oakland, T., Kranzler, J., Mohr, C. . . . & Freeman, A. (2001). Anatomical risk factors for phonological dyslexia. *Cereb. Cortex, 11*(2), 148–157.
126 Licht, R., Bakker, D., Kok, A. & Bouma, A. (1988). The development of lateral event-related-potentials (ERPs) related to word naming: A four-year longitudinal study. *Neuropsychologia, 26*(2), 327–340.
127 Licht, R., Bakker, D., Kok, A. & Bouma, A. (1992). Grade-related changes in event-related-potentials (ERPs) in primary school children: Differences between two reading tasks. *J. Clin. Exp. Neuropsychol., 14*(2), 193–210.
128 Livingstone, M., Rosen, G., Drislane, F. & Galaburda, A. (1991). Physiological and anatomical evidence for a magnocellular defect in developmental dyslexia. *Proc. Natl. Acad. Sci. USA, 88*(18), 7943–7947.
129 Lovegrove, W., Martin, F., Blackwood, M. & Badcock, D. (1980). Specific reading difficulty: Differences in contrast sensitivity as a function of spatial frequency. *Science, 210,* 439–440.
130 Lovett, M. (1992). Developmental dyslexia. In I. Rapin & S. J. Segalowitz (Eds.), *Handbook of neuropsychology, Vol. 7. Child neuropsychology* (pp. 163–185). Amsterdam, The Netherlands: Elsevier Science.
131 Lynn, K. P. (2011). Developmental malformation of the corpus callosum: a review of typical callosal development and examples of developmental disorders with callosal involvement. *J. Neurodev. Disord., 3*(1), 3–27.
132 McAnally, K. & Stein, J. (1996). Abnormal auditory transient brainstem function in dyslexia. *Proc. R. Soc., Part B, 263,* 961–965.
133 McCrory, E., Frith, U., Brunwick, N. & Price, C. (2000). Abnormal functional activation during a simple word repetition task: A PET study of adult dyslexics. *J. Cogn. Neurosci., 12*(5), 753–762.
134 Manis, F., Seidenberg, M., Doi, L., McBride-Chang, C. & Petersen, A. (1996). On the bases of two subtypes of developmental dyslexia. *Cognition, 58*(2), 157–195.

135 Marino, C., Citterio, A., Giorda, R., Facoetti, A., Menozzi, G., Vanzin, L. ... & Molteni, M. (2007). Association of short-term memory with a variant within DYX1C1 in developmental dyslexia. *Genes Brain Behav.*, *6*(7), 640–646.
136 Marsell, T. & Rajan, P. (1975). Lateral specialization for recognition of words and faces in good and poor readers. *Neuropsychologia*, *13*(4), 489–497.
137 Martinez, J. & Sanchez, E. (1999). Dichotic listening CV lateralization and developmental dyslexia. *J. Clin. Exp. Neuropsychol.*, *21*(4), 519–534.
138 Mason, A., Cornelissen, P., Fowler, M. & Stein, J. (1993). Contrast sensitivity, ocular dominance and reading disability. *Clin. Vis. Sci.*, *8*(4), 345–353.
139 Masutto, C., Bravar, L. & Fabbro, F. (1994). Neurolinguistic differentiation of children with subtypes of dyslexia. *J. Learn Dis.*, *27*(8), 520–526.
140 Matanova, V. (2001). *Dyslexia* [in Bulgarian]. Sofia, Bulgaria: Publishing House "Sofi-R".
141 Menghini, D., Finzi, A., Benassi, M., Bolzani, R., Facoetti, A., Giovagnoli, S. ... & Vicari, S. (2010). Different underlying neurocognitive deficits in developmental dyslexia: A comparative study. *Neuropsychologia*, *48*(4), 863–872.
142 Mody, M., Studdert-Kennedy, M. & Brady, S. (1997). Speech perception deficits in poor readers: Auditory processing or phonological coding? *J. Exp. Child Psychol.*, *64*(2), 199–231.
143 Moll, K., Hasko, S., Groth, K., Bartling, J. & Schulte-Körne, G. (2016). Letter-sound processing deficits in children with developmental dyslexia: An ERP study. *Clin. Neurophysiol.*, *127*(4), 1989–2000.
144 Moncrieff, D. & Black, J. (2008). Dichotic listening deficits in children with dyslexia. *Dyslexia*, *14*(1), 54–75.
145 Moore, L., Brown, W., Markee, T., Theberge, D. & Zvi, J. (1995). Bimanual coordination in dyslexic adults. *Neuropsychologia*, *33*(6), 781–793.
146 Morton, L. & Siegel, L. (1991). Left ear dichotic listening performance on consonant-vowel combinations and digits in subtypes of reading-disabled children. *Brain Lang.*, *40*(1), 162–180.
147 Murphy-Ruiz, P. C., Peñaloza-López, Y. R., García-Pedroza, F. & Poblano, A. (2013). Right cerebral hemisphere and central auditory processing in children with developmental dyslexia. *Arq Neuro-Psiquiatria*, *71*(11), 883–889.
148 Nagarajan, S., Mahncke, H., Salz, T., Tallal, P., Roberts, T. & Merzenich, M. (1999). Cortical auditory signal processing in poor readers. *Proc. Natl. Acad. Sci. USA*, *96*(11), 6483–6488.
149 Nicolson, R. & Fawcett, A. (1990). Automaticity: A new framework for dyslexia research? *Cognition*, *35*(2), 159–182.
150 Nicolson, R. I., Fawcett, A., Berry, E., Jenkins, I., Dean, P. & Brooks, D. (1999). Association of abnormal cerebellar activation with motor learning difficulties in dyslexic adults. *Lancet*, *353*(9165), 1662–1667.
151 Nicolson, R. I., Fawcett, A. & Dean, P. (1995). Time estimation deficits in developmental dyslexia: Evidence of cerebellar involvement. *Proc. R. Soc. Lond. B Biol. Sci.*, *259*(1354), 43–47.
152 Nicolson, R., Fawcett, A. & Dean, P. (2001). Dyslexia, development and the cerebellum. *Trends Neurosci.*, *24*(9), 515–516.
153 Obrzut, J. (1979). Dichotic listening and bisensory memory skills in qualitatively diverse dyslexic readers. *J. Learn Dis.*, *12*(5), 304–314.
154 Obrzut, J. (1988). Deficient lateralization in learning disabled children. In D. Molfese & S. Segalowitz (Eds.), *Brain lateralization in children* (pp. 567–589). New York: Guilford.

155 Obrzut, J., Boliek, C. & Bryden, M. (1997). Dichotic listening, handedness, and reading ability: A meta-analysis. *Dev. Neuropsychol.*, *13*(1), 97–110.

156 Obrzut, J., Mondor, T. & Uecker, A. (1993). The influence of attention on the dichotic REA with normal and learning disabled children. *Neuropsychologia*, *31*(12), 1411–1416.

157 Orton, S. (1928). A physiological theory of reading disability and stuttering in children. *NEJM*, *198*, 1045–1052.

158 Pacheco, A., Araújo, S., Faísca, L., de Castro, S. L., Petersson, K. M. & Reis, A. (2014). Dyslexia's heterogeneity: Cognitive profiling of Portuguese children with dyslexia. *Reading and Writing*, *27*(9), 1529–1545.

159 Patel, T. & Licht, R. (2000). Verbal and affective laterality effects in P-dyslexic, L-dyslexic and normal children. *Child Neuropsychol.*, *6*(3), 157–174.

160 Patterson, K., Vargha-Khadem, F. & Polbey, C. (1989). Reading with one hemisphere. *Brain*, *112*(1), 39–63.

161 Penolazzi, B., Spironelli, C. & Angrilli, A. (2008). Delta EEG activity as a marker of dysfunctional linguistic processing in developmental dyslexia. *Psychophysiology*, *45*, 1025–1033.

162 Perfetti, C. & Bell, L. (1991). Phonemic activation during the first 40ms of word identification. *J. Mem. Lang.*, *30*(4), 473–485.

163 Peterson, R. L., Pennington, B. F. & Olson, R. K. (2013). Subtypes of developmental dyslexia: testing the predictions of the dual-route and connectionist frameworks. *Cognition*, *126*(1), 20–38.

164 Pirizollo, F. & Rayner, K. (1979). Cerebral organization and reading disability. *Neuropsychologia*, *17*(5), 485–491.

165 Plaut, D., McClelland, J. M., Seidenberg, M. S. & Patterson, K. (1996). Understanding normal and impaired word reading: Computational principles in quasi-regular domains. *Psychol. Rev.*, *103*(1), 56–115.

166 Plomin, R. & Kovas, Y. (2005). Generalist genes and learning disabilities. *Psychol. Bull.*, *131*(4), 592–617.

167 Pollmann, S., Maertens, M., von Cramon, D., Lepsien, J. & Hugdahl, K. (2002). Dichotic listening in patients with splenial and nonsplenial callosal lesions. *Neuropsychology*, *16*(1), 56–64.

168 Price, C. (1998). The functional anatomy of word comprehension and production. *Trends Cogn. Sci.*, *2*(8), 281–288.

169 Pumfrey, P. & Reason, R. (1991). *Specific learning difficulties (Dyslexia)*. London & New York: Routledge.

170 Rae, C., Lee, M., Dixon, R., Blamire, A., Thompson, C., Styles, P. . . . & Stein, J.F. (1998). Metabolic abnormalities in developmental dyslexia detected by 1H magnetic resonance spectroscopy. *Lancet*, *351*(9119), 1849–1852.

171 Ramus, F. (2003). Developmental dyslexia: Specific phonological deficit or general sensorimotor dysfunction? *Curr. Opin. Neurobiol.*, *13*(2), 212–218.

172 Ramus, F. (2004). Neurobiology of dyslexia: A reinterpretation of the data. *Trends Neurosci.*, *27*(12), 720–726.

173 Ramus, F., Pidgeon, E. & Frith, U. (2002). The relationship between motor control and phonology in dyslexic children. *J. Child Psychol. Psychiatry*, *44*(5), 712–722.

174 Ramus, F., Rosen, S., Dakin, S., Day, B., Castellote, J., White, S. . . . & Frith, U. (2003). Theories of developmental dyslexia: Insights from a multiple case study of dyslexic adults. *Brain*, *126*(4), 841–865.

175 Ramus, F. & Szenkovits, G. (2008). What phonological deficit? *Q. J. Exp. Psychol.*, *61*(1), 129–141.

176 Ravich-Shcherbo, I., Maryutina, T. & Grigorenko, Y. E. (1999). *Psychogenics* [in Russian]. Moscow, Russia: Aspekt Press.
177 Robichon, F., Levrier, O., Farnarier, P. & Habib, M. (2000). Developmental dyslexia: Atypical cortical asymmetries and functional significance. *Eur. J. Neurol.*, 7(1), 35–46.
178 Robin, P. (2005). Comorbidity of dyslexia, dyspraxia, attention deficit disorder (ADD), attention deficit hyperactive disorder (ADHD), obsessive compulsive disorder (OCD) and Tourette's syndrome in children: A prospective epidemiological study. *Clin Chiropr.*, 8(4), 189–198.
179 Rojias, D., Camou, S., Reite, M. & Rogers, S. (2005). Planum temporale volume in children and adolescents with autism. *J. Autism Dev. Disord.*, 35(4), 479–487.
180 Ruff, S., Cardebat, D., Marie, N. & Demonet, J. (2002). Enhanced response of the left frontal cortex to slowed down speech in dyslexia: An fMRI study. *Neuroreport*, 13, 1285–128.
181 Rumsey, J. (1992). The biology of developmental dyslexia. *JAMA*, 268(7), 912–915.
182 Rumsey, J. (1996). Developmental dyslexia: Anatomic and functional neuroimaging. *Ment. Retard Dev. Disabil. Res. Rev.*, 2(1), 28–38.
183 Rumsey, J., Andreason, P., Zmetkin, A. & King, C. (1994). Right frontotemporal activation by tonal memory in dyslexia: An O-15 PET study. *Biol. Psychiatry*, 36(3), 171–180.
184 Rumsey, J., Horvitz, B., Donohue, B., Nace, K., Maisog, J. & Andreason, P. (1999). A functional lesion in developmental dyslexia: Left angular gyral blood flow predicts severity. *Brain Lang.*, 70(2), 187–204.
185 Rumsey, J., Nace, K., Donohue, B., Wise, D., Maisog, J. & Andreason, P. (1997). A PET study of impaired word recognition and phonological processing in dyslexic men. *Arch. Neurol.*, 54, 562–573.
186 Salmelin, R., Service, E., Kiesila, P., Uutela, K. & Salonen, O. (1996). Impaired visual and word processing in dyslexia revealed with magnetoencephalography. *Ann. Neurol.*, 40(2), 157–162.
187 Satz, P. (1990). Developmental dyslexia: An etiological reformulation. In G. Pavlidis (Ed.), *Perspective on dyslexia* (pp. 3–26). New York: John Wiley & Sons.
188 Schachter, S., Ransil, B. & Geschind, N. (1987). Association of handedness with hair color and learning disabilities. *Neuropsychologia*, 25(1B), 269–276.
189 Schmahmann, J. D. & Pandya, D. N. (2008). Disconnection syndromes of basal ganglia, thalamus, and cerebrocerebellar systems. *Cortex*, 44(8), 1037–1066.
190 Schulte-Korne, G., Deimel, W., Barting, J. & Remschmidt, H. (1999). The role of phonological awareness, speech perception, and auditory temporal processing for dyslexia. *Eur. Child Adolesc. Psychiatry*, 8(Suppl 3), III/28–III/34.
191 Schultz, R. T., Cho, N. K., Staib, L. H., Kier, L. E., Fletcher, J. M., Shaywitz, S. E. . . . & Duncan, J. S. (1994). Brain morphology in normal and dyslexic children: The influence of sex and age. *Ann. Neurol.*, 35(6), 732–742.
192 Seidenberg, M. S. & McClelland, J. L. (1989). A distributed, developmental model of word recognition and naming. *Psychol. Rev.*, 96(4), 523–568.
193 Shaywitz, S. (1998). Dyslexia. *NEJM*, 338, 307–312.
194 Shaywitz, S. & Shaywitz, B. (2005). Dyslexia (specific reading disability). *Biol. Psychiatry*, 57(11), 1301–1309.
195 Shaywitz, S., Shaywitz, B., Pugh, K., Fulbright, R., Constable, R., Mencl, W. . . . & Gore, J. C. (1998). Functional disruption in the organization of the brain for reading in dyslexia. *Proc. Natl. Acad. Sci. USA*, 95(5), 2636–2641.
196 Siegel, L. (1999). Issues in the definition and diagnosis of learning disabilities: A perspective on Guckenberger v. Boston University. *J. Learn Dis.*, 32(4), 304–319.

197 Simos, P. G., Breier, J. I., Fletcher, J. M., Bergman, E. & Papanicolaou, A. C. (2000). Cerebral mechanisms involved in word reading in dyslexic children: A magnetic source imaging approach. *Cereb. Cortex*, *10*(8), 809–816.

198 Snowling, M. J. & Hulme, C. (2005). Learning to read with a language impairment. In M. J. Snowling & C. Hulme (Eds.), *The science of reading: A handbook* (pp. 397–412). Oxford: Wiley-Blackwell.

199 Spironelli, C. & Angrilli, A. (2006). Language lateralization in phonolological, semantic and orthographic tasks: A slow evoked potential study. *Behav. Brain Res.*, *175*(2), 296–304.

200 Spironelli, C., Penolazzi, B. & Angrilli, A. (2008). Dysfunctional hemispheric asymmetry of theta and beta EEG activity during linguistic tasks in developmental dyslexia. *Biol. Psychol.*, *77*(2), 123–131.

201 Sprenger-Charolles, L., Cole, P., Lacert P & Serniclaes, W. (2000). On subtypes of developmental dyslexia: Evidence from processing time and accuracy scores. *Canad. J. Exp. Psychol.*, *54*(2), 87–90.

202 Springer, S. & Deutsch, G. (1990). *Left brain, right brain* (3rd ed.). San Francisco, CA: W. H. Freeman.

203 Stanovich, K. E. (1988). Explaining the differences between the dyslexic and the garden-variety poor reader: The phonological core variable. *J. Learn Dis.*, *21*(10), 590–604.

204 Stanovich, K., Siegel, L. & Gottardo, A. (1997). Converging evidence for phonological and surface types of reading disability. *J. Educ. Psychol.*, *89*, 114–127.

205 Stein, J. (1991). Visiospatial sense, hemispheric asymmetry and dyslexia. In J. Stein (Ed.), *Vision and visual dyslexia* (pp. 181–188). London: MacMillan.

206 Stein, J. (2001). The magnocellular theory of developmental dyslexia. *Dyslexia*, *7*(1), 12–36.

207 Stein, J. & McAnally, K. (1996). Impaired auditory temporal processing in dyslexics. *Irish J. Psychol.*, *16*, 220–228.

208 Stein, J. & Talcott, J. (1999). Impaired neuronal timing in developmental dyslexia – The magnocellular hypothesis. *Dyslexia*, *5*(2), 59–77.

209 Stein, J. & Walsh, V. (1997). To see but not to read: The magnocellular theory of dyslexia. *Trends Neurosci.*, *20*(4), 147–151.

210 Talcott, J., Hansen, P., Willis-Owen, C., McKinnell, I., Richardson, A. & Stein, J. (1998). Visual magnocellular impairment in adult developmental dyslexics. *Neuroophtalmology*, *20*(4), 187–201.

211 Tallal, P. (1980). Auditory temporal perception, phonics, and reading disabilities in children. *Brain Lang*, *9*(2), 182–198.

212 Temple, C., Jeeves, M. & Vilarroya, O. (1990). Reading in callosal agenesis. *Brain Lang.*, *39*(2), 235–253.

213 Temple, E., Poldrack, R., Salidis, J., Deutsch, G., Tallal, P., Merzenich, M. . . . & Gabrieli, J. D. (2001). Disrupted neural responses to phonological and orthographic processing in dyslexic children: An fMRI study. *Neuroreport*, *12*(2), 299–307.

214 Thompson, M. (1976). A comparison of laterality effects in dyslexics and controls using verbal dichotic listening tasks. *Neuropsychologia*, *14*(2), 243–246.

215 Trussel, L. (1998). Cellular mechanisms for preservation of timing in central auditory pathways. *Curr. Opin. Neurobiol.*, *7*(4), 487–492.

216 Turkelyaub, P., Gareau, L., Flowers, D., Zeffiro, T. & Eden, G. (2003). Development of neural mechanisms for reading. *Nat Neurosci.*, *6*(7), 767–773.

217 Van der Schoot, M., Licht, R., Horsley, T. & Sergeant, J. (2002). Fronto-central dysfunctions in reading disability depend on subtype: Guessers but not spellers. *Dev. Neuropsychol.*, *22*(3), 533–564.

218 Vellutino, F. R. (1979). *Dyslexia: Theory and research*. Cambridge, MA: MIT Press.
219 Vlachos, F., Papathanasiou, I. & Andreou, G. (2007). Cerebellum and reading. *Folia Phoniatr Logoped.*, *59*(4), 177–183.
220 Volkova, L. (1989). *Logopedics* [in Russian]. Moscow, Russia: Prosveshcheniye.
221 Waldie, K. (1999). Hemispheric specialization for reading in subtypes of children with developmental dyslexia. *Int. J. Neurosci.*, *97*(3/4), 238–238.
222 Webster, R. I. & Shevell, M. I. (2004). Neurobiology of specific language impairment. *J. Child Neurol.*, *19*(7), 471.
223 Weeks, N., Capetillo-Cunliffe, L., Rayman, J., Iacoboni, M. & Zaidel, L. (1999). Individual differences in the hemispheric specialization of dual route variables. *Brain Lang.*, *67*(2), 110–133.
224 Weinberger, D. R., Luchins, D. J., Morihisa, J. & Wyatt, R. J. (1982). Asymmetrical volumes of the right and left frontal and occipital regions of the human brain. *Ann. Neurol.*, *11*(1), 97–100.
225 Wimmer, H., Mayringer, H. & Raberger, T. (1999). Reading and dual-task balancing: Evidence against the automatization deficit explanation of developmental dyslexia. *J. Learn Dis.*, *32*(5), 473–478.
226 Witelson, S. F. (1976). Abnormal right hemisphere functional specialization in developmental dyslexia. In R. M. Knights & D. J. Bakker (Eds.), *The neuropsychology of reading disorders: Theoretical approaches* (pp. 233–255). Baltimore, MD: University Park Press.
227 Witelson, S. F. (1977). Developmental dyslexia: two right hemispheres and non-left. *Science*, *195*, 309–311.
228 Witton, C., Talcott, J., Hansen, P., Richardson, A., Griffiths, T., Rees, A. . . . & Green, G. G. (1998). Sensitivity to dynamic auditory and visual stimuli predicts nonword reading ability in both dyslexic and normal readers. *Curr. Biol.*, *8*(14), 791–797.
229 Wolf, M. & Bowers, P. (1999). The "Double Deficit Hypothesis" for the developmental dyslexias. *J. Educ. Psychol.*, *91*, 1–24.
230 Zadina, J., Corey, D., Casbergue, R., Lemen, L., Rouse, J., Knaus, T. . . . & Foundas, A. L. (2006). Lobar asymmetries in subtypes of dyslexic and control subjects. *J. Child Neurol.*, *21*(11), 922–931.
231 Zaidel, E. (1990). Language functions in the two hemispheres following complete cerebral commissurotomy and hemispherectomy. In F. Boller & J. Grafman (Eds.), *Handbook of neuropsychology* (Vol. 4, pp. 115–150). Amsterdam, The Netherlands: Elsevier.
232 Zesiger, P. & de Partz, M. (1994). Perturbations du langage ecrit: les dyslexies et les dysgraphies. In X. Seron & M. Jeannerod (Eds.), *Neuropsychologie humaine* (pp. 419–438). Leige, Belgium: Mardaga.
233 Ziegler, J. C., Castel, C., Pech-Georgel, C., George, F., Alario, F. X. & Perry, C. (2008). Developmental dyslexia and the dual route model of reading: simulating individual differences and subtypes. *Cognition*, *107*(1), 151–178.
234 Zurif, E. & Carson, G. (1970). Dyslexia in relation to cerebral dominance and temporal analysis. *Neuropsychologia*, *8*(3), 351–361.

4
INTELLECTUAL DISABILITY

Introduction

According to the new revision of the *Diagnostic and Statistical Manual-Fifth Edition* (*DSM-V*) [1], intellectual disability (ID) (Intellectual Developmental Disorder) (formerly Mental retardation) is defined as a disorder with onset during the developmental period that includes both intellectual and adaptive functioning deficits in conceptual, social and practical areas. The conceptual areas include skills in language, reading, writing, math, reasoning, knowledge and memory. The social areas refer to empathy, social judgment, interpersonal communication skills, the ability to make and retain friendships and others. The practical areas refer to self-management in different domains (personal care, job responsibilities, money management, recreation, organizing school and work tasks, etc.).

ID is considered chronic and often co-occurs with other mental conditions such as attention deficit hyperactivity disorder (ADHD) and autism spectrum disorder (ASD). *DSM-V* [1] continues the tradition by specifying ID as mild, moderate, severe or profound, but the focus is primarily on ability and needed supports rather than on IQ scores as in the *DSM-Fourth Edition*.

In addition to categorization by severity/IQ level, ID can also be subdivided into syndromic intellectual disability (S-ID) and non-syndromic intellectual disability (NS-ID), based on the presence/absence of comorbidities in addition to intellectual deficits. In S-ID, subjects exhibit one, or multiple, clinical features or comorbidities in addition to ID. Genetic syndromes such as Down syndrome, Williams syndrome, Fragile X syndrome, Rett syndrome, Turner syndrome, T 21, etc., are examples of S-ID. Traditionally, the diagnosis "NS-ID" refers to the presence of ID without accompanying additional physical, neurological and/or metabolic abnormalities [3, 34, 40].

While S-ID has a clear definition, there is a debate over the definition of NS-ID. It is thought that due to the difficulty in ruling out the presence of subtler neurological anomalies, psychiatric disorders and symptoms of some syndromes in these individuals, as they may be less apparent, or difficult to diagnose due to the cognitive impairment, the distinction between S-ID and NS-ID is often blurred [34].

Studies indicate that ID has a complex and heterogeneous aetiology, including genetic or environmental factors. More than 750 different causes have been identified. They can be organized into five general categories: (1) chromosomal abnormalities; (2) metabolic disorders; (3) embryonic teratogen exposure; (4) complications during delivery; and (5) childhood illness or injury (for details, see [36]). Although ID is one of the most frequently diagnosed heterogeneous neurodevelopmental conditions, it is reported that the causes remain unclear in more than 60 percent of cases [3, 34].

It is considered that ID exists due to a wide range of aetiologies that cause structural changes in the brain. These structural changes may vary from visible and easily distinguishable major brain malformations, to weak, sub-microscopic defects in the interneuronal connections that cannot be registered even by histopathological examination after death (for a review, see [56]). Mainly, this impossibility to define the aetiology of ID before one's death has caused the intuitive knowledge that individuals with ID must have "something different" about the structure and organization of the brain [6, 56].

The association between abnormal cerebral dominance and ID has been systematically studied for nearly a century, leading to the collection of a sufficient amount of data, which suggests that individuals with ID have a deviant cerebral organization and atypical lateralization, which is reflected in non-right-handedness and lack of, or reversed, language lateralization [20, 55, 58].

Handedness and intellectual disability

Handedness studies in subjects with ID have been systematically conducted since the 70s. There is a clear evidence for atypical hand preferences in ID. High incidence of non-right-handedness, including left-handedness and mixed-handedness, among the subjects with ID (S-ID and NS-ID) has been found by different researchers [5, 9, 24, 36, 42, 45, 50, 55, 61, 63]. These findings have been confirmed by the performance measurements of handedness in ID [2, 8, 39, 44, 49, 59]. Despite differences in data between the studies, the reported frequency of both mixed-handedness and left-handedness is approximately two to three times as high among subjects with ID compared to the general population [33, 51].

According to some studies, there is an increased prevalence of mixed-handedness and non-left-handedness among subjects with ID [24, 42, 53, 62]. Soper et al. [62] examined the handedness within a sample with ID using items appropriate for lower functioning subjects, with multiple presentations within and between sessions 1 week apart, and revealed a dramatic shift from the normal right-handedness, primarily due to the presence of a large mixed-handedness subgroup of subjects who showed inconsistent hand preference within items. Morris and Romski [42] assessed the handedness of nonspeaking or minimally speaking subjects with moderate, severe or profound ID and confirmed increased prevalence of mixed-handedness, as had been previously reported. A recent study, comprising meta-analyses of studies that have assessed the handedness in subjects with intellectual disability of unknown/idiopathic nature compared to typically developing subjects, also reported higher levels of non-right-handedness in the intellectually disabled subjects than those typically developing [47].

Generally, these findings suggested the existence of a large mixed-handedness subtype of ID that is characterized by ambiguous hand preference [42, 62] and that is not closely linked to level of cognitive impairment [29]. Moreover, based on these findings, it has been proposed that the presence of ambiguous handedness could be explained with bilateral damages that impede the establishment of cerebral dominance for motor control in either hemisphere [42, 61, 62].

The main criticism against the assumption for the existence of mixed-handedness subtype of ID is that most studies have not taken into account important methodological factors such as sensory impairments, motor impairments (especially asymmetrical ones), speech and language deficits, history of seizure conditions, especially in cases of severe and profound ID, which could significantly affect handedness [59].

There is a hypothesis that left-handedness is associated mainly with severe and profound ID [33, 37, 52]. By reviewing relevant research literature, Pipe [52] reported evidence linking left-handedness to ID in a group with more severe and generalized deficits. Examining the relationship between personal and familial hand preference and ID, Bradshaw-McAnulty et al. [8] found that 13 percent of a mildly and moderately retarded group and 28 percent of a severely and profoundly retarded group were left-handed, suggesting that right-hand preference varied inversely with severity of ID. These findings were evaluated as well, representing an excess of sinistrality in proportion to degree of ID and supporting the hypothesis that it is due to pathological left-handedness [8, 52]. Furthermore, it was proposed that the larger number of left-handers among subjects with severe and profound ID was due to a disordered development of LH systems for manual motor control [8, 32, 37, 61].

Handedness was found to be significantly related to language ability in subjects with ID. Examining a representative sample of subjects with ID, Lucas et al. [37] revealed an increased prevalence of left-handedness among those individuals with language deficits. In a later study, Groen et al. [23] found that within a group of children with Down syndrome, those who showed a stronger or more consistent hand preference had better language and memory skills.

Although lateral preferences in the use of sensory organs and limbs have been considered among the most obvious functional asymmetries in humans [31], up to this date and to our knowledge, the relation of ID to other types of sensory (eye, ear) and motor (foot) asymmetries has been examined only in two studies. Porac et al. [54] examined hand, eye, foot and ear preferences in a group with ID and in two control groups and found significantly higher incidence of left-sided or mixed-sided behaviors on each of the preference dimensions in the group with ID compared to the control groups. Furthermore, lateral preference patterns tended to be concordant only in the control groups. In a recent study, Leconte and Fagard [35] evaluated lateral preferences in two groups of children with ID of idiopathic origin (10–11 years and 12–14 years, respectively), compared to those of typically developing children. The results showed no between-group differences with regard to the occurrence of left-handedness, but higher incidence of mixed-handedness among ID than in typically developing children, and lower test-retest consistency of hand preference in the younger group with ID than in the control group. Left-eyedness and crossed hand-eye preference were also more common among ID than in typically developing children. No age-related difference in laterality was found in ID children. Findings from both studies have provided additional support to the assumption that ID is associated with atypical asymmetry.

Two theoretical perspectives have been put forward to explain atypical laterality in subjects with ID. They were developed on the basis of studies of hand preference in populations with ID. According to the first perspective, early brain damage impedes the establishment of a normal pattern of cerebral dominance for language in either hemisphere [9, 37, 54, 58, 61], or delays neurological development for normal brain functioning regarding cerebral dominance [13]. According to the other perspective, reduced lateralization is due to maturational delay in neuronal pathways [4, 41]. Furthermore, there is a suggestion that the early brain damage hypothesis is applicable to the population with severe and profound ID, while the delayed maturation hypothesis is applicable to the population with mild ID [41].

Language lateralization and intellectual disability

The conception of atypical cerebral laterality in individuals with ID has not received consistent support from the studies on language lateralization. In general, research findings obtained mainly from dichotic-listening studies comparing subjects with Down syndrome (i.e. with S-ID), subjects with ID of unknown aetiology (NS-ID) and typically developing subjects have shown that Down syndrome and ID of unknown aetiology differ regarding the pattern of hemispheric asymmetries for language perception.

Data from studies of subjects with Down syndrome are largely consistent, revealing atypical left-ear advantage (LEA)/right-hemispheric advantage (RHA) for language perception [16, 17, 22, 26, 27, 28, 50, 65, 66], or a lack of hemispheric advantage [60, 63, 65].

Two main hypotheses have been put forward to explain atypical asymmetries in populations with Down syndrome. According to the first, proposed by Hartley [28] and empirically less supported, individuals with Down syndrome exhibit reversed cerebral asymmetry, that is, typically LH functions are served by the RH and typically RH functions are served by the LH.

The second hypothesis, proposed by Elliott et al. [16, 17, 18] and more widely accepted, suggests the existence of a unique pattern of functional brain organization in right-handed subjects with Down syndrome including RH localization of speech perception and LH localization of speech expression. This hypothesis has received support from studies that have found that the reversed hemispheric specialization for speech perception in subjects with Down syndrome exists together with a common LH specialization for speech production and simple and complex manual functions [16, 29, 48, 65], and a typical RH specialization for spatial perception [15]. Furthermore, it is assumed that the pattern of anomalous cerebral laterality for language in subjects with Down syndrome is linked with the weak linguistic abilities that these subjects exhibit [30, 49].

Based on the neuropsychological disconnection model, proposed by Geschwind [20], Elliott and co-authors have interpreted these findings as evidence that some of the difficulties in the specific information processing exhibited by subjects with Down syndrome may be due to a functional disconnection of cerebral areas responsible for the receptive speech from those responsible for the organization and control of speech movements. It is thought that the unique pattern of dissociation of lateralized systems for speech perception and speech production that are typically supported by the same hemisphere in the typically developing population is specific to Down syndrome and is not observed in other populations with ID of unknown aetiology, therefore, it cannot be attributed to the ID per se [16, 17, 29, 66].

In contrast to studies of subjects with Down syndrome, the results from dichotic listening studies of subjects with ID of unknown aetiology are more inconsistent. Pipe [50] assessed language laterality in subjects with Down syndrome, subjects with NS-ID and typically developing individuals using dichotic listening tasks, and revealed the typical right-ear advantage (REA)/left-hemispheric advantage (LHA) for speech stimuli in subjects with NS-ID. Giencke and Lewandowski [22] repeated the results of Pipe exploring similar target groups – with Down syndrome, with NS-ID and controls. Using a dichotic monitoring test, Shoji et al. [57] examined linguistic lateralization in adolescents with Down syndrome, adolescents with ID of unknown aetiology and three control groups at different ages (respectively with an average age of 4.7 years, 8.5 years and 18.7 years) and found that only adolescents with Down syndrome exhibited an atypical linguistic lateralization with a reverse pattern of LEA. Hornstein and Mosley [33] did not find differences between subjects with mild ID and normal subjects regarding the pattern of ear asymmetries, but found significantly poorer performance accuracy in subjects with ID. By contrast, Pipe and Beale [53] compared children with ID and normal children and found that mean REAs were smaller for the group with ID than for the control group but absolute ear advantages were similar for the two groups, suggesting atypical, but not reduced, functional asymmetries for children with ID. On the other hand, Paquette et al. [46] documented a LEA/RHA for speech stimuli in individuals with ID of unknown aetiology and interpreted the pattern of their finding in support of the notion of atypical cerebral laterality in populations with ID as a consequence of the early brain damage.

Based on a research literature survey of findings for dichotic stimulation in the domain of ID, Mosley and Vrbancic [43] pointed out that in spite of the paucity of studies with intellectually disabled subjects with application of dichotic stimulation, three conclusions could be drawn. First, when subjects with NS-ID are compared to typically developing subjects matched for mental age, the ear asymmetries are invariably in the expected direction for the type of stimulus used; however, the magnitude is variable. Second, under dichotic monitoring, subjects with ID, including Down syndrome subjects, demonstrate the same pattern of intrusion errors from the unattended right ear as do subjects with normal intelligence matched for mental age. Third, the majority of the dichotic listening studies have focused on the "atypical" speech lateralization of Down syndrome subjects as the data received are equivocal regarding the pattern of speech lateralization in these subjects.

Summarizing the results from the above-mentioned studies, the notion of atypical cerebral dominance in individuals with NS-ID seems to be largely supported by the findings of handedness studies, but minimally supported by the findings of dichotic-listening studies.

The few studies in the area of ID of unknown aetiology which have used verbal dichotic perception and the inconsistency of their results, along with the presence of evidences for an association between atypical language lateralization and poor language skills of people with ID, irrespective of its origin [29, 30, 50], initiated the present study. Its major aim was to investigate both the degree of the reported right-hand preference and hemispheric asymmetry for speech perception in a group of children with mild NS-ID and a control group of typically developing children.

Personal research data

Subjects

Twenty-eight children with mild ID (IQ 50–70) of unknown aetiology (seventeen boys and eleven girls, age ranging from 8.7 to 16.1 years; *Mean* age = 10.7, SD = 2.2) participated in the study. All children were pupils in a special school (with first grade completed or pupils in second, third or fourth grade).

The selection of the study sample of children with ID was made on the basis of data from medical records at school and parents' reports obtained through an interview. All selected children met the following requirements:

- normal hearing;
- lack of movement disorders;
- presence of delayed or disturbed language development; and
- writing and drawing with right hand and absence of experienced pressure in childhood to switch the writing hand from the preferred left to the right.

The control group consisted of twenty-eight normally developing children matched for chronological age (*Mean* age = 9.11, SD = 1.9), sex (seventeen boys and eleven girls) and handedness. They were pupils in regular classes (with first grade completed or pupils in second, third or fourth grade), and according to the information provided by their parents, class academic advisor and school psychologist, all were right-hand writers, with normal hearing, normal intelligence and good academic skills.

All studied children were Bulgarian native speakers. Their participation was voluntary and with the consent of their parents and school institutions.

Assessment of handedness

In view of the study purpose to explore between-group differences regarding the degree of the reported right-handedness, the hand preference of each child was assessed by a performance test described in detail in Chapter 2 "Developmental stuttering", section "Assessment of handedness".

A Quotient of manual asymmetry (QMA) was calculated individually for each child. Children who scored between −70 and +70 were classified as mixed-handed, those who scored between +71 and +100 were classified as right-handed and those who scored between −71 and −100 were classified as left-handed.

In addition, familial sinistrality histories (i.e. presence/absence of first- and second-degree left-handed relatives) were also obtained for all participants.

Dichotic listening: stimuli and procedure

The used dichotic test with consonant-vowel syllables is described in detail in Chapter 2 "Developmental stuttering", section "Dichotic listening". The recall is made orally, in free condition, after playing each dichotic pair.

Data analysis and statistics

Laterality Quotient (LQ) and Perceptive performance were the main variables used for the individual and group analysis of dichotic listening scores. Their calculations are described in Chapter 2 "Developmental stuttering", section "Data analysis and statistics".

For statistical evaluation, the Crosstab chi-square test and Independent Sample t-tests in the SPSS 16.0 were applied. Also, effect size was calculated.

Results from the assessment of handedness

Table 4.1 presents the results from the assessment of handedness and familial sinistrality in the group with ID and the control group.

Although all studied children were initially determined as right-handers based on the information about preferred writing and drawing hand and the absence of pressure in childhood to switch writing/drawing hand from preferred left to right, according to the performance test scores, 78.6 percent of the control group and only 53.6 percent of the group with ID showed right-handedness. The remaining

TABLE 4.1 Distribution of participants in study groups according to the demonstrated type of handedness and the presence of familial sinistrality (in %)

	Mixed-handedness		Right-handedness		Familial sinistrality	
	n	%	n	%	n	%
Control group	6	21.4	22	78.6	8	28.6
Group with ID	13	46.4	15	53.6	8	28.6

21.4 percent of the control group and 46.4 percent of the group with ID demonstrated mixed-handedness. These between-group differences were statistically significant ($\chi^2_{[1]}$ = 3.903, p = .048, φ = 0.264).

No between-group differences were registered regarding the frequency of the reported familial sinistrality histories (M = 1.000).

Dichotic listening results

The analysis of dichotic test results found significant differences between the group with ID and the group of controls regarding the pattern of hemispheric asymmetry for dichotic speech perception.

Comparison of the mean LQ scores (M, SD; %) revealed significant between-group differences: control group – Mean LQ = +9.33, SD = 10.94; group with ID – Mean LQ = –4.01, SD = 11.13 (t (54) = 4.525, p < .000, Hedges' g = 1.208). It is evident that the mean LQs of study groups are different in value and sign, indicating between-group differences both in the direction and the magnitude of interaural asymmetry. Therefore, at a group level, while the control group demonstrated the typical REA/LHA for dichotic speech perception, the group with ID demonstrated slight LEA/RHA.

It is very important that the typical REA/LHA was founded in 75.00 percent of controls and 53.6 percent of the group with ID. Except for one child of the control group (3.6 percent) who demonstrated no-ear advantage for dichotic listening, all the rest (21.4 percent of the control group and 46.4 percent of the group with ID) showed LEA/RHA. These between-group differences did not reach statistical significance, but had practical significance with a moderate effect size ($\chi^2_{[2]}$ = 4.579, p = .089, Cramer's V = 0.286).

The received results clearly showed a significantly higher frequency of the atypical pattern of RHA for dichotic speech perception in the group of children with ID in comparison with the control group.

Since the calculation of a mean LQ for a group have taken into account the signs of the individual LQs, its value depends to a great extent on the ratio of negative and positive LQs. Due to the reported significant between-group differences in the incidence of atypical RHA, the mean absolute values of LQ of both groups were compared. The results revealed a significant between-group difference reflected in a reduced hemispheric asymmetry in the group with ID: *Mean absolute*

LQ = 13.51, SD = 6.15 for the control group and *Mean absolute* LQ = 8.76, SD = 4.95 for the group with ID (*t* (54) = 3.182; *p* < .002, Hedges' *g* = 0.851).

Extremely large between-group differences were revealed through the comparative analysis concerning perceptive performance as measured by the mean percentage of correctly reported syllables on both ears, and separately on the left and right ear, respectively (Table 4.2).

TABLE 4.2 Mean percentage of correct identified syllables (*M*; *SD*) of studied groups

	Mean overall performance		Mean of right ear		Mean of left ear	
	M	SD	M	SD	M	SD
Control group	46.3	8.7	50.8	8.1	41.7	9.0
Group with ID	26.8	8.3	25.4	10.4	28.2	9.9
t (*p*)	8.62 < .000		10.22 < .000		5.34 < .000	
Hedges' G	2.301		2.727		1.429	

The group of children with ID displayed significantly worse dichotic speech perception in comparison to the control group. As can be seen from the table, the critical decrease in the mean percentage of correctly identified syllables of the group with ID (*Mean* = 26.8, *SD* = 8.3 vs. *Mean* = 46.3, *SD* = 8.7 of the controls; *t* (54) = 8.62, *p* < .001, Hedges' *g* = 2.301) was mainly due to the much worse perception of patterns presented to the right ear (*Mean* = 25.4, *SD* = 10.4 vs. *Mean* = 50.8, *SD* = 8.1 of the control group, *t* (54) = 10.22, *p* < .001, Hedges' *g* = 2.727) than the perception of patterns presented to the left ear (*Mean* = 28.2, *SD* = 9.9 vs. *Mean* = 41.7, *SD* = 9.0 of the control group; *t* (54) = 5.34, *p* < .001, Hedges' *g* = 1.429).

The finding that 89.3 percent of studied children with ID and only one child of the controls (3.6 percent) displayed an effect of extreme neglect of one of the ears in dichotic listening conditions was of particular importance. The nature of this effect is expressed in an absolute inability to perceive both of the presented dichotic syllables. These children reproduced only one of the syllables (correctly or incorrectly) and insisted explicitly that they have not heard two syllables, or have heard the same syllables in both ears.

The observed difference in the incidence of this phenomenon in studied groups was highly significant ($\chi^2_{|1|}$ = 41.5354, *p* < .000, φ = 0.859).

Discussion

This study aimed to investigate handedness and language lateralization in children with ID of unknown aetiology and history of disturbed language development. The findings clearly demonstrated that both their pattern of manual asymmetry and their pattern of hemispheric asymmetry for speech perception deviated from the patterns observed in typically developing children of the same chronological age.

Results from the dichotic listening test showed that the study sample with ID exhibited a reduced RHA at the group level. At the individual level, half of the group demonstrated the atypical LEA/RHA for dichotic perception of speech sounds and the other half demonstrated the typical REA/LHA. However, an important finding was the significantly reduced Mean absolute LQ of the group with ID compared to the control group, suggesting a distinctly reduced hemispheric asymmetry in the group with ID, regardless of its direction (left or right). Another significant finding was the registered effect of extreme neglect of one of the ears in dichotic listening conditions in the vast majority of the group with ID (89.3 percent) versus only one child of controls (3.6 percent). In addition, the perceptive performance accuracy of all studied children with ID, without exception, was critically reduced.

In summary, the pattern of results obtained from the dichotic listening task revealed that the study sample of children with mild NS-ID and language deficits is characterized by an atypical pattern of hemispheric asymmetry for speech sound perception, including a reduced RHA and a prominent perceptive deficit. Furthermore, another important finding was that about half of the study sample with ID demonstrated mixed-handedness.

This finding regarding hand preference in subjects with ID is in accordance with laterality studies indicating increased non-right-handedness among subjects with NS-ID [24, 42, 53, 62] and supports the assumption of existence of a large mixed-handedness subtype of ID that is characterized by ambiguous hand preference [42, 62]. Lack of differences between the group with ID and the control group regarding the frequency of the reported familial sinistrality rejects the possibility that atypical cerebral laterality in subjects with NS-ID is an inherited feature of the cerebral function organization.

As far as dichotic listening results are concerned, they do not fully repeat the pattern of the results of any of the previous dichotic listening studies of subjects with NS-ID, but partly agree with the results of the few studies that have found differences in cerebral asymmetry for language perception between subjects with ID and typically developed subjects. Similar to my findings, Paquette et al. [46] found a LEA/RHA for dichotic speech perception in subjects with ID of unknown aetiology, Pipe and Beale [53] found smaller mean REAs for the group of children with ID compared to the group of normal children and Hornstein and Mosley [33] found significantly poorer performance accuracy in subjects with ID than in normal subjects.

On the other hand, the results of the current study are similar to the results obtained in studies of subjects with Down syndrome (i.e. with S-ID), suggesting lack of hemispheric advantage [60, 63, 65] or atypical RHA for speech perception [16, 17, 21, 26, 27, 28, 50, 65, 66].

In my opinion, the key cause for the pattern of results in this study was the fact that all children with ID had speech and language deficits and difficulties in literacy.

Present findings suggest atypical and reduced functional asymmetries for children with NS-ID and support the existence of a relationship between these deviations in cerebral laterality and the presence of delayed or disturbed language development.

Atypical cerebral laterality refers to the reverse or weak or bilateral representation of language in the two cerebral hemispheres [20] and this study provided reasonable evidence for its presence in subjects with NS-ID who exhibit speech and language deficits. Furthermore, an indirect connection between the causes of ID and the disturbed cerebral lateralization can be hypothesized. Based on broadly accepted views that brain abnormalities in ID vary widely in type and magnitude and are associated with a large diversity of ethiologies (for a review, see [56]), it can be supposed that brain abnormalities may cause maturational disturbances or delay of both hemispheric lateralization and hemispheric integration. The effect of extreme neglect of one of the ears in dichotic listening conditions observed in almost all studied children with ID is in my view strongly indicative for a poor bilateral integration, probably due to disturbed callosal transfer – an idea shared by other researchers of cerebral laterality in ID [4, 41].

It is completely possible that the disturbed cerebral lateralization in ID, which in turn causes a disordered language development, represents a negative consequence of a maladaptive neuroplasticity throughout recovery after an early brain damage – a suggestion relevant to the idea that neuroplasticity may also mediate the emergence of pathological symptomatology of neurodevelopmental disorders, such as autism, schizophrenia and ADHD [for a review and details, see [19]).

In general, the results of the present study suggest that there are deviations in cerebral laterality in a subgroup of population with mild NS-ID and comorbid speech and language disorders, reflected in a reduced or atypical hemispheric asymmetry and poor bilateral integration.

Furthermore, findings of the current study support the hypothesis that a lack of cerebral dominance or establishment of atypical cerebral dominance may be one cause of disordered language development in ID [29, 30, 50] and therefore allow the conclusion that atypical cerebral lateralization is linked with comorbid language disorders and not with the ID per se.

References and further reading

1. American Psychiatric Association. (2013). *Diagnostic and statistical manual of mental disorders* (5th ed.). Washington, D.C.: American Psychiatric Association.
2. Batheja, M. & McManus, I. C. (1985). Handedness in the mentally handicapped. *Dev. Med. Child Neurol.*, 27(1), 63–68.
3. Beleza-Meireles, A., Kockum, I., Qiu-Ping, Y., Picelli, S., Wetterberg, L., Gustavson, K.-H. . . . & Schalling, M. (2008). Complex aetiology of an apparently Mendelian form of mental retardation. *Med. Genet.*, 9(6), 4–9.
4. Berman, A. (1971). The problem of assessing cerebral dominance and its relation to intelligence. *Cortex*, 7(4), 372–386.
5. Bishop, D. V. M. (1990). *Handedness and developmental disorder*. Oxford: Blackwell.

6 Bodensteiner, J. B., Ellis, C. R. & Schaefer, G. B. (2005). Mental retardation. In B. L. Maria (Ed.), Current management in child neurology (3rd ed.) (pp. 285–296). London: BC Decker.
7 Bowler, D. M., Cufflin, J. & Kiernan, C. (1985). Dichotic listening of verbal and nonverbal material by Down's syndrome children and children of normal intelligence. *Cortex, 21*(4), 637–644.
8 Bradshaw-McAnulty, G., Hicks, R. & Kinsbourne, M. (1984). Pathological left-handedness and familial sinistrality in relation to degree of mental retardation. *Brain Cogn., 3*(4), 349–356.
9 Bunn, L., Simon, D. A., Welsh, T. N., Watson, C. & Elliott, D. (2002). Speech production errors in adults with and without Down syndrome following verbal written and pictorial cues. *Dev. Neuropsychol., 21*(2), 157–172.
10 Burack, J. A., Hodapp, R. M. & Zigler, E. (1988). Issues in the classification of mental retardation: Differentiating among organic etiologies. *J. Child Psychol. Psychiatry, 29*(6), 765–779.
11 Chang, B. S., Apse, K. A., Caraballo, R., Cross, J. H., Mclellan, A., Jacobson, R. D. ... & Walsh, C. A. (2006). A familial syndrome of unilateral polymicrogyria affecting the right hemisphere. *Neurology, 66*(1), 133–135.
12 Chua, R., Weeks, D. J. & Elliott, D. (1996). A functional systems approach to understanding verbal-motor integration in individuals with Down syndrome. *Down Syndr. Res. Pract., 4*(1), 25–36.
13 Delacato, C. (1974). *The ultimate stranger*. New York: Doubleday.
14 Di Nuovo, S. F. & Buono, S. (1997). Laterality and handedness in mentally retarded subjects. *Percept. Mot. Skills, 85*, 1229–1230.
15 Elliott, D., Pollock, B. J., Chua, R. & Weeks, D. J. (1995). Cerebral specialization in adults with Down syndrome. *Am. J. Ment. Retard., 99*, 605–615.
16 Elliott, D. & Weeks, D. (1993). Cerebral specialization for speech perception and movement organization in adults with Down syndrome. *Cortex, 29*(1), 103–113.
17 Elliott, D., Weeks, D. & Chua, R. (1994). Anomalous cerebral lateralization and Down syndrome. *Brain Cogn., 26*(2), 191–195.
18 Elliott, D., Weeks, D. & Elliott, C. (1987). Cerebral specialization in individual with Down syndrome. *Am. J. Ment. Retard., 92*(3), 263–271.
19 Gazzaniga, M. S. (Ed.) (2009). *The cognitive neurosciences*. (4th ed.). Cambridge, MA: MIT Press.
20 Geschwind, N. (1965). Disconnection syndromes in animals and man. *Brain, 88*(2), 237–294.
21 Geschwind, N. & Galaburda, A. S. (1987). *Cerebral lateralization*. Cambridge, MA: MIT Press.
22 Giencke, S. & Lewandowski, L. (1989). Anomalous dominance in Down syndrome young adults. *Cortex, 25*(1), 93–102.
23 Groen, M. A., Yasin, I., Laws, G., Barry, J. G. & Bishop, D. V. M. (2008).Weak hand preference in children with Down syndrome is associated with language deficits. *Dev. Psychobiol., 50*(3), 242–250.
24 Grouios, G., Sakdami, N., Poderi, A. & Alevriadou, A. (1999). Excess of non-right handedness among individuals with intellectual disability: experimental evidence and possible explanations. *J. Intellect. Dis. Res., 43*(4), 306–313.
25 Grouios, G., Ypsilanti, A. & Koidou, I. (2013). Laterality explored: Atypical hemispheric dominance in Down syndrome. In Subrata Kumar Dey (Ed.), *Down syndrome* (pp. 209–236). Rijeka, Croatia: InTech.

26 Hartley, X. Y. (1981). Lateralization of speech stimuli in young Down' syndrome children. *Cortex*, *17*(2), 341–248.
27 Hartley, X. Y. (1982). Receptive language processing of Down's syndrome children. *J. Ment. Defic. Res.*, *26*, 263–268.
28 Hartley, X. Y. (1985). Receptive language processing and ear advantage of Down' syndrome children. *J. Ment. Defic. Res.*, *29*, 197–205.
29 Heath, M. & Elliott, D. (1999). Cerebral specialization for speech production in persons with Down syndrome. *Brain and Lang.*, *69*(2), 193–211.
30 Heath, M., Grierson, L., Binsted, G. & Elliott, D. (2007). Interhemispheric transmission time in persons with Down syndrome. *J. Intellect Dis. Res.*, *51*(12), 972–981.
31 Hellige, J. B. (1993). *Hemispheric asymmetry: What's right and what's left.* Cambridge, MA: Harvard University Press.
32 Hicks, R. & Barton, A. (1975). A note on left-handedness and severity of mental retardation. *J. Genet. Psychol.*, *127*(2), 323–324.
33 Hornstein, H. A. & Mosley, J. L. (1986). Dichotic-listening task performance of mildly mentally retarded and nonretarded individuals. *Am. J. Ment. Defic.*, *90*(5), 573–578.
34 Kaufman, L., Ayub, M. & Vincent, J. (2010). The genetic basis of non-syndromic intellectual disability: A review. *J. Neurodev. Disord.*, *2*(4), 182–209.
35 Leconte, P. & Fagard, J. (2006). Lateral preferences in children with intellectual deficiency of idiopathic origin. *Dev. Psychol.*, *48*(6), 492–500.
36 Lewin, J., Kohen, D. & Mathew, G. (1993). Handedness in mental handicap: Investigation into populations of Down's syndrome, epilepsy and autism. *Br. J. Psychiatry*, *163*(5), 674–676.
37 Lucas, J., Rosenstein, L. & Bigler, E. (1989). Handedness and language among the mentally retarded: Implications for model of pathological left-handedness and gender differences in hemispheric specialization. *Neuropsychologia*, *27*(5), 713–723.
38 McManus, I. & Cornish, K. (1997). Fractioning handedness in mental retardation: What is the role of the cerebellum? *Laterality*, *2*(2), 81–90.
39 Mandal, M., Pandey, G., Tulsi, D. & Bryden, M. (1998). Handedness and mental retardation. *Laterality*, *3*(3), 221–225.
40 Mash, E. & Wolfe, D. (2015). *Abnormal child psychology* (6th ed.). Belmont, CA: Wadsworth Publishing.
41 Mohan, A., Singh, A. & Mandal, M. (2001). Transfer and interference of motor skills in people with intellectual disability. *J. Intellect Dis. Res.*, *45*(4), 361–369.
42 Morris, R. & Romski, M. (1993). Handedness distribution in a nonspeaking population with mental retardation. *Am. J. Ment. Retard.*, *97*, 443–448.
43 Mosley, J. L. & Vrbancic, M. I. (1990). Dichotic stimulation and mental retardation. *Res. Dev. Dis.*, 11(2), 139–163.
44 Mulvey, M., Ringenbach, S. D. R. & Jung, M. L. (2011). Reversal of handedness effects on bimanual coordination in adults with Down syndrome. *J. Intellect Dis. Res.*, *55*(10), 998–1007.
45 Oppewal, A., Hilgencamp, T. I., van Wijck, R. & Evenhuis, H. M. (2013). The effect of handedness on grip strength in older adults with intellectual disabilities. *Res. Dev. Disabil.*, *34*(5), 1623–1629.
46 Paquette, C., Bourassa, M. & Peretz, I. (1996). Left-ear advantage in pitch perception of complex tones without energy at the fundamental frequency. *Neuropsychologia*, *34*, 153–157.
47 Papadatou-Pastou, M. & Tomprou, D.-M. (2015). Intelligence and handedness: Meta-analyses of studies on intellectually disabled, typically developing, and gifted individuals. *Neurosci. Biobehav. Rev.*, *56*, 151–165.

48 Piccirilli, M., D'Allessandro, P., Mazzi, P., Sciarma, T. & Testa, A. (1991). Cerebral organization for language in Down syndrome patients. *Cortex*, *27*(1), 41–47.
49 Pickersgill, M. & Pank, P. (1970). Relation of age and mongolism to lateral preferences in severely subnormal subjects. *Nature*, *228*, 1342–1344.
50 Pipe, M. E. (1983). Dichotic-listening performance following auditory discrimination training in Down's syndrome and developmentally retarded children. *Cortex*, *19*(4), 481–491.
51 Pipe, M. E. (1988). Atypical Laterality and retardation. *Psychol. Bull.*, *104*(3), 343–347.
52 Pipe, M. E. (1990). Mental retardation and left-handedness: Evidence and theories. In S. Coren (Ed.), *Left handedness: Behavioral implications and anomalies* (pp. 293–318). Amsterdam, The Netherlands: North-Holland.
53 Pipe, M. E. & Beale, I. L. (1983). Hemispheric specialization for speech in retarded children. *Neuropsychology*, *21*(1), 91–98.
54 Porac, C., Coren, S. & Duncan, P. (1980). Lateral preferences in retardates: Relationships between hand, eye, foot and ear preference. *J. Clin. Neuropsychol*, *2*(3), 173–188.
55 Satz, P. (1972). Pathological left handedness: An explanatory model. *Cortex*, *8*(2), 121–135.
56 Schaefer, G. & Bodensteiner, J. (1999). Developmental anomalies of the brain in mental retardation. *Int. Rev. Psychiatry*, *11*(1), 47–55.
57 Shoji, H., Koizumi, N. & Ozaki, H. (2009). Linguistic lateralization in adolescents with Down syndrome revealed by a dichotic monitoring test. *Res. Dev. Disabil.*, *30*(2), 219–228.
58 Silva, D. & Satz, P. (1979). Pathological left-handedness: Evaluation of a model. *Brain Lang.*, *7*(1), 8–16.
59 Snell, M. (1987). *Systematic instruction of person with severe handicaps*. Columbus, OH: Merill.
60 Sommers, R. & Starkey, K. (1977). Dichotic verbal processing in Down's syndrome children having qualitatively different speech and language skills. *Am. J. Ment. Defic.*, *82*(1), 44–53.
61 Soper, H. & Satz, P. (1984). Pathological left-handedness and ambiguous handedness. A new explanatory model. *Neuropsychologia*, *22*(4), 511–515.
62 Soper, H., Satz, P., Orsini, D., van Gorp, W. & Green, M. (1987). Handedness distribution in a residential population with severe or profound mental retardation. *Am. J. Ment. Defic.*, *92*(1), 94–102.
63 Tannock, R., Kershner, J. R. & Oliver, J. (1984). Do individuals with Down syndrome possess right hemisphere language dominance? *Cortex*, *20*(2), 221–231.
64 Uecker, A., Mangan, P., Obrsut, J. & Nadel, L. (1993). Down syndrome in neurobiological perspective: An emphasis on spatial cognition. *J. Clin. Child Psychol.*, *22*(2), 266–276.
65 Welsh, T., Elliott, D. & Simon, D. (2003). Cerebral specialization and verbal-motor integration in adults with and without Down syndrome. *Brain Lang.*, *84*(2), 152–169.
66 Zekulin-Hartley, X. (1981). Hemispheric asymmetry in Down syndrome children. *Can. J. Behav. Sci.*, *13*(3), 210–217.

5
AUTISM SPECTRUM DISORDER

Introduction

Autism is a life-long, severe, complex and profound disruption of the cognitive, personal and social functioning of the individual. According to the American Psychiatric Association's (APA, 1994) definition, it is a neurodevelopmental disorder characterized by verbal and non-verbal deficiencies; poor social skills and repetitive, restrictive and stereotyped modes of behavioral responses [31].

Autism was discovered by Leo Kanner and Hans Asperger. Independently of one another, Kanner in 1943 [64] and only a year later Asperger in 1945 [4] used the term "autism" to describe similar conditions of abnormal child development, mainly affecting the behavioral sphere. In the ensuing period of attempts for clinical definition and explanation of autism, disagreements about its conceptualization have emerged and unfortunately have remained until now.

The reported wide variation in the presence and the severity of the symptoms among the subjects with a diagnosis of "autism" soon led to the birth of the concept of autism spectrum disorders, which quickly became popular and widely accepted [1, 61, 63, 102, 118]. According to this concept, autism spectrum is considered to be a continuum of disorders and conditions, ranging considerably in presence and severity of the symptoms, prognosis and perspective of development, and probably in their aetiology, and sharing many phenotypic characteristics and necessarily the "triad of impairments"– impairment in social interaction, impairment in communication and impairment in scope and range of interests and activities [7, 63, 112].

Although the concept of autism spectrum disorders has been very popular for several decades, their conceptualization and the definition of the subtypes and differentiation criteria have constantly remained debatable [21, 84, 102, 112, 118].

According to *Diagnostic and Statistical Manual-Fourth Edition (DSM-IV)*, autism spectrum disorders include autism (Kanner syndrome, classic autism, autistic disorder), Asperger disorder/syndrome (defined in the International Classification of Diseases, Tenth Edition [ICD-10] [119] and *DSM-IV* [31] as autism without language and intellectual deficits) and pervasive developmental disorder-not otherwise specified (PDD-NOS). The *DSM-IV* has been under revision for several years, and the new edition, the *DSM-fifth edition* (*DSM-V*), implemented in 2013, contained significant changes in the criteria and categories of autism spectrum disorders. One of the most significant changes was the removal of the separate diagnostic labels of autistic disorder, Asperger's disorder and PDD-NOS, and the implementation of one umbrella term "Autism Spectrum Disorder (ASD)". Further distinctions will be made according to severity levels (Level 1, Level 2 or Level 3) based on the amount of support needed. With regard to the changes of the previous diagnostic criteria, they include no emphasis on language delay and age of onset [85].

It is clear that the revisions based exclusively on research, analysis and expert opinion aim mainly to optimize the diagnosis of this condition, but it is also clear that the new *DSM-V* criteria could substantially alter the composition of the autism spectrum [77]. Despite the positive expectations (see [71]), serious concerns were already voiced and discussed in the literature, such as unintended negative consequences, including the possibility to adversely affect treatment planning, to restrict eligibility to early intervention and special education programs and limit the scope of services for affected children (for details, see [45]). In my opinion, another important concern could be put forward with regard to how these changes might impact the scientific research on autism considering the broad empirical support to the concept of autism spectrum disorders [1, 63], as well as the assumption of autism as a heterogeneous disorder comprising subtypes with different underlying pathology [87, 112].

Handedness and autism spectrum disorder

Currently the aetiology of ASD is still unknown [21, 84, 102, 112, 118], but the view that this developmental disorder has a neurobiological origin and is caused by a brain or neurological dysfunction is widely shared [13, 21, 87, 96, 97, 114]. The hypothesis postulating a connection between ASD and cerebral lateralization abnormality remains one of the most popular.

The acceptance of atypical hand preference as an indicator of possible brain damage [44] and the accumulation of evidence for greater frequency of non-right-handedness among neuropathological populations [57] both have initiated a systematic research of manual asymmetries among subjects with ASD.

The research results have clearly indicated a deviation from the typical pattern of hand preference in subjects with ASD. It is important that all handedness-related abnormalities described in the literature have greater frequency in autistic population: left-handedness and mixed-handedness [8, 10, 14, 22, 23, 43, 72, 110, 113]; weak, inconsistent or ambiguous handedness [18, 22, 36, 50, 106, 110]; and dissociation of hand preference and hand skill [77].

The increased incidence of left-handedness among autistic subjects is well-documented [23, 43, 72, 110, 114], and Satz's notion of "pathological left-handedness" [104, 105] is widely applied in the attempts for its explanation.

Most studies have reported not only a greater frequency of left-handedness but also of mixed-handedness. In a series of studies, Bishop [10] found dramatically increased incidence of left- and mixed-handedness in autistic children in comparison with typically developing children of the same age. Similar results of increased incidence of non-right-handedness (left- and/or mixed-handedness) have been obtained by other researchers [8, 14, 22, 23, 110, 113].

Escalante-Mead et al. [36] compared hand preferences of high-functioning autistic individuals with a history of disordered early language development, high-functioning autistic individuals with normal early language acquisition and typically developing children, and revealed that the autistic group with a history of early language disturbance showed more atypical cerebral dominance (significantly reduced rates of established left or right lateral hand preference) than both the healthy control group and the autistic group with normal early language development. Based on received results indicating maturational disturbances in establishing lateral preference rather than increased rates of left-handedness, researchers concluded that atypical establishment of cerebral dominance may be a cause of disordered language development in ASD.

In another interesting study, the hand preferences of nonspeaking students with ASD (determined from videotape records of their sign and non-sign actions) were compared with the hand preferences of children in two control non-autistic groups, all speaking and communicating with sign language (a "hearing children of deaf parent(s)" group and a "deaf children of hearing parents" group). The results showed that autistic children were markedly less lateralized with respect to signing, but not non-sign actions [13].

Along with the increase in the percentage of non-right-handers among the autistic subjects, an increased incidence of inconsistent handedness was reported among them (e.g. once throw the ball with the left hand and another time with the right hand) [18, 50, 110], markedly more pronounced in those with disordered early language development [32]. Soper et al. [109, 110] have suggested that this effect is specific for ASD and is due to a bilateral damage, which does not allow both hemispheres to develop manual dominance.

McManus et al. [77] first reported another type of pathological handedness in the autistic population, comprising a disassociation between manual preference and manual skill. Researchers established such a disassociation in 50 percent of studied autistic children, who demonstrated clear preference to the right hand, but no differences in the hand skill. A subsequent study failed to reveal evidence for such a disassociation, but established a greater frequency of both the weak handedness and the inconsistent handedness among autistic children in comparison with non-autistic children [22].

Although lateral preferences in the use of sensory organs and limbs have been considered among the most obvious functional asymmetries in humans [54], except for handedness, there are almost no studies examining the relation of ASD with other types of sensory (eye, ear, smell) and motor (foot) asymmetries. To date, and to my knowledge, only one study has investigated the relationship of ASD with footedness as the results received revealed greater inconsistencies in foot preference in children with high functioning autism and Asperger syndrome compared to typically developing children [80]. Likewise, only one study has examined the relation of ASD with eyedness and nasal cycle and have found significantly higher rates of left-eye preference and left nasal dominance (as well as left-hand preference) in children with ASD compared to typically developing children [26]. As far as the relation of ASD with eardness is concerned, no study to date has been conducted.

Language lateralization and autism spectrum disorder

Language deficits have been considered as a key feature of the ASD [15, 69, 89, 94, 96, 103] and as one of the three characteristics that define autistic disorder in the *DSM-IV* and ICD-10 criteria. According to the current *DSM-V*, the requirement of a delay and deviance in language development are no longer necessary for a diagnosis, that is the three areas of impairments in ASD are reduced to two areas: social-communication area and behavioral area including fixated interests and repetitive behaviors.

It is important to emphasize that the removal of delay and deviance in language development from the set of the key features defining autistic disorder does not diminish the significance of the issue concerning the relationship between poor language development and atypical cerebral dominance in autistic subjects and should not withdraw the researchers' attention and interest from its studying.

Indeed, the language skills vary widely between the cases – from complete lack of spoken language to above average development of the structural language [34, 46, 61, 106], but it is common for autistic individuals to have pervasive disorders of pragmatics and unusual forms of language [11, 89, 94].

Even the earliest studies of handedness-related abnormalities in a large number of subjects with ASD provoked the assumption that the atypical pattern of hemispheric dominance impedes the development not only of manual dominance but also of language skills [20, 27]. Furthermore, the association of left-hemispheric or bilateral damages with both an increased incidence of handedness-related abnormalities and language dysfunctions (considered as a core feature and important factor in autism and autism prognosis [75]), triggered systematic research of the hypothesis suggesting abnormal lateralization of language functions in subjects with ASD [75].

Comparative studies of the volume of the autistic brains have indicated obvious deviations from the patterns typically observed in the general population. The results of some earlier studies on the total brain volume revealed its enlargement in autism (megalencephaly) [70, 90, 91], but more recent studies showed that brain size has been enlarged only in children [5, 24]. For example, in a study of a sample with

ASD (ranging from 8 to 46 years of age), Aylward et al. [5] found out that while head size in autistic subjects was enlarged relative to controls at all ages, brain size was only enlarged in children. Adolescents and adults did not exhibit larger brains than the age-matched controls. These findings led the authors to the conclusion that while healthy adolescents and adults continue to experience slight increase in brain volume, brain volume in adolescents with ASD actually decreases during this time period [5]. In a recent study, Greimel et al. [46] examined regional grey matter volumes in a large sample of children, adolescents and adults with ASD using whole-brain voxel-based morphometry (VBM) and found that compared to controls, ASD subjects showed reduced grey matter volumes in the anterior cingulate cortex, posterior superior temporal sulcus and middle temporal gyrus. With regard to age effects on regional grey matter volume in ASD, researchers revealed complex changes in grey matter developmental trajectories of several brain regions that underpin social-cognitive and motor functions.

On the base of a meta-analysis of all brain size reports until this moment, Redcay and Courchesne [95] revealed a consistent pattern of brain size changes, namely, brain size in ASD was slightly reduced at birth but dramatically increased within the first year of life, and then plateaued so that by adulthood the majority of cases were within normal range. These findings led them to the conclusion that the period of pathological brain growth and arrest in ASD is largely restricted to the first years of life, before the typical age of clinical identification, and thus, the picture that emerges in studies of the older autistic brain reflects the outcome rather than the process of pathology.

The hypothesis that the brain in children with ASD undergoes an abnormal growth trajectory that includes a period of early overgrowth was supported by several longitudinal studies. The first one identified significantly enlarged cerebral grey and white matter in autistic children, with the most severe enlargement occurring in frontal, temporal and cingulate cortices [107]. In the analyses for age and gender effect, Schumann et al. [107] found that all regions except occipital grey developed at an abnormal growth rate in autistic children and that females with ASD displayed a more pronounced abnormal growth profile in more brain regions than males with the disorder. In the subsequent longitudinal magnetic resonance imaging (MRI) examination aiming to investigate early growth trajectories in brain volume and cortical thickness in ASD, Hazlett et al. [53] found generalized cerebral cortical enlargement in children with ASD, with a disproportionate enlargement in temporal lobe white matter, but no changes in cortical thickness. The lack of significant difference between autistic children and controls in the rate of brain growth for this age interval led authors to the assumption that brain enlargement in ASD results from an increased rate of brain growth before the age of 2. The most recent longitudinal study of the cortical thickness development in a large sample of autistic subjects and age- and gender-matched typically developing controls, conducted by Zielinski et al. [122], found many specific regional differences in age-related trajectories in cortical thickness, suggesting that abnormal cortical development in ASD undergoes three distinct phases: accelerated expansion in early childhood, accelerated thinning in later childhood and adolescence, and decelerated thinning in early adulthood.

Recently, Mottron et al. [87] have proposed the Trigger-Threshold-Target Model to describe the phenotypic, cognitive and genetic heterogeneity of autism. According to the model, upregulated synaptic plasticity due to genetic mutations triggers brain reorganization in individuals with low plasticity threshold, mostly within regions sensitive to cortical reallocations, the multimodal association cortices. Perturbation of the experience-dependent development of cortical organization and behavioral phenotypic consequences are the final results of this plasticity reaction. Differences in the target of brain reorganization, perceptual versus language regions, account for the main autistic subgroups: with and without speech onset delay. Since, in the model, non-syndromic and syndromic autism are considered as the two ends of the ASD, it is suggested that enhanced but normal plasticity may underlie non-syndromic autism, whereas altered synaptic plasticity, triggered by genetic mutation or event, may underlie syndromic autism with intellectual disability and dysmorphism in addition to autism.

Structural neuroimaging studies of the size of the brain regions with key roles in speech and language functions revealed obvious differences between controls and subjects with ASD. In an MRI study, Jou et al. [60] found enlarged right superior temporal gyrus in children and adolescents with high-functioning autism compared to controls, and no differences regarding the volume of left superior temporal gyrus – findings, interpreted as supporting the idea of neuroanatomical basis of the social perceptual deficits, characterizing this severe neurodevelopmental disorder. In contrast, measuring the planum temporale by MRI scans – an anatomical region closely related to the functional language asymmetry, Rojas and co-workers [98, 99] revealed reduced volume of the left planum temporale in autistic subjects of all ages: adults [98] and adolescents and children [99]. McAlonan et al. [74], using VBM, received similar results, with decreased grey matter volume of left superior temporal gyrus in children with ASD compared to normal controls.

In another MRI comparative investigation [9], the positive relationships between receptive language functions and superior temporal gyrus volume typically observed in the general population [42, 81] was observed in controls, but not in subjects with ASD.

Rojas et al. [99] emphasized that analyzing the results concerning planum temporale volume in ASD in combination with the recent findings on the total brain volume (enlarged in children but not in adolescents and adults) raises the important question of whether the reduced volume of the left planum temporale may be directly related to delays in language acquisition or vice versa, the reduced language competency may impact the structural development of planum temporale in a hemisphere specific way.

Early imaging studies of anatomical asymmetries, using computerized brain tomography, provided equivocal evidence for the lateralization of hemispheric deficit in ASD. For example, Hauser et al. [51] revealed left hemisphere (LH) abnormalities in the medial temporal lobe; Hier et al. [58] found reversal of left dominant parieto-occipital asymmetry (i.e. right hemispheric) in 57 percent of the autistic group and subsequent studies revealed bilateral dysfunction [25, 101, 114, 123].

Knaus et al. [68] used MRI to measure the anatomy of critical language areas in children and adolescents with ASD and typically developing individuals and found increased grey matter volume of frontal language regions in adolescents with ASD. In a subsequent study, Knaus et al. [69], using the same method, examined the relationship between language laterality, the anatomy of language regions and language abilities in right- and left-handed adolescent boys with ASD and typically developed boys. The results revealed that participants with typical left-lateralized language activation had smaller frontal language region volume and higher fractional anisotropy of the arcuate fasciculus compared to the group with atypical language laterality, across both ASD and control participants. Right-handed controls were the most prevalent among the typical laterality group and left-handers with ASD were the most prevalent among those with atypical language lateralization. Atypical language laterality was more prevalent in the group with ASD than in the control group. Researchers concluded that these findings suggest that anatomical differences may be more associated with variation in language laterality than specifically with ASD. Furthermore, they had the assumption that language laterality may provide a novel way of subdividing samples, resulting in more homogenous groups for research into genetic and neurocognitive foundations of developmental disorders.

Studying only children with ASD, Hashimoto et al. [49] established a lack of frontal lobe asymmetry, and Herbert et al. [55] identified that both frontal (Broca's area) and temporal (Wernike's area) language-related regions displayed a reversal of structural asymmetry in boys with ASD compared to normal control boys, as the frontal abnormality was substantially more extreme.

In a comparative study of the inferior frontal volumetric asymmetries in autistic boys with and without language impairment, boys with specific language impairment (SLI), and healthy controls, De Fossé et al. [30] found reversed asymmetries in a language-impaired autistic group and in a group with SLI (larger on the right side), and typical, leftward asymmetry in both unimpaired language groups (larger on the left), strengthening a phenotypic link between SLI and a subgroup of ASD. Based on these findings, the researchers concluded that the anatomical asymmetry reversal may be intimately linked with language deficit rather than ASD per se [30].

In a whole-brain MRI morphometric survey of asymmetry in boys with high-functioning ASD and boys with developmental language disorder, Herbert et al. [56] found widespread shifts in cortical asymmetry in both disorders. Asymmetry differences between groups were most significant in the higher order association areas. The authors suggested that the anatomical changes underlying these disorders were pervasive and the functional deficits might be relatively pervasive as well, although they might manifest in different domains with different degrees of severity. Moreover, Herbert et al. [56] emphasized that the great similarity between the group with ASD and the group with developmental language disorder suggested a relationship between these disorders and similar alterations in neural systems.

Recently, Yu et al. [121] carried out a meta-analysis of MRI studies of people with ASD to systematically explore the whole brain for anatomic correlates of delay and no delay in language acquisition in people with ASD. Based on the findings, the authors concluded that whereas grey matter differences in people with Asperger syndrome compared with controls are sparser than those reported in studies of people with autism, the distribution and direction of differences in each category are distinctive.

In DTI study of the anatomy of arcuate fasciculus – a white matter fibre bundle with great importance in language, Fletcher et al. [40] revealed that white matter microstructure in the arcuate fasciculus was affected in subjects with high-functioning autism. Furthermore, the language specialization apparent in the left arcuate of healthy controls was not as evident in ASD, which may suggest a relation to poorer language functioning.

In addition to the reversed anatomical asymmetry in language-related cortical regions, a number of studies have highlighted a reversed or reduced functional (language-processing) asymmetry in people with ASD. In a series of comparative studies of electroencephalography (EEG)-asymmetries to auditory speech stimuli, Dawson and her colleagues [27–29] found that the majority of children with ASD had a reversed pattern of hemispheric asymmetry (right-dominant) compared to controls. Researchers also reported a correlation between the level of language development and the magnitude of the rightward bias of the asymmetry, that is they found that autistic children with more impaired language abilities were more likely to have reversed laterality than those with less impaired language.

Recently, Stroganova et al. [111] also reported EEG-data providing evidence for abnormal functional brain lateralization in ASD. Analyzing EEG spectral power and interhemispheric asymmetry within delta, theta and alpha bands in 3- to 8-year-old boys with ASD (twenty-one from Russia and twenty-three from Sweden), and a corresponding number of age-matched typically developing boys, the researchers revealed that boys with ASD comprised a non-homogeneous group in relation to theta and alpha spectral power. Based on the pattern of the received results, Stroganova and co-workers concluded that the abnormal broadband EEG asymmetry in ASD might point to a diminished capacity of the right temporal cortex to generate EEG rhythms.

Using single positron emission computed tomography (SPECT), Chiron et al. [20] found hypofunction of the LH, and in a study with positron emission tomography (PET), Zilbovicius et al. [123] received evidence for bilateral brain dysfunction of temporal lobes in children with ASD, but no indications for more specific LH abnormalities.

In a recent study, using functional transcranial doppler sonography (fTCD) during the performance of verbal tasks, Whitehouse and Bishop [117] investigated four adult groups: (1) a group with SLI; (2) a group with a history of childhood SLI, who did not meet the criteria for language impairment in adulthood; (3) a group with ASD and a comorbid language impairment; and (4) a group with no history of developmental disorder. Except for the group with SLI, the prevalent majority of the other groups showed the typical LH dominance. In contrast, the majority of participants in the SLI group had language function lateralized to the right hemisphere (RH) or dispersed bilaterally. Based on these findings, the researchers assumed that atypical cerebral dominance is not implicated in all cases of poor language development, but may act as a biological marker of persisting SLI.

Two recent functional MRI (fMRI) studies of cortical responses to speech sounds in young children or toddlers with ASD suggested aberrant RH lateralization by demonstrating a trend towards greater recruitment of regions of the RH during speech stimulation [37, 100]. Furthermore, Eyler et al. [37] pointed that these lateralized abnormalities of temporal cortex processing of language in ASD worsen with age, becoming most severe in 3- and 4-year-old autistic children.

Using late-field magnetoencephalography (MEG) recordings to calculate a hemispheric Lateralization Index from the neuromagnetic activity evoked by passive auditory presentation of vowel stimuli, Flagg et al. [39] studied language-impaired children with ASD and typically developing controls and found that the two groups followed opposite maturational trajectories in language lateralization: LH dominance was increased in the sample of typically developing children and RH dominance was increased in the sample of children with ASD.

In order to better characterize the functional organization of language in ASD, Kleinhans et al. [67] used two frontally mediated language tasks (letter and category fluency) to measure the functional organization of language in fourteen high-functioning ASD individuals and matched controls with standard fMRI. A lateralization analysis of prefrontal activation found significantly greater leftward asymmetry in controls than in the ASD group in the letter fluency task and lack of between-group differences in lateralization in the category fluency task, indicating reduced hemispheric differentiation for verbal fluency tasks in autistic subjects. Based on these findings, the researchers hypothesized that the abnormal functional organization might be related to early, rapid overgrowth of frontal lobes and subsequent delay of brain development, as such growth dysregulation could disrupt the protracted developmental progression by which the LH becomes dominant for language, and in turn contribute to the language impairment seen in ASD [67].

Using a novel MEG approach – a custom child-sized MEG – a group of researchers conducted a series of studies with the purpose to investigate the pathophysiology of the developing ASD cortex [58, 65, 66, 120]. A study of physiological connectivity and the laterality of physiological connectivity in children with ASD and typically developing children (aged 3–4 years) revealed a rightward-lateralized neurophysiological network in conscious young children with ASD [65].

Another study examining differences in auditory cortex function that are associated with language development found less leftward lateralization of the intensity of the P50m component in response to voice stimuli in children with ASD compared with controls, suggesting atypical brain function in the auditory cortex in young children with ASD, regardless of language development [120]. In a subsequent study, researchers revealed significantly reduced connectivity between the left-anterior and the right-posterior areas in right-handed children with ASD compared with typically developed children, as the reduction in coherence was significantly correlated with clinical severity of ASD [66]. The last of the series of studies examined physiological brain lateralization in young children with ASD and found unusual lateralization of brain oscillations in young children with ASD [60].

Recently, Preslar et al. [92] conducted a systematic review and meta-analysis of the literature in order to explore the hypothesis that there would be a difference in brain lateralization between autistic and control subjects as measured by imaging techniques, and that this difference in asymmetry would be correlated with a difference in handedness. The results revealed a decrease in strength of lateralization in autistic subjects and an insignificant effect of handedness on this relationship.

Since the majority of studies on brain lateralization in ASD focus on abnormal lateralization in language-related regions, it is unclear whether lateralization abnormalities are presented across multiple brain networks or are restricted in language-related regions. To answer this question, Cardinale et al. [19] studied a small sample of autistic children and adolescents using a resting-state fMRI and found that abnormal lateralization in ASD existed across many intrinsic networks (visual, auditory, motor, executive, language and attentional), which, without exception, showed atypical rightward asymmetry shifts. Based on these findings, researchers suggested that the atypical rightward asymmetry might be a pervasive feature of functional brain organization in ASD.

In a subsequent study, Nielsen et al. [88] failed to replicate Cardinale and other colleagues' results using functional connectivity MRI from a large sample. These authors also found either a lack of left lateralization or greater right lateralization in the group with ASD, but only within isolated language-related brain regions, which led them to the conclusion that abnormal language lateralization in ASD may be due to abnormal language development rather than a deficit in hemispheric specialization of the entire brain.

Although scarce, dichotic listening studies of functional hemispheric asymmetries also provided evidences for reduced or reversed asymmetry of language processing in ASD. Prior and Bradshaw [93] found reduced right-ear advantage (REA) and a significant excess of RH dominance for verbal stimuli among autistic children. Similarly, Hayashi et al. [52] found lower advantage and clearly higher incidence of a left-ear advantage (LEA) for speech processing among high-functioning right-handed autistic children. Blackstock [12] revealed a LEA in children with ASD, and Martínez-Sanchis et al. [82] reported that children with high-functioning ASD exhibited no-ear advantage (NEA) for dichotic listening to verbal stimuli. Arnold and Schwartz [3], however, reported no differences between normal children and children with high-functioning ASD with regard to the pattern of hemispheric asymmetry for dichotic verbal listening.

Rinehart et al. [96] investigated the performances of executive function tasks (a serial choice reaction-time task and a Posner-type paradigm) and nonexecutive, visual-perceptual tasks of a group with high-functioning autism; a group with Asperger's disorder and control groups matched according to age, sex, handedness and full-scale IQ. Compared with controls, the group with ASD demonstrated deficiencies in right hemispace performance on executive function tasks, but normal lateralization on nonexecutive tasks. In contrast, the group with Asperger's disorder showed similar laterality patterns to their matched controls on both executive and nonexecutive function tasks. Rinehart et al. [96] concluded that taken together, these findings suggested a LH functional anomaly in ASD.

Autism and Asperger syndrome – separate clinical entities or not?

Most probably, the introduction of *DSM-V* will defer the controversy whether autism and Asperger syndrome deserve diagnostic status at all, but it is unlikely to weaken the researchers' interest towards the hypothesis that this neurodevelopmental condition is a heterogeneous disorder including different subtypes, given the presence of many supporting evidences.

Although inconsistent, probably due to methodological issues in research related to the lack of consensus on definition and the criteria for differentiating of the main subtypes of autism spectrum disorders, the majority of data accumulated over the years from neurobiological, neurophysiological and neuropsychological studies point to the LH as a primary site of neurobiological disruption in autism, supporting the LH dysfunction theory. The theory is based on clinical and experimental observations that individuals with autism exhibit deficits related to LH functions such as language, symbol use and sequential processing together with intact RH functions such as drawing, music and visual-spatial abilities [12, 38, 96].

The emergence of two groups of evidences moves away the focus from the LH dysfunction theory framework to neurobiological circuitry models of autism [86, 96] such as the Bradshaw's frontostriatal model of autism [17]. The first one includes the data suggesting a task-dependent, regional impairment of LH functioning rather than a global impairment affecting all LH functions (for a review, see [96]) and the second one includes the data indicating right hemispheric [43, 103] or bilateral impairments [43] in autism.

Unlike autism, Asperger's disorder is not associated with early language delay and therefore has often been imputed to RH rather than LH dysfunction [38]. But together with the neurobehavioral evidence supporting a RH deficit in Asperger's disorder [35], there are evidences (mainly from neuroimaging studies) for the existence of both RH and LH abnormalities in individuals with Asperger's disorder [25, 48, 76, 121].

Obviously, although there is a close connection between autism and Asperger's disorder and it is difficult to distinguish high-functioning autism from Asperger's disorder, there are differences in their neurobiology, reflected in the dissociations in hemispheric functioning in these disorders [20, 36, 38, 69, 96, 121].

Recent neuroimaging studies of the normal ontogenetic development of functional brain asymmetry uncovered a RH dominance between the age of 1 and 3 years, and a LH dominance after 3 years of age, suggesting that the shift to

LH dominance coincides with language development, is associated with it and is provoked by it [20]. In the context of this evidence, Rinehart et al. [96] attempted to make a complex analysis of available findings about the lateralized deficits in autism and in Asperger's disorder based on which he presumed that a number of RH anomalies are available in both disorders, while LH dysfunction is available in autism only. On this basis, the researchers hypothesized that there is a RH dysfunction in both disorders, but only in autism, there is additionally a LH dysfunction which is responsible for the impaired language development [96]. It is quite possible for LH damage to lead to anomalous language lateralization – reduced LH or reversed RH lateralization, which becomes a potential cause of autism-specific language deficits. Therefore, the establishment of LH dominance may be a significant event in the differential aetiology of autism and Asperger's disorder [96].

According to the original assumption of Escalante-Mead et al. [36], since language delay may be related to a specific genetic disturbance in autism [16], it is possible that this linkage may result from a more generalized genetically mediated disturbance in cerebral organizational events that give rise to specialization in hemispheric function.

Taken together, the above data and theoretical analyses allow the generalization for increasing empirical support and broader acceptance of the idea that the disturbance of brain lateralization development and establishment of abnormal hemispheric asymmetry may be a cause of disordered language development in ASD [30, 36, 112]. Moreover, related to this is the appealing assumption that the presence of atypical laterality may be a significant marker for the identification of neurobiological or genetically distinct subgroups of individuals with ASD [36, 38, 67, 110].

Sharing this reasoning, I have conducted my own research on the relationship between atypical cerebral asymmetries and ASD.

Personal research data

This study is intended to investigate the differences in four lateral preferences (handedness, footedness, eyedness and eardness) between typically developing children and autistic children with severe impairment of language development, in order to verify the hypothesis that subjects with ASD and early language impairment exhibit left-side preferences or anomalous dominance.

Subjects

Seventeen children with ASD and a history of severely disordered early language development (ten boys and seven girls, age ranging from 5.7 to 16.1 years, *Mean* age = 9.8 years, *SD* = 3.1) participated in the study. All autistic children met *DSM-IV* diagnostic criteria for autism [31]. At the time of the study, all attended a resource centre for autistic children.

Two children (one boy and one girl) were nonspeaking and another five children (four boys and one girl) had a heavily underdeveloped phrasal speech with their spontaneous spoken language mainly presented by stereotyped expressions and echolalias.

According to the data from anamnesis and medical records, all children with ASD had normal hearing and absence of movement disorders.

The control group consisted of seventeen typically developing children (ten boys and seven girls, age ranging from 5.3 to 12.8 years; *Mean* age = 8.10 years, SD = 2.8). All controls were pupils in mainstream school or kindergarten.

On the basis of information provided by parents, school psychologists and/or medical persons, all controls had normal hearing, normal language and intellectual development and good academic success. All children participated voluntarily and with the parents' and the school institutions' consent.

Assessment of handedness

The assessment of handedness was made by a performance test described in detail in Chapter 2 "Developmental stuttering", section "Assessment of handedness". A Quotient of manual asymmetry (QMA) was calculated individually for each child. Children who scored between −70 and +70 were classified as mixed-handed, those who scored between +71 and +100 were classified as right-handed and those who scored between −71 and −100 were classified as left-handed. These cut-off points have been established by Dragovic [33] depending on statistical criteria.

In order to assess the consistency of hand preference, each child's handedness was measured in two repeated sessions. The second testing session was done not earlier than 24 hours following the first. The handedness was determined as inconsistent when the participant showed a different type of handedness in the first and second testing sessions and as consistent in cases with lack of such a change across the sessions.

In addition, detailed pedigrees, including first- and second-degree relatives, were obtained for all participants from both of their biological parents.

Assessment of eyedness, eardness and footedness

Assessments of eyedness, eardness and footedness were made by performance tests consisting of two activities each: for eye, looking through a door's keyhole and looking through a telescope; for ear, listening to the tick-tacking of a clock closed in a small box and listening in through a wall; and for foot, kicking a ball and stepping up onto a chair. Each activity was scored as left = −1 and right = +1, so that the children who scored +2 were classified as right-eyed/eared/footed, those who scored −2 were classified as left-eyed/eared/footed and those who scored 0 were classified as mixed-eyed/eared/footed.

In order to assess the consistency of lateral preferences, the eyedness, eardness and footedness of each child were measured in two repeated sessions. The second testing sessions were done not earlier than 24 hours following the first ones. The eyedness, eardness and footedness were determined as inconsistent when the child showed different scores for the first and the second testing sessions.

For statistical evaluation, the Crosstab chi-square test and Independent Sample *t*-tests in the SPSS 16.0 were applied. Also, effect size was calculated.

Results

An overview of the results from the comparative handedness measurements of the group with ASD and the control group is presented in Table 5.1.

As shown, each of the studied groups demonstrated very similar patterns of distribution of the participants according to the type of manual preference in both handedness measurements. The obtained results revealed that a significantly higher percentage of controls exhibited right-handedness in comparison with the group with ASD ($p < .05$), and in contrast, a significantly higher percentage of children with ASD showed mixed-handedness in comparison with the control group ($p < .05$). No significant between-group differences were found with respect to left-handedness ($p > .05$). For type of handedness, there were significant differences between control and autistic groups in first ($\chi^2_{|2|} = 10.431$, $p = .005$, Cramer's $V = 0.554$) and second ($\chi^2_{|2|} = 8.667$, $p = .013$, Cramer's $V = 0.505$) testing sessions.

With respect to the handedness inconsistency, the between-groups' comparison again found significant differences: only one child (5.9 percent) from the control group versus six children (35.3 percent) from the group with ASD demonstrated different type of handedness across testing sessions ($\chi^2_{|1|} = 4.497$, $p = .034$, $\varphi = 0.364$).

Finally, regarding the frequency of presence of familial sinistrality, there were no significant differences between autistic and control groups. Almost equal small percentages of both groups (17.65 percent of the control group and 23.53 percent of the group with ASD) reported a presence of left-handed relative/s of the first and/or second degree ($p > .05$).

Results from the assessment of eyedness are presented in Table 5.2. Their analysis did not reveal significant between-group differences ($p < .05$). Nevertheless, it is noteworthy that while in the first measurement, both groups demonstrated very similar patterns of the results, as the majority of the participants showed right-

TABLE 5.1 Distribution of participants in study groups according to the demonstrated type of handedness in the first and second testing sessions

	First testing session						Second testing session					
	LH		MH		RH		LH		MH		RH	
	n	%	n	%	n	%	n	%	n	%	n	%
Control group	1	5.9	2	11.8	14	82.4	1	5.9	2	11.8	14	82.4
Group with ASD	0	0.0	11	64.7	6	35.3	0	0.0	10	58.8	7	41.2

LH, left-handedness; MH, mixed-handedness; RH, right-handedness.

TABLE 5.2 Distribution of participants in study groups according to the demonstrated type of eyedness in the first and second testing sessions

	First testing session						Second testing session					
	LE		ME		RE		LE		ME		RE	
	n	%	n	%	n	%	n	%	n	%	n	%
Control group	1	5.9	3	17.6	13	76.5	1	5.9	6	35.3	10	58.8
Group with ASD	2	11.8	3	17.6	12	70.6	0	0.0	10	58.8	7	41.2

LE, left-eyedness; ME, mixed-eyedness; RE, right-eyedness.

eyedness (76.47 percent of the control group and 70.59 percent of the group with ASD), a strong reduction of the proportion of participants with right-eyedness was observed in both groups in the second measurement: from 76.47 percent to 58.82 percent in the control group and from 70.59 percent to 41.18 percent in the group with ASD.

This reduction was more distinct in the group with ASD, so that the percentage of children with right-eyedness (41.2 percent) became less than the percentage of children with mixed-eyedness (58.8 percent). Nevertheless, for type of eyedness, there were insignificant differences between control and autistic groups in the first ($\chi^2_{|2|} = 0.373$, $p = .830$, Cramer's $V = 0.105$) and second ($\chi^2_{|2|} = 2.529$, $p = .282$, Cramer's $V = 0.273$) testing sessions.

Statistically significant between-group differences and a moderate effect size were found regarding the inconsistency of eyedness. The obtained results revealed that higher percentages of the group with ASD (58.8 percent) showed eyedness inconsistency in comparison with the control group (23.6 percent) ($\chi^2_{|1|} = 4.371$, $p = .037$, $\varphi = 0.359$).

Results from the assessment of eardness are presented in Table 5.3.

In the first testing session, both groups demonstrated absolutely identical patterns of the results as 88.2 percent of the children in each study group showed right-ear preference ($\chi^2_{|1|} = 0.000$, $p = 1.000$). In the second testing session, the

TABLE 5.3 Distribution of participants in study groups according to the demonstrated type of eardness in the first and second testing sessions

	First testing session						Second testing session					
	LEr		MEr		REr		LEr		MEr		REr	
	n	%	n	%	n	%	n	%	n	%	n	%
Control group	0	0.0	2	11.8	15	88.2	0	0.0	2	11.8	15	88.2
Group with ASD	0	0.0	2	11.8	15	88.2	3	17.6	5	29.4	9	52.9

LEr, left-eardness; MEr, mixed-eardness; REr, right-eardness.

TABLE 5.4 Distribution of participants in study groups according to the demonstrated type of footedness in the first and second testing sessions

	First testing session |||||| First testing session |||||| First testing session					
	LF		MF		RF		LF		MF		RF	
	n	%	n	%	n	%	n	%	n	%	n	%
Control group	0	0.0	5	29.4	12	70.6	0	0.0	5	29.4	12	70.6
Group with ASD	0	0.0	4	23.5	13	76.5	0	0.0	6	35.3	11	64.7

LF, left-footedness; MF, mixed-footedness; RF, right-footedness.

control group entirely retained the results, but the group with ASD demonstrated strong decrease in the percentage of children with right-eardness, from 88.2 percent to 52.9 percent. Nevertheless, the between-group differences with respect to the frequency of right-eardness did not reach statistical significance ($\chi^2_{|2|}$ = 5.786, p = .055), but had practical significance with a large effect size (Cramer's V = 0.413).

Statistically significant difference was found regarding the inconsistency of eardness. Results revealed that a higher percentage of children in the group with ASD (47.1 percent) showed eardness inconsistency, changing the type of ear preference across testing sessions, compared with the control group (11.8 percent) ($\chi^2_{|1|}$ = 5.100, p = .024, φ = 0.387).

Only the assessment of footedness did not show any differences between the control group and the group with ASD (Table 5.4).

The majority of the control group (70.6 percent in both testing sessions) and the group with ASD (76.5 percent in the first testing session and 64.7 percent in the second one) showed right-footedness. The rest of the groups demonstrated mixed-footedness. In summary, there were no significant differences between the two groups with respect to the demonstrated type of footedness in the first ($\chi^2_{|1|}$ = 0.151, p = .697, φ = 0.067) and second ($\chi^2_{|1|}$ = 0.134, p = .714, φ = 0.063) testing sessions.

No differences were also found with regard to the inconsistency of footedness: one-third of both groups (at 33.5 percent in each group) changed the type of foot preference across testing sessions ($\chi^2_{|1|}$ = 0.000, p = 1.000).

Discussion

This study aimed to provide data on lateral preferences among children with ASD and comorbid severe language impairment, compared to age- and gender-matched typically developing children, in order to test the hypothesis that autistic individuals with history of severe early language disturbance exhibit an abnormal cerebral dominance.

Two sensory asymmetries (eyedness and eardness) and two motor asymmetries (handedness and footedness) were explored in two repeated sessions. The obtained results showed that the group with ASD demonstrated atypical patterns of hemispheric dominance for all investigated modalities, except the footedness.

In this study, the incidences of mixed handedness and ambiguous handedness were significantly higher in autistic children compared to typically developing children. These findings are in agreement with previous observations on the disturbances in hand preference in ASD [8, 10, 36, 50, 110]. Soper et al. [110] reported a dramatic shift away from right-handedness in lower functioning autistic subjects due to an increased frequency of two phenotypes, manifesting left-handedness and ambiguous handedness, as the ambiguously handed were found to exhibit much lower intellectual scores. Hauck and Dewey [50] found that the lack of a definite hand preference in children with ASD was linked with poorer performances on motor, language and cognitive tasks. Escalante-Mead et al. [36] compared high-functioning autistic individuals with and without early language impairment and healthy individuals on an assessment of manual preference by the Edinburgh Handedness Inventory and found an increased rate of left-handedness among autistic individuals with a history of early language disturbance, and a higher incidence of mixed-handedness in all autistic individuals with and without early language impairment. In a recent study, Scharoun and Bryden [106] assessed three measures of handedness (Waterloo Handedness Questionnaire, Annett pegboard and WatHand Cabinet Test) in two repeated sessions and reported that although no differences were revealed between children with ASD and normal children, children with ASD demonstrated variable performance of the Annett pegboard, providing partial support for literature describing autistic individuals as having a weak hand preference.

The above-mentioned results of previous studies suggested that the increased incidences of mixed or ambiguous handedness were due to maturational delay [8] or disturbances [36] in establishing lateral preferences and were interpreted as supporting the bilateral brain dysfunction hypothesis [50, 110]. Present results completely support these speculations.

With regard to the other lateral preferences evaluated in this study, the rates of inconsistent or ambiguous eardness and eyedness were significantly higher in autistic children compared to typically developing children. In addition, a slight tendency towards increased incidences of non-right ear and eye preferences was also detected in the autistic group. No between-group differences were found with respect to the footedness.

Present findings concerning eyedness and footedness are not consistent with the findings reported by Markoulakis et al. [80], Scharoun and Bryden. [106] and Dane and Balci [26]. Markoulakis et al. reported greater inconsistencies in foot dominance, and Dane and Balci reported higher rates of left-eyedness in autistic children compared to normal children. Possible reasons for these discrepancies could include methodological differences, and differences in characteristics of the studied samples: Markoulakis et al. examined twelve children with high-functioning autism and Asperger syndrome, aged 6–9 years, and assessed motor control skills through a variety of footedness tasks; Dane and Balci investigated thirty-seven subjects with autism, aged 5–20 years, and used only one activity to define the dominant eye; and in the present study, seventeen children with ASD and severe language impairment, aged 5–16 years, were assessed for their eye, ear, and foot preferences by performance tests each of which included two activities.

To sum up, what differentiates the present study about the relationship between ASD and laterality from previous similar studies is the fact that our study sample consisted only of low-functioning autistic subjects with severely disordered early language development. This subgroup of ASD has the most severe clinical manifestations and the worst prognosis compared to all the rest with ASD diagnosis. Moreover, language deficits, and particularly deficits of the structural language – a function which is a priority of the LH – are its key characteristic.

Strict selection of studied samples of autistic children and established clear evidences for the existance of specific deviations in all examined modalities of cerebral laterality except footedness, that is handedness, eardness and eyedness, substantiate the conclusion that the disturbed lateralization of cerebral functions with an insufficient, incomplete or absent hemispheric dominance is typical for the language-impaired subgroup of ASD, and could be relevant to the presence and persistence of a part of its typical cognitive and behavioral deficits. Moreover, it seems more likely that atypical pattern of cerebral laterality is linked with the comorbid-specific language disorder rather than with the autism itself – an idea shared by other researchers [12, 27, 28, 29, 30, 36, 70].

Functional brain organization is thought to be shaped by a complex interaction between multiple genes, in particular their expression, hormonal and environmental influences (for details, see [115]). Present results do not give any grounds for assumptions about the origin of the observed deviations in the patterns of functional asymmetries in children with ASD, although the lack of differences between autistic and control groups with regard to familial sinistrality does not support the suggestion for a possible inheritance of the pattern of aberrant dominance [83] and rather supports the hypothesis that the disturbed cerebral lateralization in ASD may be due to a maladaptive neuroplasticity, which may be triggered by both genetic (mutations) and environmental factors [41, 87].

As a general conclusion, based on present findings, it can be stated that ASD with comorbid early language impairment may be associated with weak or ambiguous laterality and lack of hemispheric dominance, probably due to a bilateral brain dysfunction. Also, present results provided additional support to the assumption that the atypical pattern of cerebral laterality can be linked with the comorbid language disorder rather than with the ASD per se [12, 27, 28, 29, 30, 36, 70].

References and further reading

1. Akshoomoff, N. (2005). The neuropsychology of autistic spectrum disorders. *Dev. Neuropsychol.*, 27(3), 307–310.
2. Akshoomoff, N., Lord, C., Lincoln, A., Courchesne, E., Carper, R., Townsend, J. . . . & Courchesne, E. (2004). Outcome classification of preschoolers with autism

spectrum disorders using MRI brain measures. *J. Am. Acad. Child Adolesc. Psychiatry*, *43*(3), 349–357.
3   Arnold, G. & Schwartz, G. E. (1983). Hemispheric lateralization of language in autistic and aphasic children. *J. Autism Dev. Disord.*, *13*(2), 129–139.
4   Asperger, H. (1944/1991). "Autistic psychopathy" in childhood (U. Frith, Trans., Annot.). In U. Frith (Ed.), *Autism and Asperger syndrome* (pp. 37–92). New York: Cambridge University Press.
5   Aylward, E., Minshew, N., Field, K., Sparks, B. & Singh, N. (2002). Effects of age on brain volume and head circumference in autism. *Neurology*, *59*(2), 175–183.
6   Bachevalier, J. (1994). Medial temporal lobe structures and autism: A review of clinical and experimental findings. *Neuropsychologia*, *32*(6), 627–648.
7   Baron-Cohen, S. (1995). *Mindblindness: An essay on autism and theory of mind*. Boston, MA: MIT Press.
8   Barry, R. & James, A. (1978). Handedness in autistic, retardates, and normal of a wide age range. *J. Autism Child. Schizophr.*, *8*(3), 314–323.
9   Bigler, E., Mortensen, S., Neeley, S., Ozonoff, S., Krasny, L., Johnson, M. . . . & Lainhar, J. E. (2007). Superior temporal gyrus, language function, and autism. *Dev. Neuropsychol.*, *31*(2), 217–238.
10 Bishop, D. V. M. (1990). *Handedness and developmental disorder*. Oxford: Blackwell.
11 Bishop, D. & Norbury, C. (2005). Executive functions in children with communication impairments, in relation to autistic symptomatology: 2: Response inhibition. *Autism*, *9*(1), 29–43.
12 Blackstock, E. (1978). Cerebral asymmetry and the development of early infantile autism. *J. Autism Child. Schizophr.*, *8*(3), 339–353.
13 Bonvillian, J., Gershoff, E., Seal, B. & Richards, H. (2001). Hand preferences in sign-learning students with autistic disorder. *Laterality*, *6*(3), 261–281.
14 Boucher, J. (1977). Hand preference in autistic children and their parents. *J. Autism Child. Schizophr.*, *7*(2), 177–187.
15 Boucher, J. (2003). Language development in autism. *Int. J. Pediatr. Otorhinolaryngol.*, *6751*, S159–S163.
16 Bradford, Y., Haines, J., Hutcheson, H., Gardiner, M., Braun, T., Shefield, V. . . . & Piven, J. (2001). Incorporating language phenotypes strengthens evidence of linkage to autism. *AJMG*, *105*(6), 539–547.
17 Bradshaw, L. L. (2001). *Developmental disorders of the fronto-striatal system: Neuropsychological, neuropsychiatric and evolutionary perspectives*. Hove, UK: Psychology Press.
18 Bryson, S. (1990). Autism and anomalous handedness. In S. Cohen (Ed.), *Left handedness* (pp. 441–456). Amsterdam, The Netherlands: Elsevier.
19 Cardinale, R. C., Shih, P., Fishman, I., Ford, L. M. & Muller, R. A. (2013). Pervasive rightward asymmetry shifts of functional networks in autism spectrum disorder. *JAMA Psychiatry*, *70*, 975–982.
20 Chiron, C., Leboyer, M., Leon, F., Jambaque, I., Nuttin, C. & Syrota, A. (1995). SPECT of the brain in childhood autism: Evidence for a lack of normal hemispheric asymmetry. *Dev. Med. Child Neurol.*, *37*(10), 849–860.
21 Cohen, D. & Volkmar, F. (Eds.). (1997). *Handbook of autism and pervasive developmental disorders* (2nd ed.). New York: John Wiley & Sons.
22 Colby, K. & Parkison, C. (1977). Handedness in autistic children. *J. Autism Child. Schizophr.*, *7*(1), 3–9.
23 Cornish, K. & McManus, I. (1996). Hand preference and hand skill in children with autism. *J. Autism Dev. Disord.*, *26*(6), 597–609.

24 Courchesne, E., Carper, R. & Akshoomoff, N. (2003). Evidence of brain overgrowth in the first year of life in autism [Comment]. *JAMA*, *290*(3), 337–344.
25 Damasio, H., Maurer, R., Damasio, A. & Chui, H. (1980). Computerized tomographic scan findings in patients with autistic behavior. *Arch. Neurol.*, *37*(8), 504–510.
26 Dane, S. & Balci, N. (2007). Handedness, eyedness and nasal cycle in children with autism. *Int. J. Dev. Neurosci.*, *25*(4), 223–226.
27 Dawson, G., Finley, C., Phillips, S. & Galpert, L. (1986). Hemispheric specialization and the language abilities of autistic children. *Child Dev.*, *57*(6), 1440–1453.
28 Dawson, G., Finley, C., Phillips, S. & Lewy, A. (1989). A comparison of hemispheric asymmetries in speech-related brain potentials of autistic and dysphasic children. *Brain Lang.*, *37*(1), 26–41.
29 Dawson, G., Warrenburg, S. & Fuller, P. (1982). Cerebral lateralization in individuals diagnosed as autistic in early childhood. *Brain Lang.*, *15*(2), 353–368.
30 De Fossé, L., Hodge, S., Makris, N., Kennedy, D., Caviness, V., McGrath, L. . . . & Harris, G. J. (2004). Language-association cortex asymmetry in autism and specific language impairment. *Ann. Neurol.*, *56*(6), 757–766.
31 APA. (1994). *Diagnostic and statistical manual of mental disorders, fourth edition*. Washington, D.C.: American Psychiatric Association.
32 APA. (2013). *Diagnostic and statistical manual of mental disorders, fifth edition*. Arlington, VA: American Psychiatric Association American Psychiatric Publishing.
33 Dragovic, M. (2004). Categorization and validation of handedness using latent class analysis. *Acta Neuropsychiatr.*, *16*(4), 212–218.
34 Dunn, M. & Bates, J. (2005). Developmental change in neutral processing of words by children with autism. *J. Autism Dev. Disord.*, *35*(3), 361–376.
35 Ellis, H., Ellis, D., Fraser, W. & Deb, S. (1994). A preliminary study of right hemisphere cognitive deficits and impaired social judgments among young people with Asperger syndrome. *Eur. Child Adolesc. Psychiatry*, *3*(4), 255–266.
36 Escalante-Mead, P., Minshew, L. & Sweeney, J. (2003). Abnormal brain lateralization in high-functioning autism. *J. Autism Dev. Disord.*, *33*(5), 539–543.
37 Eyler, L. T., Pierce, K. & Courchesne, E. (2012). A failure of left temporal cortex to specialize for language is an early emerging and fundamental property of autism. *Brain*, *135*, 949–960.
38 Fein, H., Humes, M., Kaplin, E., Lucci, D. & Waterhouse, L. (1984). The question of left hemisphere dysfunction in infantile autism. *Psychol. Bull.*, *95*(2), 258–281.
39 Flagg, E. J., Cardy, J. E. O., Roberts, W. & Roberts, T. P. L. (2005). Language lateralization development in children with autism: Insights from the late field magnetoencephalogram. *Neurosci. Lett.*, *386*(2), 82–87.
40 Fletcher, P., Whitaker, R., Tao, R., DuBray, M., Froehlich, A., Ravichandran, C. . . . & Lainhart, J. E. (2010). Microstructural connectivity of the arcuate fasciculus in adolescents with high-functioning autism. *Neuroimage*, *51*(3), 1117–1125.
41 Gazzaniga, M. S. (Ed.) (2009). *The cognitive neurosciences. (4th edition)*. Cambridge, MA: MIT Press.
42 Gernbacher, M. & Kaschak, M. (2003). Neuroimaging studies of language production and comprehension. *Ann. Rev. Psychol.*, *54*, 91–114.
43 Gillberg, C. (1983). Autistic children's hand preferences: Results from an epidemiological study of infantile autism. *Psychiatry Res.*, *10*(1), 21–30.
44 Goldstein, K. (1948). *Language and language disturbances*. New York: Grune & Statton.
45 Grant, R. & Nozyce, M. (2013). Proposed changes to the American Psychiatric Association diagnostic criteria for autism spectrum disorder: Implications for young children and their families. *Matern. Child Health J.*, *17*(4), 586–592.

46 Greimel, E., Nehrkorn, B., Schulte-Rüther, M., Fink, G. R., Nickl-Jockschat, T., Herpertz-Dahlmann, B. . . . & Eickhoff, S. B. (2013).Changes in grey matter development in autism spectrum disorder. *Brain Struct. Funct.*, *218*(4), 929–942.

47 Hale, C. & Tager-Flusberg, H. (2005). Social communication in children with autism: The relationship between theory of mind and discourse development. *Autism*, *9*(2), 157–178.

48 Happe, F., Ehlers, S., Fletcher, P., Frith, U., Johansson, M. & Billberg, C. (1996). Theory of mind in the brain: Evidence from a PET scan study of Asperger syndrome. *Neuroreport*, *8*(1), 197–201.

49 Hashimoto, T., Tayama, M., Mori, K., Fujino, K., Miyazaki, M. & Kuroda, Y. (1989). Magnetic resonance imaging in autism: preliminary report. *Neuropediatrics*, *20*(3), 142–146.

50 Hauck, J. & Dewey, D. (2001). Hand preference and motor functioning in children with autism. *J. Autism Dev. Disord.*, *31*(3), 265–277.

51 Hauser, S., DeLong, G. & Roman, N. (1975). Pneumographic studies in the infantile autism syndrome. *Brain*, *98*(4), 667–688.

52 Hayashi, M., Takamura, I., Kohara, H. & Yamazaki, K. (1989). A neurolinguistic study of autistic children employing dichotic listening. *Tokai J. Exp. Clin. Med.*, *14*(4), 339–345.

53 Hazlett, H. C., Poe, M. D., Gerig, G., Styner, M., Chappell, C., Smith, R. G. . . . & Piven, J. (2011). Early brain overgrowth in autism associated with an increase in cortical surface area before age 2 years. *Arch. Gen. Psychiatry*, *68*(5), 467–476.

54 Hellige, J. B. (1993). *Hemispheric asymmetry: What's right and what's left*. Cambridge, MA: Harvard University Press.

55 Herbert, M., Harris, G., Adrien, K., Ziegler, D., Makris, N. & Kenedy, D. (2002). Abnormal asymmetry in language association cortex in autism. *Ann. Neurol.*, *52*(5), 588–596.

56 Herbert, M. R., Ziegler, D. A., Deutsch, C. K., O'Brien, L. M., Kennedy, D. N., Filipek, P. A. . . . & Caviness, V. S. Jr. (2005). Brain asymmetries in autism and developmental language disorder: A nested whole-brain analysis. *Brain*, *128*(Pt 1), 213–226.

57 Hicks, R. & Barton, A. (1975). A note on left-handedness and severity of mental retardation. *J. Gen. Psychol.*, *127*(2), 323–324.

58 Hier, D., LeMay, M. & Rosenberger, P. (1979). Autism and unfavorable left-right asymmetries of the brain. *J. Autism Dev. Disord.*, *9*(2), 153–159.

59 Hiraishi, H., Kikuchi, M., Yoshimura, Y., Kitagawa, S., Hasegawa, C., Munesue, T. . . . & Minabe, Y. (2015). Unusual developmental pattern of brain lateralization in young boys with autism spectrum disorder: Power analysis with child-sized magnetoencephalography. *Psychiatry Clin. Neurosci.*, *69*(3), 153–160.

60 Jou, R., Minshew, N., Keshavan, M., Vitale, M. & Hardan, A. (2010). Enlarged right superior temporal gyrus in children and adolescents with autism. *Brain Res.*, *1360*, 205–212.

61 Jou, R., Jackowski, A., Papademetris, X., Rajeevan, N., Staib, L. & Volkmar, F. (2011). Diffusion tensor imaging in autism spectrum disorders: Preliminary evidence of abnormal neural connectivity. *Aust. N. Z. J. Psychiatry*, *45*(2), 153–162.

62 Joseph, R., Steele, S., Meyer, E. & Tager-Flusberg, H. (2005). Self-ordered pointing in children with autism: Failure to use verbal mediation in the service of working memory? *Neuropsychologia*, *43*(10), 1400–1411.

63 Kabot, S., Masi, W. & Segal, M. (2003). Advances in the diagnosis and treatment of autism spectrum disorders. *Prof. Psychol. Res. Pr.*, *34*(1), 26–33.

64 Kanner, L. (1943). Autistic disturbances of affective contact. *Nerv. Child*, *2*, 217–250.

65 Kikuchi, M., Shitamichi, K., Yoshimura, Y., Ueno, S., Hiraishi, H., Hirosawa, T. . . . & Minabe, Y. (2013). Altered brain connectivity in 3-to 7-year-old children with autism spectrum disorder. *Neuroimage: Clinical, 2,* 394–401.
66 Kikuchi, M., Yoshimura, Y., Hiraishi, H., Munesue, T., Hashimoto, T., Tsubokawa, T. . . . & Minabe, Y. (2015). Reduced long-range functional connectivity in young children with autism spectrum disorder. *Soc. Cogn. Affect Neurosci., 10*(2), 248–254.
67 Kleinhans, N. M., Müller, R.-A., Cohen, D. N. & Courchesne, E. (2008). Atypical functional lateralization of language in autism spectrum disorders. *Brain Res., 1221,* 115–125.
68 Knaus, T. A., Silver, A. M., Dominick, K. C., Schuring, M. D., Shaffer, N., Lindgren, K. A. . . . & Tager-Flusberg, H. (2009). Age-related changes in the anatomy of language regions in autism spectrum disorder. *Brain Imaging Behav., 3*(1), 51–63.
69 Knaus, T., Silver, A., Kennedy, M., Lindgren, K., Dominick, K., Siegel, J. . . . & Tager-Flusberg, H. (2010). Language laterality in autism spectrum disorder and typical controls: a functional, volumetric, and diffusion tensor MRI study. *Brain Lang., 112*(2), 113–120.
70 Lainhart, J., Piven, J., Wzorek, M., Landa, R., Santangelo, S., Coon, H. . . . & Flostein, S. E. (1997). Macrocephaly in children and adults with autism. *J. Am. Acad. Child Adolesc. Psychiatry, 36*(2), 282–290.
71 Lauritsen, M. B. (2013). Autism spectrum disorders. *Eur. Child Adolesc. Psychiatry, 22*(1), 37–42.
72 Leboyer, M., Osherham, D., Nostem, N. & Robertoux, P. (1988). Is autism associated with anomalous dominance? *J. Autism Dev. Disord., 18,* 539–551.
73 Lotspeich, L., Kwon, H., Schumann, C., Fryer, S., Goodlin-Jones, B., Buonocore, M. . . . & Reiss, A. L. (2004). Investigation of neuroanatomical differences between autism and Asperger syndrome. *Arch. Gen. Psychiatry, 61*(3), 291–298.
74 McAlonan, G. M., Cheung, V., Cheung, C., Suckling, J., Lam, G. Y., Tai, K. S. . . . & Chua, S. E. (2005). Mapping the brain in autism. A voxel-based MRI study of volumetric differences and intercorrelations in autism. *Brain, 128*(Pt 2), 268–276.
75 McCann, B. S. (1981). Hemispheric asymmetries and early infantile autism. *J. Autism Dev. Disord., 11*(4), 401–411.
76 McKelvey, J., Lambert, R., Mottron, L. & Shevell, M. (1995). Right-hemisphere dysfunction in Asperger'syndrome. *J. Child Neurol., 10*(4), 310–314.
77 McManus, I., Murray, K., Doyle, K. & Baron-Cohen, S. (1992). Handedness in childhood autism shows a dissociation of skill and preference. *Cortex, 28*(3), 373–381.
78 McManus, I., Silk, G., Cole, D., Mellon, A., Wong, J. & Kloss, J. (1988). The development of handedness in children. *Br. J. Dev. Psychol., 6*(3), 257–273.
79 McPartland, J. C., Reichow, B. & Volkmar, F. R. (2012). Sensitivity and specificity of proposed DSM-5 diagnostic criteria for autism spectrum disorder. *J. Am. Acad. Child Adolesc. Psychiatry, 51*(4), 368–383.
80 Markoulakis, R., Scharoun, S. M., Bryden, P. J. & Fletcher, P. C. (2012). An examination of handedness and footedness in children with high functioning autism and Asperger syndrome. *J. Autism Dev. Disord., 42*(10), 2192–2201.
81 Martin, R. C. (2003). Language processing: Functional organization and neuro-anatomical basis. *Ann. Rev. Psychol., 54,* 55–89.
82 Martínez-Sanchis, S., Bernal, M. C., Costa, A. & Gadea, M. (2014). Abnormal linguistic lateralization and sensory processing in high functioning children with autism spectrum conditions. *J. Behav. Brain Sci., 4*(9), 432–442.
83 Martínez-Sanchis, S., Santacreu, M. C. B., Sancho, R. C. & Domenech, M. G. (2014). Language laterality, handedness and empathy in a sample of parents of children with autism spectrum disorder. *Psicothema, 26*(1), 17–20.

84 Matanova, V. (2003). *Psychology of anomalous development* [in Bulgarian]. Sofia, Bulgaria: Publishing House "Nemezida".
85 Michael, B. & First, M. D. (Eds.). (2013). *DSM-5. Handbook of differential diagnosis*. Arlington, VA: American Psychiatric Pub.
86 Minshew, N., Sweeney, J. & Bauman, M. (1997). Neurological aspect of autism. In D. Cohen & F. Volkmar (Eds.), *Handbook of autism and pervasive developmental disorders* (2nd ed., pp. 344–370). New York: John Wiley & Sons.
87 Mottron, L., Belleville, S., Rouleau, G. A. & Collignon, O. (2014). Linking neocortical, cognitive, and genetic variability in autism with alterations of brain plasticity: The Trigger-Threshold-Target model. *Neurosci. Biobehav. Rev.*, 47, 735–752.
88 Nielsen, J. A., Zielinski, B. A., Fletcher, P. T., Alexander, A. L., Lange, N., Bigler, E. D. . . . & Anderson, J. S. (2014). Abnormal lateralization of functional connectivity between language and default mode regions in autism. *Mol. Autism*, 5, 8.
89 Noens, I. & van Berckelaer-Onnes, I. (2005). Captured by details: Sense-making, language and communication in autism. *J. Commun. Disord.*, 38(2), 123–141.
90 Piven, J., Arndt, S., Bailey, J. & Andreasen, N. (1996). Regional brain enlargement in autism: A magnetic resonance imaging study. *J. Am. Acad. Child Adolesc. Psychiatry*, 35(4), 530–536.
91 Piven, J., Arndt, S., Bailey, J., Havercamp, S., Andreasen, N. & Palmer, P. (1995). An MRI study of brain size in autism. *Am. J. Psychiatry*, 152(8), 1145–1149.
92 Preslar, J., Kushner, H. I., Marino, L. & Pearce, B. (2014). Autism, lateralisation, and handedness: A review of literature and meta-analysis. *Laterality*, 19(1), 64–95.
93 Prior, M. R. & Bradshaw, J. L. (1979). Hemisphere functioning in autistic children. *Cortex*, 15(1), 73–81.
94 Rapin, I. & Dunn, M. (2003). Update on the language disorders of individuals on the autistic spectrum. *Brain Dev.*, 25(3), 166–172.
95 Redcay, E. & Courchesne, E. (2008). Deviant functional magnetic resonance imaging patterns of brain activity to speech in 2–3-year-old children with autism spectrum disorder. *Biol. Psychiatry*, 64(7), 589–598.
96 Rinehart, N. J., Bradshaw, J. I., Brereton, A. V. & Tonge, B. J. (2002). Lateralization in individuals with high-functioning autism and Asperger's disorder: A Frontostriatal Model. *J. Autism Dev. Disord.*, 32(4), 321–332.
97 Rinehart, N. J., Bradshaw, J. I., Brereton, A. V. & Tonge, B. J. (2002). A clinical and neurobehavioural review of high-functioning autism and Asperger's disorder. *Aust. N. Z. J. Psychiatry*, 36(6), 762–770.
98 Rojias, D., Bawn, S., Benkers, T., Reite, M. & Rogers, S. (2002). Smaller left hemisphere planum temporale in adults with autistic disorder. *Neurosci. Lett.*, 323(3), 237–240.
99 Rojias, D., Camou, S., Reite, M. & Rogers, S. (2005). Planum temporal volume in children and adolescents with autism. *J. Autism Dev. Disord.*, 35(4), 479–487.
100 Redcay, E. & Courchesne, E. (2005). When is the brain enlarged in autism? A meta-analysis of all brain size reports. *Biol. Psychiatry*, 58(1), 1–9.
101 Rumsey, J., Creasey, H., Stepanck, J., Dorwart, R., Patronas, N. & Hamburger, S. (1988). Hemispheric asymmetries, four ventricular size, and cerebellar morphology in autism. *J. Autism Dev. Disord.*, 18(1), 127–137.
102 Rutter, M. (2005). Aetiology of autism: Findings and questions. *J. Intellect Disabil. Res.*, 49(4), 231–238.
103 Sabbagh, M. (1999). Communicative intentions and language: Evidence from right-hemisphere damage and autism. *Brain Lang.*, 70(1), 29–69.

104 Satz, P. (1972). Pathological left handedness: An explanatory model. *Cortex*, *8*(2), 121–135.
105 Satz, P., Orsini, D., Saslow, E. & Henry, R. (1985). The pathological left handedness syndrome. *Brain Cogn.*, *4*(1), 27–46.
106 Scharoun, S. M. & Bryden, P. J. (2015). Is strength of handedness reliable over repeated testing? An examination of typical development and autism spectrum disorder. *Front. Psychol.*, *6*, 17.
107 Schumann, C. M., Bloss, C. S., Barnes, C. C., Wideman, G. M., Carper, R. A., Akshoomoff, N. . . . & Courchesne, E. (2010). Longitudinal magnetic resonance imaging study of cortical development through early childhood in autism. *J. Neurosci.*, *30*(12), 4419–4427.
108 Sigman, M. & McGovern, C. (2005). Improvement in cognitive and language skills from preschool to adolescence in autism. *J. Autism Dev. Disord.*, *35*(1), 15–23.
109 Soper, H. & Satz, P. (1984). Pathological left handedness and ambiguous handedness: A new explanatory model. *Neuropsychologia*, *22*(4), 511–515.
110 Soper, H., Satz, P., Orsini, D., Henry, R., Zvi, R. & Schulman, M. (1986). Handedness patterns in autism suggest subtypes. *J. Autism Dev. Disord.*, *16*(2), 155–167.
111 Stroganova, T. A., Nygren, G., Tsetlin, M. M., Posikera, I. N., Gillberg, C., Elam, M. . . . & Orekhova, E. V. (2007). Abnormal EEG lateralization in boys with autism. *Clin. Neurophysiol.*, *118*(8), 1842–1854.
112 Tonn, R. & Obrzut, J. (2005). The neuropsychological perspective on autism. *J. Dev. Physic. Dis.*, *17*(4), 409–419.
113 Tsai, L. Y. (1982). Brief report: Handedness in autistic children and their families. *J. Autism Dev. Disord.*, *12*(4), 421–423.
114 Tsai, L., Jakoby, C. & Stewart, M. (1983). Morphological cerebral asymmetries in autistic children. *Biol. Psychiatry*, *18*(8), 317–327.
115 Vallortigara, G., Rogers, L. J. & Bisazza, A. (1999). Possible evolutionary origins of cognitive brain lateralization. *Brain Res. Rev.*, *30*(2), 164–175.
116 Wallace, G., Dankner, N., Kenworthy, L., Giedd, J. & Martin, A. (2010). Age-related temporal and parietal cortical thinning in autism spectrum disorders. *Brain*, *133*(12), 3745–3754.
117 Whitehouse, A. & Bishop, D. (2008). Cerebral dominance for language function in adults with specific language impairment or autism. *Brain*, *131*(12), 3193–3200.
118 Woodbury-Smith, M. & Voikmar, F. (2009). Asperger syndrome. *Eur. Child Adolesc. Psychiatry*, *18*(2), 2–11.
119 World Health Organization. (1993). *The ICD-10 classification of mental and behavioral disorders: Diagnostic criteria for research*. Geneva, Switzerland: WHO.
120 Yoshimura, Y., Kikuchi, M., Shitamichi, K., Ueno, S., Munesue, T., Ono, Y. . . . & Minabe, Y. (2013). Atypical brain lateralisation in the auditory cortex and language performance in 3- to 7-year-old children with high-functioning autism spectrum disorder: A child-customised magnetoencephalography (MEG) study. *Mol. Autism*, *4*, 38.
121 Yu, K. K., Cheung, C., Chua, S. E. & McAlonan, G. M. (2011). Can Asperger syndrome be distinguished from autism? An anatomic likelihood meta-analysis of MRI studies. *J. Psychiatry Neurosci.*, *36*(6), 412–421.
122 Zielinski, B. A., Prigge, M. B., Nielsen, J. A., Froehlich, A. L., Abildskov, T. J., Anderson, J. S. . . . & Lainhart, J. E. (2014). Longitudinal changes in cortical thickness in autism and typical development. *Brain*, *137*(Pt 6), 1799–1812.
123 Zilbovicius, M., Boddaert, N., Belin, P., Poline, J.-B., Remy, P., Mangin, J.-F. . . . & Samson, Y. (2000). Temporal lobe dysfunction in childhood autism: A PET Study. *Am. J. Psychiatry*, *157*(12), 1988–1993.

CONCLUSION

Over the last 25 years, I have been actively engaged in research of human laterality and especially of functional hemispheric asymmetries in children with developmental disorders. Starting with my dissertation that aimed to investigate hemispheric asymmetries in subtypes of DS, I progressively extended my knowledge of the relationships between hemispheric lateralization and developmental disorders which, in turn, led to increasing my "professional sensitivity" to signs indicating atypical asymmetries in all the children whom I have consulted or worked with as a neuropsychologist and speech therapist. All this shaped the focus and parameters of my scientific searches over the years as a researcher who never lost connection with practice. All my studies were united under the hypothesis that the presence of language impairment is the key element in the relationship of "atypical lateralization – developmental neuropathology".

The hypothesis that the development of atypical hemispheric asymmetries due to genetic, hormonal or pathological factors may increase vulnerability to developmental disorders, and especially to language disorders, is present in many etiological theories: the Orton–Travis theories of DS and DD [25, 30], the more recent theory of Crow [10] for DD, the Right Shift Theory of Annett [1, 2] and the Hormonal Theory of Geschwind and Galaburda [16] for the genesis of the cerebral lateralization, the Soper and co-workers' theory [28] and McCann's theory [21] of ASD, as over the years this hypothesis has found growing empirical support from studies using a variety of research methods.

My own research findings concerning functional hemispheric asymmetries in children suffering from the most common developmental disorders – DS, DD, ID, and ASD – provided new evidence for the relationship between atypical cerebral lateralization and impaired language development. The results revealed that all studied samples of children with these developmental disorders had underlying differences in functional hemispheric asymmetries from the matched control groups.

Supporting the opinion that the clinical and etiological heterogeneity of developmental disorders may be a source of contamination in the research on laterality [12, 11, 35], I conducted two separate studies with the aim to examine hemispheric asymmetries in the subtypes of DS and DD, respectively, comparing them with matched controls, in order to verify the hypothesis that both stutterers and dyslexics represent heterogeneous populations in terms of auditory processing, language lateralization and manual preference. I went further, assuming that abnormal hemispheric lateralization is causally linked only to HSS, especially for DS, based on findings of Boyanova [6] that hereditary stuttering, which is characterized by an increased incidence of positive family history of both stuttering or other speech and language disorders and left-handedness, and less expressed right-hand preference, emerges as an independent subtype of DS, other than PSS (also called functional or neurotic stuttering, or logoneurosis) and OSS (also called neurotiform stuttering).

The comparative analysis confirmed that DS and DD are not unitary disorders regarding language lateralization, handedness and auditory processing and clearly showed how the study of populations with developmental disorders as homogeneous groups could mask the real status of studied phenomena and lead to incorrect interpretations of the results.

Analyzing results at a group level, it is evident that total stuttering and dyslexia samples did not differ from their matched control samples in direction and magnitude of hemispheric asymmetry for speech perception. Between-subgroup comparative analyses within both the DS and DD samples, however, revealed specific differences between the results of each subgroup and the relevant control group, suggesting subgroup differences in the causes of observed deviations in hemispheric asymmetry and interhemispheric interaction during speech perception.

With regard to DS, the results of the current study revealed a relation between HSS, mixed-handedness and weak or reversed lateralization for speech perception. Groups with PSS and OSS demonstrated normal hemispheric asymmetry for both speech perception and manual preference. Furthermore, findings not only confirmed a close relationship between the auditory processing deficit and DS but also suggested obvious differences between the DS subtypes regarding the strength and underlying mechanisms of the auditory processing deficit.

Possible interpretations of these results are that:

- stutterers with PSS exhibit slight deficiency in auditory processing due to weak RH dysfunction, probably triggered by situational precursors or emotional factors;
- stutterers with OSS exhibit prominent auditory processing deficit due to auditory dysfunction of both hemispheres and probably paralleled by insufficient interhemispheric cooperation during auditory processing; or
- stutterers with HSS exhibit auditory processing deficit most probably due to weak and incomplete, or reversed, lateralization of speech perception.

Conclusion

To sum up, the present study supports the hypothesis that atypical lateralization of speech processing is causally linked only to HSS. The highest incidence of mixed-handedness and familial history of both stuttering and sinistrality suggests that the abnormal cerebral organization, including weak or reversed language lateralization and mixed-handedness, considered as a risk factor for stuttering, could be a hereditable feature for this DS subgroup. Moreover, these findings support to a greater extent the assumption that genetic risk factors for atypical cerebral asymmetry are not separate from genetic risk factors for language impairment, rather than the assumption about their separate influences (for a review of genetic models of the association between weak cerebral lateralization for language and language/literacy disorders, see [5]).

The observed deviations in interhemispheric interaction during auditory processing in the PSS and OSS, but not in language lateralization which is typically left-hemispheric, are not causally linked to the emergence of these DS subtypes and are rather a consequence of their underlying pathology.

With regard to DD, the results showed that all three DD subgroups exhibited some kind of deviations from the pattern of hemispheric asymmetries observed in the control sample of normal readers. An important finding was that the DD subgroups' deviations outline opposite tendencies, shaping three distinct patterns of abnormal hemispheric asymmetry and interhemispheric interaction.

The first one, which was typical for the group with SDS, includes mixed-handedness and unstable, weak or reversed lateralization of speech sound perception. The normal overall perceptive performance indicates a lack of phonological deficit and probably a non-phonological underlying deficit of the reading difficulties in this DD subtype, although the observed significantly reduced right-ear performance could suggest the existence of a slight LH deficit to compensate for the excessive involvement of the RH in auditory processing. Taken together, the results lead to the suggestion that this pattern, indicating lack of cerebral dominance and exuberant RH language processing, is causally related to the emergence of the SDS.

The second pattern, which was observed in PDS and nearly half of the MDS, consists of excessively strong and stable LH asymmetry for speech perception, strong auditory processing deficit reflecting auditory dysfunction of both hemispheres and a normal pattern of manual asymmetry (or right-handedness). These results suggest that despite the typical LH lateralization of language, the lack of necessary interhemispheric cooperation, especially during phonological processing, may contribute to reading difficulties in PDS and a subgroup of MDS without being causally linked with the emergence of these DD subtypes.

The third pattern of aberrant lateralization was observed in a subset of the subgroup with MDS and includes lack of asymmetry, or extremely reduced LH asymmetry, for speech perception and a strong auditory processing deficit, paralleled by mixed-handedness and familial sinistrality. I presume that this pattern of weak cerebral lateralization, including bilateral representation of language and lack of hemispheric dominance, which most probably is a hereditable trait, is causally linked with the reading difficulties of this subset of MDS.

The next step of my research on laterality in neurodevelopmental pathology was to verify the hypothesis that atypical asymmetry observed in developmental disorders which are not essentially linguistic in nature, such as NS-ID and ASD, is involved causally in the emergence of the comorbid language deficit, rather than with the developmental disorders themselves [11, 14, 20]. For this purpose, two separate studies were conducted. The first one aimed to investigate both the degree of the reported right-hand preference and hemispheric asymmetry for dichotic speech perception in a group of children with mild NS-ID and comorbid speech and language disorders and an age- and gender-matched control group. In the second study, a group of low-functioning autistic children with severely disordered early language development was compared to an age- and gender-matched control group only to their lateral preferences (or handedness, footedness, eyedness and eardness), because of the inapplicability of the dichotic listening task due to the severe language disorder of the autistic sample.

With regard to ID, the results showed that the group with NS-ID exhibited strong auditory processing deficit and atypical cerebral lateralization including reverse, weak or bilateral representation of speech perception and mixed-handedness.

With regard to ASD, the study results revealed that the autistic sample exhibited atypical patterns of lateral preferences reflected in mixed and ambiguous handedness and inconsistent or ambiguous eardness and eyedness.

Taken together, the results from these two studies support the hypothesis that atypical cerebral lateralization is causally related to the comorbid language impairment in ID and ASD rather than to the disorders themselves [11, 14, 20]. Lack of higher incidence of familial sinistrality in both pathological groups in comparison to their relevant control groups rejects the possibility that aberrant cerebral dominance is a hereditable feature and supports the assumption for an indirect relation between the causes of NS-ID and ASD and disturbed cerebral lateralization. As the two samples in the current studies had lots of shared features including intellectual deficit, language impairment and abnormal functional lateralization, although ASD and ID constitute two separate diagnoses, this similarity not only implies a relationship between the disorders, but also suggests similar brain structural and functional changes.

Several main conclusions can be drawn based on the present series of studies.

- The findings support the suggestions that handedness and language lateralization are context-specific, vary in strength and have developmental trajectories [4], and that the association between handedness and language lateralization is a natural phenomenon [1, 2, 5]. Though indirectly, the hypotheses that manual preference and language lateralization have shared genetic factors, and the strength of their relationship, may also be under genetic influence [24], also finds support.
- The pattern of the results suggests that non-right-handedness observed in populations with neurodevelopmental disorders may be an indicator of atypical language lateralization.

- The findings give strong support to the association between atypical cerebral lateralization and language impairment and have implications for laterality theories of developmental disorders.
- The studies provide evidence that heterogeneity of developmental disorders may be a serious source of contamination in the research examining the link between cerebral lateralization and developmental pathology.
- The results support the suggestion that atypical cerebral lateralization can be identified as a subtype within each neurodevelopmental disorder. Similar suggestions have been proposed by Zadina et al. [35] only for the DD; by Escalante-Mead et al. [14], Fein et al. [15], Knaus et al. [20] and Soper et al. [28] only for the ASD; by Morris and Romski [22] and Soper et al. [29] only for ID and by Rosenfield and Goodglass [26] only for DS.

There are some deviations in all subtypes of DS and DD from the pattern of cerebral lateralization observed in typically developing children. Patterns of these deviations, however, differ across the developmental disorders' subtypes in size, scope and direction. My main suggestion is that only some of them are involved causally in the emergence of specific subtypes of disorders and the rest are rather a consequence of the underlying pathophysiological mechanisms. Moreover, if we consider the positive history of familial sinistrality as a reliable indicator of genetic origin, I would further suppose that patterns of aberrant cerebral lateralization which are involved causally in the emergence of specific subtypes of developmental disorders may differ in origin – genetic versus non-genetic.

NS-ID and ASD have multiple overlapping phenotypic characteristics and language abnormalities are one of them [19]. Related to this, samples of children with NS-ID and low-functioning autism in the current studies represent subgroups within the ID and ASD populations because all participants had comorbid structural language impairment – a feature very often present in these disorders without being their core symptom. Therefore, the two samples initially had two common features: structural language impairment and intellectual deficiency. Present findings extended their overlap, revealing that atypical cerebral lateralization is another shared feature.

Thus, considering that studied ID and ASD groups represent subgroups of the general ID and ASD populations because of their comorbid language impairment, present findings evidence a phenotypic link between these NS-ID and ASD subgroups, the HSS, the SDD and a subset of the MDD. All these developmental disorders' subgroups share mixed-handedness and atypical cerebral lateralization for speech perception, leading me to the conclusion that they all could have overlapping aetiologies.

I dare say that my suggestions concerning the relationship between aberrant cerebral lateralization and neurodevelopmental pathology based on my research over four developmental disorders could be extended to all other forms of developmental disorders.

The assumption that each population of persons with developmental speech, language or literacy disorders contains a subgroup for which the aberrant cerebral lateralization is causally related to the emergence of the disorder receives support from a large number of studies that have found a connection between SLI and aberrant language lateralization [3, 9, 12, 11], as well as from studies reporting a higher incidence of atypical asymmetries in polymorphic dyslalia [7] and learning disabilities [23]. Also, the assumption that each population of persons with developmental disorders that are not linguistic in nature contains a subgroup with comorbid language impairment that might be caused by the aberrant cerebral lateralization receives support from studies that have found a connection between ADHD [17, 18], cerebral palsy [8], epilepsy [27] and schizophrenia [10].

In summary, the current studies uncovered important findings supporting the hypothesis that atypical cerebral lateralization reflects a general risk factor that can be seen across all (or at least multiple) neurodevelopmental disorders [5, 13, 31, 22]. In my opinion, the origin of this risk factor might be well understood in the context of the two-factor Developmental Instability (DI) model, proposed by Yeo and co-researches, for the aetiology of neurodevelopmental disorders [33].

DI is conceptualized as a vulnerability factor for variation in brain development across both the normal spectrum and that of neurodevelopmental pathology, and refers to the inability of the developing brain to buffer the negative effects of genetic or environmental perturbations [34, p. 246].

So, the first factor in the two-factor DI model refers to the generalized effects of DI. It is hypothesized that mutations at different loci throughout the genome, as well as other genetic factors, contribute to DI. Also, as the impact of DI is not specific to a particular developmental pathway, subjects with perturbed development of one phenotypic characteristic may also demonstrate perturbed development of other characteristics. Therefore, high DI could lead to "correlated atypicalities" or comorbidity.

The second factor refers to genetic or environmental causes that are specific to particular disorders. These factors may include certain mutations or other genetic variants affecting only particular developmental processes, gene-by-gene interactions or environmental factors such as infections, intoxications, etc. As DI disrupts mechanisms maintaining the integrity of developmental processes, the greater the instability is, the greater the impact of environmental stressors will be.

The key postulate of the DI model is that "causal factors that have relatively generalized effects exert them through DI, and these interact with both specific genetic and environmental effects to give rise to atypical neurodevelopmental outcomes" [34, p. 247]. Thus, DI may result in neurodevelopmental disorders, but the precise outcomes vary according to the interactions of DI with factors specific to particular disorders.

Present series of research provided empirical support for the DI model in four specific neurodevelopmental disorders: DS, DD, ID and ASD, through the observed greater incidence of known correlates of DI, such as atypical handedness and language lateralization in DS, DD, ID and atypical handedness, eardness and eyedness in the ASD sample.

I consider the DI model much more promising and I believe that future empirical studies of developmental disorders' subtypes inspired by the DI theory could find key answers concerning the etiopathogenetic mechanisms of different forms of neurodevelopmental pathology, and in particular, the role of the atypical asymmetrical development of the cerebral cortex in their origin.

Also, I completely agree with the assumption of Knaus et al. [20] that language lateralization may provide a novel way of subdividing samples, resulting in more homogenous groups for research into genetic and neurocognitive foundations of neurodevelopmental disorder.

Present studies have certain limitations. First, studies are designed to assess differences in functional lateralization of auditory speech perception between developmental disorders' samples and matched controls. Therefore, I am limited in proposing claims about the other language modalities (visual speech perception and language expression) and future studies need to confirm speculations regarding the other language modalities, as well.

Second, there are differences in the methodology of the ASD sample study because of the inapplicability of the dichotic listening task due to the severe language disorder of all participants with ASD.

Third, the relatively small sample size of the studied ID and ASD samples, as well as non-matched size of the dyslexia and stuttering subgroups, is also a limitation since it impacts the statistical power of the pairwise comparisons. Replications with larger samples are needed to assure the validity of the current findings.

Fourth, both tests of manual preference and dichotic listening used in the present series of studies are behavioral methods that provide an indirect measure of brain lateralization. This necessitates that the effectiveness of the approach for studying brain lateralization in the subtypes of developmental disorders is verified in studies that provide its direct measure.

In spite of these limitations of the present studies, I hope that the hypothetical models and tentative hypotheses offered in this book could guide future research.

References and further reading

1. Annett, M. (1985). *Left, right hand and brain: The right shift theory*. London: Erlbaum Associate.
2. Annett, M. (2002). *Handedness and brain asymmetry: The right shift theory*. Hove, UK: Psychology Press.
3. Badcock, N., Bishop, M., Hardiman, M., Barry, J. G. & Watkins, K. (2011). Co-localisation of abnormal brain structure and function in specific language impairment. *Brain Lang.*, *120*(3), 310.
4. Bishop, D. V. M. (2009). Genes, cognition and communication: Insights from neurodevelopmental disorders. *Ann. N. Y. Acad. Sci.*, *1156*(1), 1–18.

5 Bishop, D. V. M. (2013). Cerebral asymmetry and language development: cause, correlate or consequence? *Science*, *340*(6138), 1230531.
6 Boyanova, V. (1990). Anatomic-physiological peculiarities of children who stutter [in Bulgarian]. Blagoevgrad, Bulgaria: South-West University "Neofit Rilski" Publishing House.
7 Boyanova, V. & Kalonkina, A. (1999). Genesis of the articulatory disorders [in Bulgarian]. In V. Boyanova, V. Matanova & D. Doskov (Eds.), *Proceedings: Logopedics and Phoniatrics* (pp. 216–220). Sofia, Bulgaria: Heron Press.
8 Brizzolara, D., Pecini, C., Brovedani, P., Ferretti, G., Cipriani, P. & Cioni, G. (2002). Timing and type of congenital brain lesion determine different patterns of language lateralization in hemiplegic children. *Neuropsychologia*, *40*(6), 620–632.
9 Cohen, M., Riccio, C. & Hynd, G. (1999). Children with specific language impairment: Quantitative and qualitative analysis of dichotic listening performance. *Dev. Neuropsychol.*, *16*(2), 243–252.
10 Crow, T. (1997). Schizophrenia as failure of hemispheric dominance for language. *Trends Neurosci.*, *20*(8), 339–343.
11 De Fossé, L., Hodge, S., Makris, N., Kennedy, D., Caviness, V., McGrath, L. . . . & Harris, G. J. (2004). Language-association cortex asymmetry in autism and specific language impairment. *Ann. Neurol.*, *56*, 757–766.
12 De Guibert, C., Maumet, C., Jannin, P., Ferré, J.-C., Tréguier, C., Barillot, C. . . . & Biraben, A. (2011). Abnormal functional lateralization and activity of language brain areas in typical specific language impairment (developmental dysphasia). *Brain*, *134*(10), 3044–3058.
13 Edgar, J., Yeo, R., Gangestad, S., Blake, M., Davis, J., Lewine, J. . . . & Carñive, J. M. (2006). Reduced auditory M-100 asymmetry in schizophrenia and dyslexia: An application of an approach of the developmental instability for assessment of the atypical brain asymmetry. *Neuropsychologia*, *44*(2), 289–299.
14 Escalante-Mead, P., Minshew, L. & Sweeney, J. (2003). Abnormal brain lateralization in high-functioning autism. *J. Autism Dev. Disord.*, *33*(5), 539–543.
15 Fein, H., Humes, M., Kaplin, E., Lucci, D. & Waterhouse, L. (1984). The question of left hemisphere dysfunction in infantile autism. *Psychol. Bull.*, *95*(2), 258–281.
16 Geschwind, N. & Galaburda, A. (1987). *Cerebral lateralization*. Cambridge, MA: MIT Press.
17 Hale, T. S., McCracken, J. T., McGough, J. J., Smalley, S. L., Philips, J. M. & Zaidel, E. (2005). Impaired linguistic processing and atypical brain laterality in adults with ADHD. *Clin. Neurosci. Res.*, *5*(5–6), 255–263.
18 Hale, T. S., Smalley, S. L., Walshaw, P. D., Hanada, G., Macion, J., McCracken, J. T. . . . & Loo, S. K. (2010). Atypical EEG beta asymmetry in adults with ADHD. *Neuropsychologia*, *48*(12), 3532–3539.
19 Kaufman, L., Ayub, M. & Vincent, J. (2010). The genetic basis of non-syndromic intellectual disability: A review. *J. Neurodev. Disord.*, *2*(4), 182–209.
20 Knaus, T., Silver, A., Kennedy, M., Lindgren, K., Dominick, K., Siegel, J. . . . & Tager-Flusberg, H. (2010). Language laterality in autism spectrum disorder and typical controls: A functional, volumetric, and diffusion tensor MRI study. *Brain Lang.*, *112*(2), 113–120.
21 McCann, B. S. (1981). Hemispheric asymmetries and early infantile autism. *J. Autism Dev. Disord.*, *11*(4), 401–411.
22 Morris, R. & Romski, M. (1993). Handedness distribution in a nonspeaking population with mental retardation. *Am. J. Ment. Retard.*, *97*(4), 443–448.
23 Obrzut, J. (1988). Deficient lateralization in learning disabled children. In D. Molfese & S. Segalowitz (Eds.), *Brain lateralization in children* (pp. 567–589). New York: Guilford.

24 Ocklenburg, S., Beste, C., Arning, L., Peterburs, J. & Güntürkün, O. (2014). The ontogenesis of language lateralization and its relation to handedness. *Neurosci. Biobehav. Rev.*, *43*, 191–198.
25 Orton, S. (1928). A physiological theory of reading disability and stuttering in children. *NEJM*, *198*, 1045–1052.
26 Rosenfield, D. & Goodglass, H. (1980). Dichotic testing of cerebral dominance in stutterers. *Brain Lang.*, *11*(1), 170–180.
27 Slezicki, K. I., Cho, Y. W., Yi, S. D., Brock, M. S., Pfeiffer, M. H., McVearry, K. M. ... & Motamedi, G. K. (2009). Incidence of atypical handedness in epilepsy and its association with clinical factors. *Epilepsy Behav.*, *16*(2), 330–334.
28 Soper, H., Satz, P., Orsini, D., Henry, R., Zvi, R. & Schulman, M. (1986). Handedness patterns in autism suggest subtypes. *J. Autism Dev. Disord.*, *16*(2), 155–167.
29 Soper, H., Satz, P., Orsini, D., van Gorp, W. & Green, M. (1987). Handedness distribution in a residential population with severe or profound mental retardation. *Am. J. Ment. Defic.*, *92*(1), 94–102.
30 Travis, L. (1978). The cerebral dominance theory of stuttering 1931–1978. *JSHD*, *43*(3), 278–281.
31 Yeo, R. A., Gangestad, S., Steven, W., Thoma, R., Shaw, P. & Repa, K. (1997). Developmental instability and cerebral lateralization. *Neuropsychology*, *11*(4), 552–561.
32 Yeo, R. A. & Gangestad, S. (1998). Developmental instability and phenotypic variation in neural organization. *Adv. Psychol.*, *125*, 1–51.
33 Yeo, R. A., Gangestad, S. W., Edgar, C. & Thoma, R. (1999). The evolutionary-genetic underpinnings of schizophrenia: The developmental instability model. *Schizophr. Res.*, *39*(3), 197–206.
34 Yeo, R. A., Thoma, R. & Gangestad, S. (2007). Developmental instability and individual variation in brain development: Implications for the origin of neurodevelopmental disorders. *Curr. Direct Psychol. Sci.*, *16*(5), 245–249.
35 Zadina, J., Corey, D., Casbergue, R., Lemen, L., Rouse, J., Knaus, T. ... & Foundas, A. L. (2006). Lobar asymmetries in subtypes of dyslexic and control subjects. *J. Child Neurol.*, *21*(11), 922–931.

INDEX

acoustic dyslexia 98
activity-dependent synaptic plasticity 17
ADHD 170
age-related changes 17–18
alpha rhythm 11
Amunts, K. 9
amygdala activation 13
analytic-synthetic theory of language lateralization 20
anatomical data for differences in structure 8–10
angular gyrus 90
Annett, M. 15, 16, 79, 98, 165
Annett pegboard 157
anterior cingulate cortex 145
anterior middle frontal gyrus 44
arcuate fasciculus 148
Arnold, G. 150
Asperger, H. 141
Asperger syndrome 141–142, 151–152
attentional lability 52
attentional model 20–21
Attentional Theory of Developmental Dyslexia 94
auditory cortex 44
auditory dyslexia 98
auditory perceptive processing 65
autism spectrum disorder: Asperger syndrome and 151–152; handedness and 142–144; language lateralization and 144–151; lateral preference and 168; NS-ID and 169; overview of 141–142; personal research data on 152–158
Automaticity/Cerebellar Theory of Developmental Dyslexia 90–91
Aylward, E. 145

Bakker, D. 95–96, 99, 109, 110–111
Balci, N. 157–158
Beal, D. S. 44, 46, 48
Beale, I. L. 131, 136
Behan, P. 98
behavioural studies 13–14
Belyakova, L. 65
Berson, J. 49
beta rhythm 11
bilateral transcranial Doppler sonography 12
binaural integration deficit 86–87
bioelectric activity 11–12
birth, complications during 128
Bishop, D. 85, 98, 143, 148–149
Blackstock, E. 150
Blood, G. 49
Blood, I. 49
Bloodstein, O. 40
Boberg, E. 52
Boder, E. 95, 99
Boyanova, V. 54–55, 56, 166
Bradshaw, L. L. 150, 151
Bradshaw-McAnulty, G. 129
Brady, J. P. 49
brain asymmetries, normal 81

brain-damaged patients 13
brain size, autism spectrum disorder and 144–145
Branch, C. 43
Broca, P. 7
Broca's area 8, 9–10, 23, 47, 90, 147
Broca-Wernicke-Lichtheim-Geschwind Model 23
Brown, W. 82
Brunswick, N. 84, 85, 98
Bryden, P. J. 157

Cardinale, R. C. 150
cerebellum 90–91
cerebral blood flow 12
cerebral cortex 145
Cerebral Dominance Model 40
Cerebral Dominance Theory of Developmental Dyslexia 86
Cerebral Dominance Theory of Stuttering 41, 42, 43–51, 52, 56
cerebral palsy 170
cerebrocortical microdysgenesis 80
Chang, E. F. 24
Chang, S. E. 45
childhood illness/injury 128
Chiron, C. 148
Choo, A. L. 45, 46
chromosomal abnormalities 128
Cimmorell-Strong, J. 49
classical lesion studies 10
Cohen, M. 99
contralateral cortex 80
corpus callosum 21–22, 45, 46, 79, 87, 90, 110
Courchesne, E. 145
Crow, T. 165
Crow, T. J. 15
Curry, F. 49

Daly, D. 51, 54
Dane, S. 157–158
Dawson, G. 148
De Fossé, L. 147
Dell, C. 52, 64, 67
developmental dyslexia *see* dyslexia, developmental
Developmental Instability (DI) model 170–171
developmental stuttering *see* stuttering, developmental
Dewey, D. 157
Dextral/Chance Theory 16

Diagnostic and Statistical Manual-Fifth Edition (DSM-V) 127, 142, 144, 151
Diagnostic and Statistical Manual-Fourth Edition (DSM-IV) 141, 144
dichotic listening: description of 13–14; developmental dyslexia and 84, 86–87, 99, 103–104, 105–108, 109; developmental stuttering and 48–49, 51, 53, 58, 60–61, 64–65, 66; intellectual disability and 130–132, 133, 134–136; perceptual asymmetry and 19; right-ear advantage (REA) and 21
diffusion tensor imaging (DTI) 9, 44, 45, 53, 148
dihaptic paradigm 14
Dorman, M. F. 51
Dorsaint-Pierre, R. 9
dorsal pathway 24
Down syndrome 129, 130–131, 136
Dragovic, M. 58
Dual Route Cascaded (DRC) model 96–97, 111
dual route model of reading 78, 102
Dual Stream Model of Language 24
Duara, R. 82
dyseidetic dyslexia 95, 98, 99
dyslexia, developmental: Attentional Theory and 94; atypical cerebral dominance as etiological factor of 77–80; atypical structural and functional asymmetries in 80–88; Automaticity/Cerebellar Theory and 90–91; comorbidity and 98; current perspectives on 88; dichotic listening and 103–104, 105–108; handedness and 103, 104–105, 166, 167; Magnocellular Theory and 91–94; overview of 77; personal research data on 100–114; Phonological Theory and 88–90; studying 94–99; typologies of 95–98
dysphonetic dyslexia 95, 98, 99

eardness 144–145, 153–154, 155–156, 157–158
ectopias 80–81
Edinburgh Handedness Inventory 157
Eglinton, E. 98
electroencephalography (EEG) 11, 46, 82–83, 148
Elliott, D. 130–131
embryonic teratogen exposure 128
epilepsy 170
Epstein, R. 99

Escalante-Mead, P. 143, 152, 157, 169
event-related potentials (ERPs) 46–47, 84, 85, 110–111
evoked potentials (EPs) 11–12, 84
eyedness 144, 153–155, 157–158
Eyler, L. T. 149

Fagard, J. 130
Fein, H. 169
Flagg, E. J. 149
Fletcher, P. 148
footedness 144, 153–154, 156, 157–158
Foundas, A. L. 9, 50
frontal lobe 81, 147
frontostriatal model of autism 151
functional MRI (fMRI) 12–13, 22, 85, 90–91, 149, 150
functional neuroimaging 12–13
functional specialization of the brain: bioelectric activity differences and 11–12; brain-damaged patients and 10; empirical basis for 7–8; genesis of 14–18; healthy subjects and 12–14; hemispheric interaction and 21–23; language lateralization and handedness and 24–26; language organization and 23–24; perceptual asymmetry and 19–21; structural differences and 8–10; theoretical framework of 18–19
functional transcranial Doppler sonography (fTCD) 85, 148–149
functional transcranial Doppler ultrasonography (fTSD) 13
fusiform gyrus 90

Galaburda, A. 79, 165
Galin, D. 83
Gazzaniga, M. S. 18
gender: abnormal growth trajectory and 145; developmental stuttering and 50; dyslexia and 80– 81; structural differences and 9
genetic theories of lateralization 16
Georgiewa, P. 85
Geschwind, N. 79, 98, 131, 165
Geschwind-Behan-Galaburda Theory 16–17
Giencke, S. 131
Good, C. D. 9
Goodglass, H. 51, 169
grapheme-phoneme conversion 89, 90, 96
graphemic parsing 89
Gregory, H. 49

Greimel, E. 145
Groen, M. A. 129
Gross-Glenn, K. 85
Gruber, L. 51
gyrus angularis 79

handedness: autism spectrum disorder and 142–144, 147, 153, 154, 157, 168; developmental dyslexia and 98, 99, 103, 104–105, 108–110, 111, 112–113, 166, 167; developmental stuttering and 40–42, 50, 57–58, 59–60, 63–67, 166–167; functional differentiation and 7; genetic theories and 16; intellectual disability and 128–130, 133–134, 135–136; language dominance and 2; language lateralization and 24–26; reading disorders and 78, 79; right-ear advantage (REA) and 14; structural differences and 8–9; testosterone exposure and 16–17
Harm, M. W. 97, 112
Hartley, X. Y. 130
Hartman, B. 40
Hashimoto, T. 147
Haslam, R. 81
Hauck, J. 157
Hauser, S. 146
Hayashi, M. 150
Hazlett, H. C. 145
healthy subjects, data from 12–14
Heim, S. 84
Helland, T. 98
hemispheric interaction 21–23
Herbert, M. 147
hereditary component for stuttering 39–40, 54–55, 60, 61–62, 63, 66–67
hereditary subtype of stuttering (HSS) 55, 56–57, 166–167
Heschl's gyrus 8, 9
heterozygote advantage 79
Hickok, G. 24
Hier, D. 81, 146–147
high temporal resolution magnetoencephalography (MEG) 84
hippocampal formation 8
Hiscock, M. 21
homozygote disadvantage 79
Hormonal Theory of Cerebral Lateralization 79, 165
Hornstein, H. A. 131, 136
Hugdahl, K. 21
Hynd, G. 82

Illingworth, S. 85
Index of Differential Diagnosis 57
inferior frontal gyrus 44
Ingham, R. J. 47
intellectual disability: handedness and 128–131; language lateralization and 130–132; overview of 127–128; personal research data on 132–137
ipsilateral cortex 80

Janke, L. 44, 46
Jariabkova, K. 98
Jones, R. 42–43
Jou, R. 146

Kanner, L. 141
Keller, S. S. 9
Kelly, E. 54
Kilshaw, D. 98
Kimura, D. 19
Kinsbourne, M. 20, 21
Kleinhans, N. M. 149
Klimesch, W. 83
Knaus, T. 147, 169, 171
Kulynych, J. J. 9

Lamm, O. 99
language dominance 2, 9
language lateralization: analytic-synthetic theory of 20; autism spectrum disorder and 144–151; handedness and 24–26; intellectual disability and 130–132; sensorimotor theory of 19; stuttering, developmental and 42–43
language organization 23–24
language processing 1
laryngeal reflex mechanisms 52
lateral preference 143–144, 152, 153–158, 168; *see also* handedness
lateralized task performance, evidence from 86–88
learning disabilities (LD) 77, 170
Leconte, P. 130
left-ear advantage (LEA) 49–51, 61–64, 99, 107, 111, 130–131, 134, 136, 150
left-hemispheric advantage (LHA) 50, 62, 66, 86, 106–107, 110, 131, 134, 136
lesion-deficit relationships 10
Levy, J. 20
Lewandowski, L. 131
lexical (orthographical) route 78
Liebetrau, R. 51
linguistic dyslexia 95–96, 98

Lokhov, M. 52
long-term vocational training 18
Lucas, J. 129

McAlonan, G. M. 146
McCann, B. S. 165
McClelland, J. L. 97
McManus, C. 15, 16
McManus, I. 143
magnetic resonance imaging (MRI) studies 81–82, 146–148
magnetoencephalography (MEG) 48, 84, 149
Magnocellular Theory of Developmental Dyslexia 91–94
maladaptive plasticity 18, 137
Markoulakis, R. 157
Martinez, J. 99, 109
Martínez-Sanchis, S. 150
masking level difference tasks 51
metabolic disorders 128
methodology, for book 2
Michigan Neuropsychological Test Battery 54
middle temporal gyrus 90, 145
mixed dyslexia subtype (MDS) 95, 102, 106–108, 109, 112–113, 167
Mohr, B. 22–23
Moll, K. 84
Moore, W. 52, 63
Morozov, V. P. 50, 53, 63–64, 66, 67
morphological differences 8
Morris, R. 128–129, 169
Mosley, J. L. 131–132, 136
Mottron, L. 146

nasal cycle 144
neural plasticity 17–18, 137, 146
neuroanatomic data 80–82
neurogenesis 17
neurophysiological evidence 82–85
neuropsychological assessment 10
neurotic (psychogenic) subtype of DS 54
neurotiform (organic) subtype of DS 54
Nielsen, J. A. 150
no-ear advantage (NEA) 49, 87, 150
Noehr, B. 51
non-lexical (sublexical or phonological) route 78
non-syndromic intellectual disability (NS-ID) 127–128, 131–132, 136–137, 168, 169

Obrzut, J. 99
occipital lobes 81
Ocklenburg, S. 24, 25
orbital frontal cortex 81
organic subtype of stuttering (OSS) 55, 56–57, 61–62, 63, 65–66, 166–167
Orton, S. 1, 40, 52, 56, 63, 78, 87
Orton-Travis theories 165

Paquette, C. 131, 136
pars opercularis 8
pars triangulais 8, 9
partial pleiotropy model 25
passive oddball paradigm 84
perceptual asymmetry 19–21
perceptual dyslexia 95–96, 98
pervasive developmental disorder-not otherwise specified (PDD-NOS) 142
Peterson, R. L. 97
phonematic dyslexia 98
phoneme integration 89, 95
phonological dyslexia subtype (PDS) 97, 98, 102, 107–108, 109, 110–111, 112, 113, 167
Phonological Theory of Developmental Dyslexia 88–90
phylogenetic development 24–25
Piorkowski 57
Pipe, M. E. 129, 131, 136
planum parietale 8
planum temporale 8, 9–10, 44, 79, 81, 90, 146
Poeppel, D. 24
polymorphic dyslalia 170
Porac, C. 129–130
Porter, R. J. 51
positron emission tomography (PET) 12, 84–85, 148
posterior superior temporal sulcus 145
Poulos, M. 52
Powell, R. L. 51
prenatal testosterone exposure 16–17
Preslar, J. 150
primary visual cortex 80
Prior, M. r. 150
programmed cell death 17
psychic dominance 41
psychogenic subtype of stuttering (PSS) 55, 56–57, 61–63, 64–65, 166–167
psychomotor reactivity 57
psychotrauma 56

Quinn, P. 51

Ramus, F. 88, 91, 94, 114
Rapid Auditory Processing Theory of Developmental Dyslexia 92
Rastatter, M. 52, 64, 67
Rauschecker, J. P. 24
Raven 100
reading 77–78; *see also* dyslexia, developmental
Redcay, E. 145
right-ear advantage (REA) 14, 21, 49–50, 61–63, 66, 86–87, 99, 106–107, 110, 131, 134, 136, 150
right-hemisphere advantage (RHA) 64–65, 107, 111, 130, 131, 134, 136
Right Shift Theory 16, 79, 165
Riley, G. 54
Riley, J. 54
Rinehart, N. J. 150–151, 152
Rippon, G. 84, 98
Robb, M. 50
Rojas, D. 146
Rolandic operculum 44
Romski, M. 128–129, 169
Rosenfield, D. 51, 52, 169
Rumsey, J. 85

Sanchez, E. 99, 109
Sato, Y. 48
Satz, P. 143
Schachter, S. 98
Scharoun, S. M. 157
schizophrenia 170
Schumann, C. M. 145
Schwartz, G. E. 150
Scott, S. K. 24
Seidenberg, M. S. 97, 112
sensorimotor syndrome 89
sensorimotor theory of language lateralization 19
Shaywitz, S. 85
Shklovsky, V. 51
Shoji, H. 131
Simos, P. G. 84
single positron emission computed tomography (SPECT) 148
Slorach, N. 51
Smith, A. 54
somatosensory area 44
Sommer, M. 44, 53
Sommers, R. 49
Soper, H. 128, 143, 157, 165, 169
Sowman, P. F. 48
specific learning disabilities (SLD) 77

split-brain studies 21–22
Standard Progressive Matrices (SPM) 100
Stein, J. 94
Steinmetz, H. 9
Stroganova, T. A. 148
structural differences 8–10
stuttering, developmental: atypical cerebral dominance for speech and 40–41; Cerebral Dominance Theory of 43–51; current perspectives on 53–55; differential diagnosis of 56–57; handedness and 41–42, 166–167; language lateralization and 42–43; overview of 39–40; personal research data on 56–68; theoretical models of 52–53
superior temporal gyrus 44, 90, 146
supramarginal gyrus 90
surface (orthographic) dyslexia subtype (SDS) 97, 98, 102, 106–108, 109, 111–112, 113, 167
Sviderskaya, N. 11
Sylvian parietotemporal region 24
syndromic intellectual disability (S-ID) 127–128
Szenkovits, G. 114

tachistoscopic paradigm 14, 19, 86
Talcott, J. 94
temporal lobe 145, 147
temporo-frontal language system 53
testosterone exposure, prenatal 16–17, 42, 79
thalamus 80

theoretical assumptions and conceptions 2
Travis, L. 41, 52, 56, 63
Trigger-Threshold-Target Model 146

unitary theory of stuttering 54

Van Borsel, J. 43
ventral pathway 24
visual (optic) dyslexia 98
Visual Theory of Dyslexia 92
vocalization-induced suppression 48
voxel-based morphometry (VBM) 44, 45, 46, 145, 146
Vrbancic, M. I. 131–132

Wada test 13, 42
Waldie, K. 86
Weber-Fox, C. M. 46–47
Webster, W. 52, 64, 67
Wernicke, C. 7
Wernicke-Lichtheim Model 23
Wernicke's area 8, 23, 24, 47, 81, 85, 147
Whitehouse, A. 148–149
Witelson, S. F. 86
word identification models 96

Yeo, R. A. 170
Yu, K. K. 148

Zadina, J. 82, 169
Zhu, D. C. 45
Zielinski, B. A. 145–146
Zilbovicius, M. 148
Zimmermman, G. N. 54